JADE LINDGAARD is a journalist for the news site *MediaPart*, and she coedited *La France invisible*, with Stéphane Beaud and Joseph Confavreux (2006); XAVIER DE LA PORTE is a journalist for the radio station France Culture.

COUNTERBLASTS

COUNTERBLASTS is a series of short, polemical titles that aims to revive a tradition inaugurated by Puritan and Leveller pamphleteers in the seventeenth century, when, in the words of one of their number, Gerard Winstanley, the old world was "running up like parchment in the fire." From 1640 to 1663, a leading bookseller and publisher, George Thomason, recorded that his collection alone contained over twenty thousand pamphlets. Such polemics reappeared both before and during the French, Russian, Chinese and Cuban revolutions of the last century.

In a period where politicians, media barons and their ideological hirelings rarely challenge the basis of existing society, it is time to revive the tradition. Verso's Counterblasts will challenge the apologists of Empire and Capital.

The Impostor: BHL in Wonderland

Jade Lindgaard and Xavier de la Porte

Translated by John Howe

London • New York

This English-language edition first published by Verso 2012

First published as *Le B.A. BA du BHL: Enquête sur le plus grand intellectuel français*

1 3 5 7 9 10 8 6 4 2

Verso
UK: 6 Meard Street, London W1F 0EG
US: 20 Jay Street, Suite 1010, Brooklyn, NY 11201
www.versobooks.com

Verso is the imprint of New Left Books

ISBN-13: 978-1-84467-748-1

British Library Cataloguing in Publication Data
A catalogue record for this book is available from the British Library

Library of Congress Cataloging-in-Publication Data
A catalog record for this book is available from the Library of Congress

Typeset in Minion Pro by MJ Gavan, Cornwall
Printed in the US by Maple Vail

On the one occasion on which I met the author, I was immediately struck by the thought that here there was a very poor man's Albert Camus: he is ever such a pretty boy, acutely conscious of this fact, with exceedingly expensive clothes deployed with an infinitely careful consciousness. My intuition proved correct, in as far as there is a long message conveying an eager identification with Camus and the conviction that if only Camus had lived, they would have been chums, liking the same kind of women, loving to live it up, and so on. Now, sartorial affectations are his own business, but the corresponding conscious-casual style of writing affects the quality of what he has to say. A random casualness is presented as being, really, an elegant form of profundity. In fact, it is simply random casualness.

Ernest Gellner

From a review (unpublished due to his untimely death) of Bernard-Henri Lévy's *Adventures on the Freedom Road: French Intellectuals in the Twentieth Century*

CONTENTS

PREFACE: WHO'S AFRAID OF BHL?

Any British or American reader who picks up this book is more than likely to have come across a sort of joke French intellectual called Bernard-Henri Lévy, usually known as BHL in France, where the acronym has become his signature. They may have come across his name during the recent Dominique Strauss-Kahn (DSK) affair; or perhaps seen him photographed among rebel combatants in Libya or arm-in-arm with a glamorous blonde in the hall of a five-star hotel. Perhaps some have seen his articles in the *Huffington Post*, or read his book on the death of the *Wall Street Journal* writer Daniel Pearl or the diary of his journey across the US in the footsteps of Tocqueville.

Naturally, foreign newspapers and journals sometimes poke fun at him for being so very French, so Parisian. But he knows a lot, cites three philosophers in a sentence, and is said to be highly respected in France. And the man looks good. His expensively dishevelled hair frames a handsome aquiline face, which is usually sun-tanned and set off by an impeccably white unbuttoned shirt. He is always keen to denounce injustice and new 'barbarisms': the stoning of women for adultery, the repression of Iranian demonstrators in 2009, genocide in Darfur, the rise of nationalisms. To all appearances, he is a militant democrat, a moral authority; a committed left intellectual, like Jean-Paul Sartre.

So non-French readers may well perceive him as a courageous European philosopher, vigilant in seeking to awaken sleeping consciences and oppose the abuse of power. A sort of new dissident, a Parisian Vaclav Havel, an Old World Chomsky, a Sean Penn of journalism, a French-style Norman Mailer.

But BHL is not really like that. Not exactly.

Let's start with a spot of history. This is not the first time that we have written about Bernard-Henri Lévy. In 2004, we published the first investigative book on Bernard-Henri Lévy, *Le B.A. BA du BHL*, in which we exposed the underside of his work and his little compromises with the truth: the cracks in his so-called investigation of the murder of Daniel Pearl, the falsehood of his meeting with Major Massoud in the Afghan mountains in the early 1980s, the constant back-scratching between him and the circle of those in his debt. We tracked the unsuccessful attempts made by the philosophers Gilles Deleuze and Cornelius Castoriadis, as well as the historian Pierre Vidal-Naquet, to denounce the intellectual fraud they saw in BHL. And we collected many testimonies from close and remote observers on his dexterity in using his adopted causes to serve his own ends.

When we started our research, there were two main reactions. Intellectuals, academics and researchers tended to say things like: 'Why get so worked up over that fellow? Everyone knows he's awful. He's a clown. He's been talking rubbish for the last thirty years.' As this broadly updated edition appears in France and the English-speaking world, our answer is still the same: BHL may well leave no mark on the history of thought, but his role is not negligible. He is read; he speaks up everywhere, about everything, all the time. Some people, through ignorance or self-interest, take him seriously. Why should the critique of Bernard-Henri Lévy be reserved for the knowledgeable? How come a newspaper editor, who speaks freely in private of the limitations he sees in BHL, nevertheless gives him space in the paper? What personal, political and ideological interests does Bernard-Henri Lévy serve? These questions lead back to French intellectual history since the 1970s.

The other reaction, often but not always from journalists, was one of alarm: 'Are you crazy? You'll never work again after that, anywhere. He'll crush you.' Strange as it may seem, Bernard-Henri Lévy inspires fear in France – not through the power of his thought, but through that of his network. He is close to most of the bosses and editors in publishing and the press, and has a propensity for making threatening phone calls when he feels ill-treated; he launches reprisals in response to articles hostile to him. We found repeated evidence of this fear during our first investigation in 2003–2004, and we noted it again during the months working on this edition. How many informants told us of overbearing, fatuous or reprehensible acts, while refusing to be quoted … Why risk getting his management or friends on your back just to denounce what is after all a minor fraud, a limited menace? 'BHL is hardly Bin Laden,' we were told. Well, no. But in some circles, to criticize him is to risk being 'asked to leave'; it shows that one rejects the way a certain world functions. That world is our world.

Are we crazy? Did he crush us? No, not any more than he crushed others who have since repeated the exercise.[1] But when the first edition of this book came out, we observed a distinct rattling of his networking machinery. We had been working discreetly and had opted not to ask Bernard-Henri Lévy for an interview (we did request one when preparing this new edition, but received no response), exploiting the fact that other investigations were under way to operate unnoticed. When our book was announced, a few days before it appeared, there were some slight signs of anxiety. Phone calls to the printer attempting to get hold of our manuscript, something the printer said had never happened to him before. A letter from Bernard-Henri Lévy's lawyer to our publisher. Then a call from the editor one of us worked for, urging us to contact Bernard-Henri Lévy, who had told her he was afraid for the safety of people who had worked with him in Pakistan. We reassured her, but did nothing further. Three days later, another phone call from the same editor warned that our publisher was going to receive another letter from Bernard-Henri Lévy's lawyer, which through some telecommunications sorcery she already had in front of her. But when the book appeared, Bernard-Henri Lévy did not sue. Because what we were saying was true; because our book was based in large part on his own texts and public utterances, and because, contrary to what he declared everywhere, we had not pried into his private life. And also because polemic serves his purposes. A constant of his career is that he has always managed to take advantage of criticisms against him: they enable him to appear as one who shakes things up, who upsets people; they keep him in the public eye.

When the book came out, we were able to ascertain that most journalists had freedom to deal with it as they pleased. Nevertheless, some of them reported phone calls from highly placed friends of Bernard-Henri Lévy, urging them not to write about it – phone calls followed by another to the editor, if the journalist remained obdurate. With television it was tougher: we were invited to appear, then disinvited a few hours later. One TV journalist put it like this: 'We called BHL to organize a debate. He refused and said he would start a nuclear war if you were in the studio.' Well of course, if it's a matter of avoiding nuclear war …

All this is rather pathetic and would even have amused us, had we not subsequently learned that some highly estimable people had suffered directly because of accusations of betrayal made by Bernard-Henri Lévy, that great defender of freedom.

If we are back on the case seven years later, it's not out of undying spite but because, what with his role in the launch of the war in Libya, his defence of an Israeli State under increasing criticism for its blockade of Gaza and its colonization policy, his championing of Dominique Strauss-Kahn and Roman Polanski, and his new US career, he has become omnipresent. A new debugging operation is called for. It has already begun in America, to expose (in the words of Katha Pollitt writing in the *Nation*) a man 'whose pretentious drivel has to be the worst thing you've exported to us since pizza-flavored La Vache Qui Rit.'[2]

1 THE POPE OF SAINT-GERMAIN-DES-PRÉS

Bernard-Henri Lévy reigns over a territory much bigger than the Vatican. The great family of those obliged to him gathered for a memorable party in November 2010. There he unleashed the full power of his aura as a star among stars, publisher of friends and of the powerful and multi-media diarist.

THE SOIRÉE AT THE FLORE: A CARTOGRAPHY OF DEBTORS

On Tuesday 30 November 2010, *La Règle du jeu* – the review founded and edited by Bernard-Henri Lévy – celebrated its twentieth anniversary at the Café de Flore in the boulevard Saint-Germain, Paris. The event could easily have passed unnoticed. *La Règle du jeu* is not a major landmark in the French intellectual landscape.

AN AWESOME PARTY FOR AN UNREAD REVIEW

The names on the editorial board look impressive: Mario Vargas Llosa (recent Nobel Prize for literature), the Israeli Amos Oz, American writers Jonathan Safran Foer and Adam Gopnik, British novelist Salman Rushdie, Bei Dao from China, Carlos Fuentes of Mexico, Eduardo Manet from Cuba, Fernando Savater from Spain … But those on the editorial committee, which keeps the review alive from day to day, are somewhat more obscure. They comprise some of the most loyal of the loyalists: the companion of all his travels and friend from the word go, Gilles Hertzog (who is also the publication's managing editor); Philippe Boggio, Bernard-Henri Lévy's official biographer; Liliane Lazar, an American academic, early fan and the first to open a website dedicated exclusively to the greater glory of Bernard-Henri Lévy,[1] and Marc Villemain, a young disciple who has also written a reverent book on the master.[2]

For twenty years, the output of the review has reflected that incongruity. At its foundation it paraded high-flown and noble ambitions: to restore 'the circuits of communication and dialogue interrupted, in Europe, by nearly half a century of totalitarian glaciation'; to 'reconcile literature with itself'; to 'ponder the barbarisms of the time', and to 'discover new authors'.[3] In practice, it has followed twenty years of struggles waged by its founder, featuring Algeria, Bosnia, Sartre or America in synchrony with Bernard-Henri Lévy's causes and books. And it marshalls his rearguard with skill and finesse. 'A spectre is haunting Europe, and even its American excrescence: the spectre of BHLophobia,' wrote Laurent Dispot in the anniversary issue, brazenly adapting the opening sentence of the *Communist Manifesto* to begin an article developing the idea that to criticize Bernard-Henri Lévy is somehow anti-Semitic.[4] The piece was embellished with pointed quotations from prestigious pens. *La Règle du jeu* is doubtless an elegant publication, but in twenty years it has not brought a single idea to prominence or discovered one author of note; in consequence, it has never managed to impose itself as a significant arena of French intellectual debate.

Nevertheless, on that evening of 30 November, 'le Tout-Paris' gathered to celebrate its twentieth anniversary. It is pointless to give a detailed account of the party. For a start, we were not present. And in any case, the *Règle du jeu* website soon performed that duty. On 2 December a blow-by-blow account appeared online, accompanied by numerous snapshots in the style of society or celebrity magazines, giving us the guests, the order of their arrival and some alleged snippets of conversation.[5] It was picked up by the press and was all over the web in no time, making a major event out of what a series of interviews with Bernard-Henri Lévy had struggled to bring to life. The anniversary of *La Règle du jeu* was only a date for socialites, after all.

The great birthday party took place in the Café de Flore, on the boulevard Saint-Germain, where Bernard-Henri Lévy – along with a segment of the Paris intelligentsia – is a habitual presence. But on this occasion, to celebrate a supposedly campaigning review, the first-floor front bore a photo of Sakineh Mohammadi Ashtiani, an Iranian woman condemned to stoning for adultery (see below, Chapter 7). Under the Madonna's gaze of the potential Iranian martyr, a mass of people swarmed for several hours (if the accounts are to be believed) in hopes of getting inside to 'the place to be', or where it was for the space of an evening. The list of individuals named as guests by the review constitutes a kind of atlas of its founder's influence.

A few intellectuals of world stature had flown in: Milan Kundera, Umberto Eco, Jorge Semprún. The others were familiar personalities on the French scene: the writer Philippe Sollers, the psychoanalyst Jean-Claude Milner, the philosophers Catherine Clément and Sylviane Agacinski (wife of former Socialist prime minister Lionel Jospin), the essayist Pascal Bruckner, the film-maker Claude Lanzmann. Among the authors was a Prix Goncourt (Atiq Rahimi), an ex-scandalous writer (Christine Angot), the biggest-selling French writer of police thrillers of the past ten years (Fred Vargas), a rugby-loving serial biographer (Jean Lacouture), and an esteemed comic-strip author and film-maker (Marjane Satrapi). Several of the novelists present were regulars on the best-seller lists. But you'd have searched in vain for any young authors or thinkers discovered by *La Règle du jeu*.

The publishing world sent a few delegates. A large part of the upper management of Grasset, where Bernard-Henri Lévy has officiated since the mid-1970s and whose CEO also runs Éditions Fayard, turned up; so did the CEO of Éditions Plon, the boss of Éditions de l'Olivier and the director of Éditions Stock. The most influential agent in French publishing was also there.

A handful of actors managed to get in, Alain Delon among them, as well as some film-makers (Roman Polanski's arrival caused one of the biggest stirs of the evening) and producers. Theatre directors and producers, a few singers, the *great* French architect Jean Nouvel, the *great* French designer Philippe Stark, a photographer, a luxury jeweller and a dancer from the Crazy Horse completed the artsy line-up.

However, representatives of other spheres outweighed the world of culture and ideas. The slew of lawyers, for example, among them several 'stars of the Bar'. Above all, a hefty contingent from the world of business and finance. We read that Arnaud Lagardère (head, as his father's heir, of Lagardère SCA, the holding company controlling the Lagardère Group which owns, among others, the Europe 1 radio station, *Le Journal du Dimanche* and the Hachette Group including Grasset and *Paris Match*) had telephoned to make his excuses, but the co-manager of the Lagardère Group was there to represent him. Also mentioned were the L'Oréal heiress's daughter, the non-executive president of Sanofi-Aventis (French and European leader of the pharmaceutical industry) and holder of multiple directorships, the development director of Areva (an industrial group specializing in nuclear technology), the associate managing director of the Rothschild Bank, the CEO of the Publicis Group (third biggest public relations group in the world) as well as, among others, the director general of a 'taxi-jet' outfit and the influential chairwoman of Image7, a PR firm.

On the political side, the government had to be present, in the persons of the minister of culture (Frédéric Mitterrand, nephew of the late former president of the Republic) and the minister of agriculture (Bruno Le Maire). The centre had sent François Bayrou (chairman of Mouvement Démocratique) and the Europe Écologie-Les Verts party its most flamboyant spokesman, the May '68 student leader Daniel Cohn-Bendit. But the most impressive contingent was provided by the Socialist Party: two former first secretaries and prime ministers (Lionel Jospin and Laurent Fabius), a former foreign minister (Hubert Védrine), a former culture and national education minister (Jack Lang), the mayor of Paris (Bertrand Delanoë) and his culture adviser (David Kessler), a member of parliament and candidate in the first stage of the presidential election (Arnaud Montebourg), a member of parliament close to François Hollande (Aurélie Filipetti) and a national secretary (Malek Boutih). Simone Veil, former president of the European Parliament, was there, as were various representatives of anti-racist groups (Sihem Habchi, president of the feminist campaign 'Ni putes ni soumises', and the president of SOS Racisme, Dominique Sopo) and Jewish associations: l'Union des étudiants juifs de France (Arielle Schwab and Raphael Haddad) and the Conseil représentatif des institutions juives de France (Richard Prasquier).

Before delving any deeper into the occasion, we would remind the reader that what was being celebrated was the twentieth anniversary of *La Règle du jeu*, a review which no one reads or cites.

'BRANDING LIVESTOCK'

The press having apparently decided to cover the event on a scale to match the occasion, the weekly journals dispatched the flower of their mastheads. The centre-left *Le Nouvel Observateur* was on hand in the persons of its proprietor, its founder, its director of external relations and a journalist. *Le Point*, right of centre, where Bernard-Henri Lévy permanently hovers in the form of a weekly 'bloc-notes', sent its editor and an eminent member of the culture desk; *L'Express*, its editorial director (who doubles as a daily interviewer on the LCI TV channel); *Marianne*, a left-populist publication, its CEO, its deputy director (also director of the monthly *Le Magazine littéraire*) and one of its star editorialists; *Le Journal du Dimanche*, its director. Even the muckraking *Le Canard Enchainé* – a historic enemy of Bernard-Henri Lévy – was at the party.

Of the dailies, *Le Monde* was represented by two of its three new proprietors, flanked by the chairman of the board and the publication's managing editor; the right-wing daily *Le Figaro* by its group editorial director and editorialist, backed by a member of its editorial committee and its society columnist. *Libération*, the left-wing daily, sent its managing editor and two journalists. The radio stations were not to be outdone. Radio France, the company that manages the publicly-owned radio stations, sent its CEO and the directors of two networks, France Inter and France Culture, the latter also represented by a programme adviser, two producers and two radio pundits. The early morning show presenter on Europe 1 gave up some sleep time to be there, accompanied by the presenter of the 6-8 p.m. slot and a heavyweight political interviewer. The director of broadcasting at RCJ, the Jewish community's radio station, showed up too. As for the TV channels, Canal Plus contributed a presenter and the Franco-German channel Arte its new chairwoman. Also in attendance were the monthly women's magazine *Elle*, the very right-wing journal *Ring*, the online news website *Mediapart*, the monthly *Lire*, the cultural magazine *Transfuge* and the journal *L'Égoïste* ... trawling for material, perhaps.

The varied and intermingled reasons for the presence of all these personalities speak volumes about the sort of relations that Bernard-Henri Lévy maintains with their different milieus. There are old friendships, working relationships, campaigning companions, favour-seekers (one journalist who was there told us he needed Bernard-Henri Lévy's help to mount an office putsch). Motives range from allegiance, curiosity, or the need to be seen in a place deemed important, right down to false naivety, the pose of the singer Jacques Higelin who confided to the cameras of TV Saint-Germain: 'I don't know what I'm doing pissing about here.'[6] Some, upset not to see their names in the list posted on the review's website, later asked for them to be added.

It takes a peevish character indeed to come up with a radical interpretation of the function of such a party. One woman journalist, who would never dream of attending, explained: 'A party like that brands the livestock in a herd.' To understand how that herd is made up, we need to detail the different facets of the grandee being fêted that evening: BHL.

BHL THE CELEB

THE END OF 'THE MOST FAMOUS COUPLE IN FRANCE'?

June 2010, with the gazettes all of a flutter: Bernard-Henri Lévy and Arielle Dombasle appeared to have split up. What *Vanity Fair* had dubbed in 2003 'the most famous couple in France'[7] was no more. It seems that everyone knew. Undeterred, the international press hastened to introduce us to the 'glamorous blonde' who was succeeding the 'vanished actress'.[8] She was Daphne Guinness, 42, a member of the famous brewing family, divorced from a Greek businessman, mother of three, and so on. In February 2011 she unbosomed herself to *Harper's Bazaar*.[9] She and BH – her pet name for him – had met five years before at a party in Paris. It was not memorable (we are not told whether she meant the meeting or the party), but they got in touch again anyway, because 'he was so fascinating and had the best sense of humour. He made me laugh and think in equal measure.' They had become 'something more' than friends. She's tried to be 'as elegant [about the situation] as possible', Daphne explained. Had someone told her this would happen, she would have said 'you were out of your mind, because I don't date married men'.[10]

Two months later, the monthly gossip magazine *Voici* gave Dombasle space for the riposte. 'All that was just Anglo-Saxon gossip and trash. Rest assured, we are not leaving each other and are living under the same roof. ... My passion is intense and complete. I can live no other way. And Bernard-Henri has an adoration for me that he proves every day. These rumours are pure poison. ... He swore me this oath of mad love.'[11]

What attracts the media to all this? Why is Bernard-Henri Lévy a recurrent figure in the celebrity press and gossip columns? Because Bernard-Henri Lévy is more noted for his image than for his oeuvre. His books, his films, his political causes are largely obscured by his open-necked shirt, his hairdo and the novel of his life. Over the years, Bernard-Henri Lévy has become a 'celeb'. He is famous for being famous.

What the celebrity press loves about Bernard-Henri Lévy is his intellectual image in a thoroughly airheaded environment. Even when he has just made a fool of himself by trying to dance for the cameras on the red carpet of the Marrakesh film festival, as he did in 2001, he manages to look weighty again as he murmurs into the TF1 camera that intercepts him: 'It's important to be here, in a country like Morocco that practises a moderate Islam.'[12]

Bernard-Henri Lévy displays tireless diligence in providing himself with opportunities to appear. For as a celeb, Bernard-Henri Lévy frequents celeb hangouts. In Paris it's Saint-Germain-des-Prés, and in particular the Brasserie Lipp and the Café de Flore, which has a 'table I like a lot, just on the way in'.[13] At Saint-Paul-de-Vence it's La Colombe d'Or, where he tells us that he always eats the same thing: 'It isn't just a way of simplifying my life, it's a question of morality, or style: I can't stand to see a guy poring over the menu, hesitating, pondering, commenting, hesitating some more, as if this were some essential matter of life or fate.'[14]

But most of all he hangs out in Marrakesh, Morocco, the ultimate place to have a house. Marrakesh, a new exotic cocktail of Geneva and Saint-Tropez, desirable for the fiscal advantages available to residents and the impunity with which the most outrageous luxury can be displayed, and where Bernard-Henri Lévy owns a magnificent villa next door to one of the residences of King Mohammed VI. Staff costs there are very reasonable, and sumptuous palaces in the Medina are still within reach of anyone with a fortune.[15] The fashion was started by Pierre Bergé and Yves Saint-Laurent in the 1970s. Then the Fiat-owning Agnelli family bought an immense property and a polo ground there, and Jean-René Fourtou (of Vivendi) a villa. Albert Frère, Belgian billionaire and chairman of the supervising council of the French TV channel M6, also owns a property. They are in good company: the stylist Jean-Paul Gaultier, the journalist Anne Sinclair and her husband Dominique Strauss-Kahn (the former Socialist minister who came to grief in New York in May 2011), the politician Jean-Louis Borloo, the ex-*Vogue* boss Prince Jean Poniatowski and the principal shareholder in the L'Oréal Group Liliane Bettencourt, among others. Bernard-Henri Lévy goes to Marrakesh to relax and to write. And he entertains there, lavishly.

More recently, Bernard-Henri Lévy bought another Moroccan pied-à-terre, this time in Tangiers. Looking over the sea, next to the famous Café Hafa, the house was renovated and decorated by the architect Andrée Putman. The work was considered so important to the history of art that France 5 broadcast a film directed by Benoît Jacquot on the house restoration.[16]

ARIELLE AND BERNARD-HENRI: SELF-MYTHOLOGIZATION OF A LEGENDARY COUPLE

'I'm often seen in the media; it amuses me, I enjoy it,' Bernard-Henri Lévy confessed to the chat-show host Michel Drucker at the end of 2001.[17] He is seen an enormous amount on television, casually combining seriousness of discourse with frivolity of context. He is still the only founder-editor of a review, to the best of our knowledge, to have been honoured with a TV broadcast from a hip Paris nightclub to announce the launch of said publication. It was in 1990, for *La Règle du jeu*. 'The role of the intellectual is to complexify,' the guest bawled learnedly over the background clamour of the club, between a little game entitled 'Who's who' and some remarks on the vandalization of the Jewish cemetery at Carpentras.

Ardisson's next guest was Arielle Dombasle. 'Is it true what people say, that Bernard-Henri Lévy is in love with you?' the presenter sniggered, amused by the actress's circumlocutions. Bernard-Henri Lévy was married at the time and his relationship with Dombasle, although of six years' standing, was completely unofficial. 'Well, couples who place themselves in the public eye always suffer greatly for it,' she sighed. Placing themselves in the public eye would nevertheless become a constant with this couple.

In June 1993, in a fairytale wedding at Saint-Paul-de-Vence, the 'prince of philosophers' married the actress. It was mainstream public TV news,[18] with photos in *Paris Match*.[19] Of course there were echoes of Yves Montand and Simone Signoret, married in the same Saint-Paul-de-Vence town hall in December 1951. One might recall the words of Jean-Paul Enthoven, his old friend and colleague from Grasset, who compared Bernard-Henri Lévy and Arielle Dombasle to the legendary couple F. Scott and Zelda Fitzgerald: 'Arielle and Bernard are Scott and Zelda, it's all there: the backdrops, the South of France, the sense of revelry, the unconcealed passion.'[20] You might think Bernard-Henri Lévy was joking when, imagining that people disapproved of his marrying an actress, he quoted Arthur Miller in reference to his marriage with Marilyn Monroe: 'A writer who marries an actress should understand that he is handing a grievance to his detractors on a plate.'[21]

But Arielle Dombasle is not Marilyn Monroe, or Zelda Fitzgerald, or Simone Signoret. Arielle Dombasle is an oddity in the French artistic landscape. Part singer (free-style soprano, with a predilection for baroque pieces in techno arrangements and cover versions of standards) and part film director (the wacky *Les Pyramides bleues*), she is primarily an actress. Her career has been split since the early 1980s between the rigours of art cinema (four films by Eric Rohmer including the 1983 *Pauline à la plage*; Karim Dridi's *Hors jeu* in 1997, Cédric Kahn's *L'Ennui* in 1998) and occasional experimental films (Alain Robbe-Grillet's *La*

Belle captive in 1982 and *Un bruit qui rend fou* in 1995), and major commercial productions (Claude Zidi's *Astérix et Obélix*, 1998) or television films (*Sissi impératrice*). What binds this somewhat heterogeneous list together is a standard performance which, with a few adjustments, she gives in film after film: as an affected ingénue with an obsolete manner of speaking and the figure of a teenager.

Something Dombasle has in common with her partner of twenty years is that she enjoyed from a very early stage a celebrity out of all proportion with her standing in French cinema. All through the 1980s she was regularly seen in *Paris Match*, as the muse of the couturier Jean-Louis Scherrer ('She lives my dresses as she lives her roles'[22]), at Fouquet's in the arms of Frédéric Mitterrand,[23] photographed in blurry soft focus à la David Hamilton before a jaunt to Hollywood,[24] at home with her cat Slooghi ...[25]

As part of an admirable effort to set the couple up in legend, Bernard-Henri Lévy seldom writes the word 'Arielle', although he often mentions her in his articles. He refers to her as 'A.', which has a more mysterious ring.[26] 'A.' and 'I' lead an intense life: 'I have been to Beni-Saf, that small port in the Oranais where I was born but have never lived; A. was with me; she had a video camera, charged with recording the slightest tremor of my visible being.'[27] In any case, if 'I' is what he is, it's thanks to 'A.'. 'I too – thank you, A.! – have become an other.'[28] Despite A.'s presence, though, 'I.' and 'S.' should not be forgotten: 'Not only would it not enter my head to stop writing because of a woman, but it is for women, for I. at the time of *Les Indes rouges*, for S. when I was writing my first essays and from now on for her, for A., that I have always written. I can write only by loving,'[29] wrote Bernard-Henri Lévy in 1994 in the Italian daily *La Stampa*.

The couple's use of the press as a place for self-mythologization has not ceased for nearly twenty years. It's there that we read about how they met for the first time when Dombasle was very young, then again by chance in Milan, opposite the Scala (he emerging from a seminar on psychoanalysis, she from a shoe shop[30]), how they had a long, secret, torrid affair conducted largely in hotel rooms ('for years, the only witnesses of my love for Bernard-Henri were hotel bellhops'[31]), how they address each other with the formal 'vous', how he forbids her to smoke or listen to loud music ... We learn from the papers, too, that she is considered to have the finest figure in Paris and that unkind commentators have nicknamed them 'ass and shirt'.

None of which prevents him from declaring, with regard to his relationship with 'A.', 'I speak about it very little, you know. I don't like talking about that ... But as in all great love stories, there's a secret, mysterious part, and a public part.'[32] Dombasle on her side never misses an opportunity to mention 'Bernard-Henri'. Just before their wedding she was quoted in *Le Figaro Madame*, the weekly women's supplement of the right-wing daily, as saying: 'Ever since the day we met, Bernard-Henri has appeared to me as the very face of love, of destiny.' 'He tells me about his days, reads me what he has written ... he's tactful enough to let me believe that he values my opinion.'[33]

He has rather less to say, but then he's pretty busy with pulling out all the stops to boost his wife's career. He hires halls for her to give concerts and rounds up his friends. And when Dombasle performed for three nights in a Broadway cabaret in September 2006, he got everyone he knew onto it. He sent personal emails to journalists soliciting coverage, he got her to be a guest on Charlie Rose,[34] he invited friends, and friends of friends.[35] Thus the first-night audience included Michael Douglas, Diane von Fürstenberg, John Malkovich, Lauren Bacall and Salman Rushdie. Also present was a *New York Times* journalist attracted by all the ballyhoo, but clearly underwhelmed by Arielle Dombasle. 'Don't believe the hype,' begins his review of the 'sloppy, poorly sung concert'. 'Ms. Dombasle's small wavery voice has about six stable notes in its middle range. When she pushes her singing up, it goes excruciatingly flat.' All in all, 'she demonstrated a complete absence of interpretive depth or indeed any sense that these songs might be connected to people's personal experience.'[36]

A cruel panning, but the important thing is to be talked about. That Charlie Rose should lose interest in her relationship with music after a few minutes, and revert to asking her about her relationship with her 'friend' Bernard-Henri Lévy: that's the essential thing. The romance has to cross the Atlantic, it's part of the game.

'HE WHO KNOWS ALL THE GAMES PLAYED BY PRESSMEN AND PUBLISHERS'

Making a display of the private is not restricted to BHL's own love life. In 1977, aged two and a half, his daughter Justine was already bouncing on his knee in *Paris Match*;[37] aged twenty-two, in September 1996, she was married in it.[38] 'It was BHL in all his pomp who gave away his daughter last weekend at the town hall of the 6th arrondissement in Paris,' ran the lead of an article that went on to describe the reception at Chez Castel, the smart nightclub in Saint-Germain-des-Prés, mentioning some 'very hot smooching' by Bernard-Henri and Arielle and enumerating the star cast: the writer Jorge Semprún, the former chief reporter of *France-Soir* Lucien Bodard, Jack Lang, the Gaullist Debré brothers, Alain Delon, Anne Sinclair and Dominique Strauss-Kahn … and since nothing is wasted in that sort of article, the journalist used it to announce the forthcoming appearance of Bernard-Henri Lévy's latest film, *Le Jour et la nuit*.

The committed reader would even have been able to follow the wedding preparations. *Le Figaro* detailed them in a rag-bag piece: 'In the middle of a fitting – with Lolita Lempicka, who is creating her wedding dress – Justine tells us: "In two days' time, I move on from dream to reality. I still can't quite believe it." Sure enough, this romance is from a different era. For Justine is marrying her first love, met four years earlier, Raphäel [the son of Jean-Paul Enthoven, he who said that Bernard-Henri and Arielle were 'Scott and Zelda']. "It's crazy, our fathers have been friends for ever, our grandfathers were, too. And now, in two days, it's our wedding, mine and Raphaël's. In our time it's unimaginable, isn't it, we almost seem like story-book characters."'[39]

What followed was in the papers too. First came a book, Justine Lévy's second novel *Rien de grave* (*Nothing Serious*), which appeared in 2004.[40] It tells the story of a young girl, Louise, who has married the son of her father's best friend, then gets hooked on amphetamines before being unceremoniously dumped by her husband, who has fallen in love with his own father's bit on the side. A cruel portrait of the husband, still more cruel of the mistress. *The Atrides* rewritten for *Voici*.

The book sold very well. But ill-intentioned people without any understanding of literature recognized themselves in it: Raphaël Enthoven, Justine Lévy's ex-husband, who then went to stay at the family villa in Marrakesh with his father's bit on the side, Carla Bruni (Nicolas Sarkozy's bride in 2008). There followed a press war. Raphaël and Carla Bruni – at that time a fashion model turned singer, and author of a hit record entitled 'Raphaël' – posed for the cover of *Paris Match*.[41] They then denied that they had authorized publication of the photo. Justine Lévy replied in *Le Nouvel Observateur*.[42] Television got involved.[43] The affair even became the subject of a debate in the 'Horizons' section of *Le Monde*. And continued in *La Revue des deux mondes*, in a text by Raphaël Enthoven entitled 'L'endroit du décor',[44] part of a survey on 'the power of discretion'.

Bernard-Henri Lévy was not left out. He too got to be a character in his daughter's novel (for a novel is what it is, of course). In it he is called 'Papa' and he is terrific. 'Papa, as always, looks deep into my eyes. He guesses everything, usually. He understands and sees it all.'[45] 'Papa' does the craziest things: 'The flat in rue Monge for example, the one where I was born, that you sold in ten minutes to the agency on the ground floor, just so you could afford to go skiing with Maman' (p. 67). And he isn't perfect: it is in Papa's office that Louise finds her first tabs of speed. 'I knew he took them sometimes, to work, to stay awake, to finish his books. I knew they made him jumpy, concentrated, irascible, rapid. I had always known they were there, in Ali-Papa's cave' (p. 98). But 'he had always had the strength to know when it was time to stop. He doesn't take them any more' (p. 113). And when Louise is in detox, 'Papa came to see me. He caused a flap, that first time in the hall, with his shades and his rock-star look, surrounded by patients in tracksuits and my new zombie friends' (p. 123).

Only an evil mind would see the slightest resemblance between Papa and Bernard-Henri Lévy. Yet that is what a number of journalists did, in *Le Monde*, for example: 'Finally, it is Bernard-Henri Lévy who is the book's most moving character, he who also knows all the games played by pressmen and publishers, and who came up with the right question. "Are you sure you're strong enough to face consequences?" BHL asked his daughter, after reading her book.'[46]

The 'games played by pressmen and publishers' says it all. The whiff of scandal surrounding Justine's book perfumed 'Ali-Papa' all over. Never mind the amphetamines, it's a novel. In the end, Bernard-Henri Lévy gained a new image: that of the father of the girl who was dumped for Carla Bruni. Notoriety was maintained. That's all that matters.

Whether literature or the intellectual world gained anything is another matter. Bernard-Henri Lévy seemed to think so. On 8 May 2004, invited by the chat-show host Thierry Ardisson to discuss the launch of his book *Récidives* on 'Tout le monde en parle', the author spoke of his pride in the success of his daughter's book. He added that it is rare to see the children of writers becoming writers themselves. 'There are the Dumas, all the same,' someone interrupted impertinently. 'That's true, there are the Dumas,' Bernard-Henri Lévy conceded with great seriousness.

No French intellectual before him has benefited from this type of notoriety. It is a peculiarity of Bernard-Henri Lévy to have constructed that image, and to have carefully maintained it over the years. He owes it to his physique, to his style of dress, to the fact that he looks good even in tabloid snapshots. He owes it to the frequentation of a circle that spawns gossip almost automatically. He owes it to his aptitude for being at ease on a TV set where nothing is being said, or what is said is said very fast. He also owes it, paradoxically, to the fact that he is not just a celeb.

BHL THE PUBLISHER

Since 1973 Bernard-Henri Lévy has been a publisher at Grasset, one of the leading French houses. Given the way French publishing works historically, the singularity of Éditions Grasset and his standing within the firm, his role is not a negligible one.

Publishing books, in its nobler aspect, means bringing to public notice ideas considered important. To issue texts by the philosopher Emmanuel Lévinas or by Benny Lévy, published respectively in 1991 and 2002 by Bernard-Henri Lévy in his 'Figures' series, or in 2011 the previously unpublished correspondence between Louis Althusser and his wife Hélène, are unarguably examples of that aspect of the métier. But publishing can also be a powerful tool in the management of social relations. In a country where doing one's book has become a principle of intellectual self-legitimization, it is important – irrespective of potential economic returns – to be able to give that pleasure to people for whom one has an obviously disinterested esteem.

When Bernard-Henri Lévy, in 1994, enabled Nicolas Sarkozy, then budget minister in Édouard Balladur's government, to publish his biography of Georges Mandel (a politician under the Third Republic, killed during the Nazi occupation);[47] or in 2002 permitted Xavier Couture, then director of broadcasting at TF1 and husband of Claire Chazal, presenter of the evening news on that channel, to excrete a novel entitled *Coma* before being appointed chairman of the board of Canal Plus a month later, he was doubtless aware that he was not doing much to advance the history of ideas or contemporary literature. When Bruno Le Maire, the minister of agriculture, felt obliged to justify his presence at the twentieth anniversary party for *La Règle du jeu* in 2010, he said: 'I've known BHL for a very long time. He helped me to get my first book published by Grasset.'[48]

Apart from that, Grasset provides a base, sensibly enough, for the publication of Bernard-Henri Lévy's personal work. *La Règle du jeu* benefits from the firm's infrastructures. And BHL is also served where necessary by another distinctive aptitude of Éditions Grasset: its capacity to advance as a team, at least in appearance. Edmonde Charles-Roux, a Grasset author and also president of the Prix Goncourt jury since

2002, summarized it in 2001: 'The interests of each are the interests of all. What's good for the house is good for us.'[49] Hence the long-standing support given by François Nourissier (who died in February 2011), a historic Grasset author and influential figure in Parisian literary life. Hence the support he can expect from Yann Moix, whom he published first in *La Règle du jeu*, before bringing him into the firm in 1996 and putting him on the road to success. Hence the support of Marc Lambron, another author in whose arrival he had a hand and who is not the least grateful: 'Lévy has this property that the great ecclesiastical organizations ought to envy: he unleashes waves of virtue; but, let's be clear, of that secretly rancorous, sexually decorous virtue stirred up by men who are too attractive to women,' Lambron wrote in *Le Point* in 2002.[50]

And Grasset was also that faithful friend, Jean-Paul Enthoven, first met in 1974, a journalist with *Le Nouvel Observateur* until 1984, who ended by joining the firm (and then the journal *Le Point*). When Enthoven's position at Grasset was under threat in the mid 1990s, Bernard-Henri Lévy weighed in with everything he had, to the extent of suggesting that the firm might have to do without him as well.[51] Unthinkable!

BHL THE DIARIST

Featured in every issue of the weekly *Le Point* since 1993, the 'bloc-notes de Bernard-Henri Lévy' is another strategic emplacement. Such a page, published in a very widely read magazine, is ideal for promoting Grasset's output, as in this entry from 2001: 'I am not too keen, in principle, on talking up things published by Grasset, my publishing house for nearly thirty years (even though I ought perhaps to force myself in the case of the Lambron, which I have just finished and which, with the Houellebecq, ought by rights to dominate this literary season). I don't really go in for that. But just this week, what could be more newsworthy than Claude Askolovitch's book on Jospin ...'[52] In rhetoric this is called a 'preterition': saying you do not like talking up Grasset books, and then doing it twice in a sentence. One mention, in passing, was of the ever-grateful Marc Lambron, who so often contrives to express – again in *Le Point* – his warm feelings about BHL's own works.[53]

A year later, at the opening of the 2002 literary season, he mentions two novels. One by Yann Moix, of which he says: 'This is the season when Yann Moix publishes a "Claude François story" which will one day be recognized as a pastiche of the Gospels and Don Quixote.'[54] And one by another Grasset author: 'This is the season when Élisabeth

Quin becomes a novelist: *Bridget Jones* à la française.'[55] He's no longer bothering to squirm about displaying Grasset's catalogue for the season. For the 2003 season, just one novel is mentioned, that of Frédéric Beigbeder, a Grasset author.[56]

When the sociologist Pierre Bourdieu died, in February 2002, he wrote: 'About that mandarin who spoke in the name of the "lower intelligentsia", about that pure product of the elite who denounced "distinction", about that media star who tirelessly theorized his allergy to "television", I only ever really wondered one thing: was he Alceste or Tartuffe?'[57] The description of Bourdieu's contribution to contemporary thought is cursory, to put it mildly. Bernard-Henri Lévy detested Pierre Bourdieu, who always treated him with disdain. But never has he addressed in any way anything the sociologist might have written. He keeps to the safer waters of invective, something the 'bloc-notes' is also handy for: unreasoned disqualification. Sometimes this produces mind-boggling indictments, for example when writing of Jacques Derrida and his book *Le Concept de 11 Septembre*: 'Where did this major, demanding thinker acquire such a mania for gathering up his own leavings? Why, in this master of my generation and a few others ... this temptation to pantheonize himself in his own lifetime?'[58]

But the 'bloc-notes' resound mainly with eulogies of journalists possessing some slight influence. When Jérôme Garcin (*Le Nouvel Observateur*, France Inter) published in 2001 a book on the 1789 French revolutionary Marie-Jean Hérault de Séchelles (1759–1794), BHL gushed: 'A book that has all the sonorities of the Grand Siècle. But in so modern a moral tone that one is – that I am – dumbfounded by it.'[59] Similar puffs appeared for books by Guy Konopniki (*Marianne*) in 2002 and 2003,[60] by Edwy Plenel (then at *Le Monde*) in 2002,[61] and by Jérôme Béglé (*Paris Match*) in 2003.[62]

What Bernard-Henri Lévy is mainly doing in his 'bloc-notes' is politicking. He uses this platform to dispense opinions on the way the world is going and on the men who govern us. We have been treated to his view of Nicolas Sarkozy, for example, for quite some time. He paid him homage after a televised swearing-in in December 2002, exalting the 'passion for public life' of that 'monk in the service of the State.'[63] And, as early as 1999: 'Sarkozy the unloved. Sarkozy, tomorrow's [Laurent] Fabius of the Right. From my pen, that's a compliment.'[64]

Useful as they are in Bernard-Henri Lévy's strategy of interventions on all fronts, these 'bloc-notes' are sometimes written quite hastily. Dictated over the phone or arriving at *Le Point* without anyone there having the right to change a single comma, they often contain disconcerting howlers. Thus, on 23 December 2010, Bernard-Henri Lévy tackled a subject close to his heart, the 'new red-brown alliance'. In response to an improbable and ultra-marginal 'International court on the Islamization of Europe', projected by the Bloc Identitaire neo-nazis and the former republican leftist militants of Riposte Laïque, he sought to condemn an alliance of extreme-left and extreme-right activists brought together by their hatred of Islam. He saw the threat as serious, since alongside the 'Bloc Identitaire skinheads' stood 'a veteran of *Le Monde diplo*, Bernard Cassen.' It was a heaven-sent opportunity for Bernard-Henri Lévy to maul *Le Monde diplomatique*, the monthly journal of the *altermondialiste* left, doubly at fault in defending positions he has always seen as suspect and in treating him with scant tenderness.

Except for a slight confusion. Bernard Cassen was indeed president of the alterglobalization movement ATTAC and director general of *Le Monde diplomatique* until 2008, but has no connection at all with Riposte Laïque. One of the founder members of Riposte does have the surname Cassen, but his first name is Pierre. Carried away by his theory, Bernard-Henri Lévy had confused the two Cassens. Taken up by the website of the weekly *Les Inrockuptibles* and prompting a libel suit from Bernard Cassen, the error did not seem to embarrass Bernard-Henri Lévy. He placed a perfunctory apology on the *Le Point* website: 'A mistake has found its way into this bloc-notes. Where I list the protagonists of the new axis between Riposte Laïque and Bloc Identitaire, Pierre Cassen should be named and not Bernard Cassen. This erratum will be printed in the next number of *Le Point*. And the sentence stands henceforth corrected here. BHL.'

At least that confusion was rectified. Not all are. Bernard-Henri Lévy had already made the surname mistake a few months earlier. In a bloc-notes dated 1 July 2010, he had savaged the journalist Frédéric Taddéi. Presenter on France Télévisions of the programme 'Ce soir ou jamais', Taddéi was accused by Bernard-Henri Lévy of partiality for a notorious anti-Semite, the humorist Dieudonné. The argumentation was solid, the indignation resounding: 'What would become of us if the public television had not just, in its very great wisdom, extended the bail of this resistant until 2014?' wrote Bernard-Henri Lévy ironically. Except that Frédéric Taddéi's contract with France Télévisions had not been extended until 2014. Bernard-Henri Lévy had manifestly confused him with Rodrigo Taddei: a Brazilian midfield footballer who had in fact had his contract with the Italian club A.S. Roma renewed until 2014.

Any old rubbish, near-misses and promotion of cronies may well supply the ballast for these 'bloc-notes', but their real importance lies in the regular platform they provide for praise, banishment, meddling and politicking.

2 AN IMPRESSIVE NETWORK OF INFLUENCE

The astonishing Areopagus gathered for the party at the Flore in November 2010 shows that Bernard-Henri Lévy is not just the 'Pope of Saint-Germain-des-Prés' and a friend to celebrities. He is also on the best terms with eminences in the political world, where he has been an adviser to politicians of every stripe, ranging from the Socialist Ségolène Royal to the herald of the hard right Nicolas Sarkozy. He is equally at ease with those in the economic world, due in particular to his activities and connections as a prosperous businessman, as a producer of films with or without his wife Arielle Dombasle and an omnipresent pressman. All in all, it is a fine network of influential contacts.

BHL THE PRINCE OF ADVISERS

In 1977 Bernard-Henri Lévy wrote in *Barbarism with a Human Face*: 'It goes without saying that never again will we be counselors to Princes.'[1] Ten years later, in 1987, he said: 'It's a matter of constantly saying no to those who, on the right as on the left, try to recruit us, to enrol us.'[2] For he likes to present himself as a free man, keeping his distance from the political authorities; a militant for causes, not for parties. This freedom distinguishes him, in his own view, from all those intellectuals who at some time in their lives have found themselves 'enrolled' so comprehensively as to cloud their judgment.

Bernard-Henri Lévy seeks to make out that having no connection with a particular party preserves him from a partisan outlook and bondage to the political authorities. In so doing he has invented a new form of 'intellectual': one who, desperate not to be here or there, is everywhere. One who despises the base backroom deals of parties but dines at the chiefs' tables, on the right as on the left.

Bernard-Henri Lévy's friendships sweep generously across the spectrum of French political life. From the Mitterrand Socialist Party – Laurent Fabius, Dominique Strauss-Kahn, Hubert Védrine, Jack Lang, Julien Dray – to figures on the right including Nicolas Sarkozy, Alain Carignon, Édouard Balladur (met through Marie-Hélène de Rothschild, a friend of Arielle Dombasle[3]), Dominique de Villepin, Bruno Le Maire. This list is certainly not exhaustive.

More interesting is the role – the posture – which he adopts in relation to political power. Firstly, Bernard-Henri Lévy is very fond of saying that he hobnobs with politicians. *Le Lys et la Cendre: Journal d'un écrivain au temps de la guerre en Bosnie*, published in 1996, is littered with these name-droppings, not always useful to the narrative, but flattering. The evening before his first departure for Sarajevo in June 1992, he dined at the Opéra comique with Bernadette Chirac, of whom he observes – surprise, surprise – that she knew nothing of the Bosnian situation.[4] At the very end of 1992, he admits to guilty pleasure on seeing François Mitterrand arrive discreetly to see his play *Le jugement dernier* – leading to this very lucid reflection complete with demure scare quotes: 'Is this the way princes "buy" writers?' (p. 114). He has lunch with Balladur (p. 166). Gets a phonecall from Sarkozy who has glimpsed him on the TV news (p. 271). And when invited to dinner by François Léotard, he comes up with a grand observation worthy of Saint-Simon: 'He is in form, Léotard' (p.171).

But the position in which Bernard-Henri Lévy best likes to describe himself is one of shrewd proximity, a knowing, finger-wagging familiarity with the great and good. Thus he can display considerable effrontery: '4 December (1992): Luncheon with Prince Charles. Conversation on Salman Rushdie. He says he's a bad writer – which is his right. But he adds that he's costing the taxpayer a lot – which seems to me a bit rich under the circumstances. This answer, then, which I let out as it came to me: "And the crown of England? You've never wondered what *that* costs the taxpayer, that dear crown of England?"'[5] Poor old Charles did not know who he was dealing with…

Bernard-Henri Lévy has a somewhat romantic conception of politics. The sort of politician he likes is the Great Man. He only likes the ones he sees – or perhaps only sees the ones he likes – and any political sympathies tend to take second place.

One might see that as an attitude softened by time and by repeated contact with the political class. But no: Bernard-Henri Lévy has always been like that. In 1977, aged twenty-nine, he made the peremptory assertion: 'Like all intellectuals I remain, whatever I may say about it, and to the precise extent that I forbid myself to get involved, fascinated by power, by its trappings and its holders.'[6] Hence the fascination with men who embody that power, such as Valéry Giscard d'Estaing, then president of the Republic:

> There is something troubling about that lunar prince, whom all commentators agree in calling fragile and lost in the incoherent imbroglio of his own machinations, but who perhaps conceals the hardest and coldest sort of determination. Is he a sort of Louis XI walking up the Champs-Élysées on foot, as his predecessor rode through Paris on a mule in arrogant defiance of convention and tradition? Or is he on the contrary a sort of Shakespearean monarch, whom a courtier from 600 years ago, an Alexandre Sanguinetti of the time, would have had quietly suffocated with a pillow?'[7]

By chance or coincidence, he was invited to the Élysée by Giscard a few months later. And he went.

Bernard-Henri Lévy likes politicians who have a kingly aura. This vassal's attitude, despite the odd squabble adeptly staged by the writer (on Communist participation in the government in 1981, on the Gulf war in 1991), marked his relationship with François Mitterrand into the early 1990s. He first met Mitterrand in 1971, aged twenty-three, when Mitterrand was first Secretary of the Socialist Party, and became one of his advisers (on the same basis as Jacques Attali) charged with the question of (worker) self-management. He might have felt tempted to enter politics proper. But what was proposed was not appropriate to the scale of his ambitions: 'François Mitterrand had even found me a constituency in Manche – on examination, the lousiest in all the kingdom [*sic*]'.[8] The direct collaboration did not last long, but the relationship endured. Mitterrand was a witness at his second marriage in 1980 and continued throughout the 1980s to make use of the talents of his former, ephemeral adviser. In the pages of the weekly journal *Globe*, for example, where the young author was one of the star writers, and which, on the eve of the 1988 presidential election, served as a conduit for Mitterrand's ideas.

A relationship based on self-interest and reciprocal instrumentalization is characteristic of the relations Bernard-Henri Lévy has maintained with the political world from the beginning. Even when he started to fantasize about himself as minister of foreign affairs.

In February 2002, Bernard-Henri Lévy was asked to lead a mission to Afghanistan by the (right-wing) president of the Republic, Jacques Chirac, and the (left-wing) prime minister Lionel Jospin. The object of the mission was to 'identify the priorities of the new Afghan authorities and define likely areas for French cooperation'.[9] It is quite rare for a mission of this sort to be entrusted to an 'intellectual' (although in 2003, the following year, Régis Debray was given a mission to Haiti). Bernard-Henri Lévy said he would accept this 'great honour'. He wrote in *Le Figaro* at the time: "The idea, in the first place, came from the president of the Republic. But it was very important that it was being co-sponsored, with similar enthusiasm, by the prime minister as well as by Hubert Védrine (the former foreign minister in Jospin's government). Not, it goes without saying, because of my own political choices, but because it was necessary to cut across party divisions. Because the Afghan cause deserved better than to be taken hostage by our national political differences, no matter how legitimate.'[10] And added, to disarm the objections that might be made to this new appointment: 'As to whether there is something paradoxical in the picture of a government entrusting a mission of this sort to a critical (Chirac, Jospin: I owe nothing to either), uncontrollable … even hostile … intellectual, there probably is.'[11]

In fact, ever since the (seemingly false) announcement of the end of the American war in Afghanistan, Bernard-Henri Lévy has been critical of the lack of French involvement in that country's reconstruction effort. And according to a former member of Védrine's staff, those same criticisms were what persuaded Jospin and Chirac to give him the mission: 'It was to make him stop insulting France. And anyway, the president and Lionel Jospin agreed with him … Intellectuals adore missions, and Bernard-Henri Lévy was cock-a-hoop.'[12] The former member of the foreign minister's staff also mentioned 'interests well understood by both sides'.

BHL AND SÉGOLÈNE ROYAL: 'ADVISER TO THE PRINCESS'

THE 'INTELLECTUAL' AND THE 'ALICE IN IDEOLOGICAL WONDERLAND'

Five years later, the 2007 presidential election gave Bernard-Henri Lévy the chance to play a new role: that of campaign director in the shadows for the Socialist candidate Ségolène Royal. From February 2007 he intervened regularly in the media on her behalf. But his role went well beyond public backing. In their book *La Femme fatale*, Ariane Chemin and Raphaëlle Bacqué write: 'How many are aware that since January, the philosopher and the candidate telephoned each other several times a day? Before every TV appearance, she consults him. After each meeting, she calls him. In cases of emergency or major turbulence in the sky over the campaign, he receives her unannounced at home, on the same side of boulevard Saint-Germain and a few doors along from her campaign HQ.'[13] Bernard-Henri Lévy as confidant to Ségolène Royal… surprising to say the least, for when the (party) president of the Poitou-Charentes region was vying with Laurent Fabius and Dominique Strauss-Kahn for investiture as the Socialist Party candidate, it was the latter who enjoyed Bernard-Henri Lévy's favour. He knew him well, saw him regularly in Marrakesh and published him at Grasset: Dominique Strauss-Kahn was the one 'who, I still think, even if it displeases those who have already turned their coats, would have been best at reinventing the left for government', he wrote in *Le Point* in 2006.[14]

When the Socialist militants designated Ségolène Royal, Bernard-Henri Lévy put a brave face on it and supported her, but at arm's length. As he also wrote in the article quoted above: 'I pass over the personality of Ségolène Royal herself, that unstable composite of demagogy and character, of extreme narcissism and genuine political boldness – I pass over the Snow White and White Lady side of this Joan of Arc for the cathode age, this neo-socialist Immaculate Conception.' Even if the rest of the article gives, among many reasons to fear her, some reasons for high hopes of her candidature, it cannot be said to show great enthusiasm.

So something must have happened to make Bernard-Henri Lévy suddenly decide, weeks later, to devote time and energy to a candidature so little suited to him.

> One day I will tell. One day I will explain the reasons (first fundamental, then circumstantial – yes, in that order) why I rallied with such strength, such determination, to her side. One day too I will speak of the good candidate she was, in a campaign strewn with landmines, littered with traps. … One day, but a long time hence, I will tell of the unease that pervaded me on the two or three occasions when I could see that woman's extreme solitude, and her courage in that solitude: her veiled gaze in those moments; her voice becoming flatter, almost toneless.[15]

What the devil could have happened, what could be so extraordinary that we must wait until 'a long time hence' to know what it was? The unbearable suspense! The mystery!

In the meantime, we must make do with what Bernard-Henri Lévy is good enough to share with us. As so often, he says a fair amount. 'That dinner, to begin with, in the restaurant of the Raphaël hotel, where we met for the first time.' Organized by the thriller writer Fred Vargas, who found her friend a little hard on the Socialist candidate, the dinner took place in early 2007. Hardly had it ended when Bernard-Henri Lévy slipped the details, that very day, into *Le Point* and the *Wall Street Journal*. The convivial trio were sitting at the back of that hotel dining room, 'the nearly empty and perhaps too solemn place chosen for our meeting', tucking into 'salad, fillets of sole, a dry white wine'.[16] They prattled about China and argued over the expression 'human rights', preferred by Ségolène Royal to the usual French term 'rights of man'. They were discussing the beaten rivals, Strauss-Kahn and co., but then 'the sommelier pours more wine. I observe she eats and drinks with hearty gusto, like Mitterrand did before he became ill ...'. They were talking about Lionel Jospin when 'a man at a neighbouring table comes over to tell her he admires her. She stands, oddly moved, blushing a deeper pink than her suit, happy, her long, pretty neck rippling with pleasure.' They moved on to the socialist defeat in 2002, then Europe, Iran, the end of (Ségolène's 'trademark') white suits, the suburbs, the role of intellectuals: 'I tell her again why the role of the intellectual is not to join in, rather it is to ask the tough questions, to lay out the issues, to – at the end, as late as possible – finally articulate his opinion. And she listens to me with a humility which belies her image, that of a strict, distant schoolteacher.'

Perhaps the key to the mystery of Bernard-Henri Lévy's rapprochement with Royal can be found here, in the intellectual's impression that the Socialist candidate was listening 'humbly' to his words. In *Ce grand cadavre à la renverse* [*Left in Dark Times: A Stand Against the New Barbarism*, translated by Benjamin Moser, Random House, 2008], published a few months after the Socialist defeat, Bernard-Henri Lévy gives another account of the dinner and describes Royal's 'way, very Alice in ideological Wonderland, of nibbling her ballpoint when she stops taking notes and of looking into her interlocutor's eyes with a touch of effrontery'.[17] We have moved from humility to effrontery, but the set-up is the same: Ségolène Royal listens, Bernard-Henri Lévy talks, and he is satisfied: 'I take my leave, still somewhat puzzled, but with the feeling that people may have been unfair to this woman—myself included.'[18]

'Within a few months,' wrote Bacqué and Chemin in *La Femme fatale*,

> the intellectual has won her friendship. He reads her poetry – not a habit of hers –, sends her the film-maker Josée Dayan to lend a hand with her official campaign ads. 'Only a woman,' he explains, 'knows how to film women.' He understands the fatigues of a campaign, the moments of lassitude, the anxieties, and compliments her gracefully. … One day he allows himself to recommend a chignon hairdo, which she wears the following day in the Europe 1 studio. To his intimates, Bernard-Henri sometimes confides: 'She's very lonely. Emotionally as well.'[19]

Politically, the intellectual's influence is not all that apparent. A few mentions of the Russian journalist Anna Politkovskaya, a reference to the Armenian genocide, commitment on Darfur: here and there in Ségolène Royal's campaign elements crop up that could suggest a Lévy input. All that was in it for Bernard-Henri Lévy was a new function, that of 'adviser to the princess', and the press accounts of it, in which he revelled. And when, in 2010, he made a fool of himself by citing in a book, in all seriousness, a non-existent philosopher (see below, chapter 9), Ségolène Royal was the first to come to his rescue.

ON THE ART OF DEFENDING POLITICAL LEADERS, RIGHT AND LEFT ALIKE

Political friendships have other benefits, for example access to the possibility of influential appointments. Early in 1991 Jack Lang, an old pal from the Mitterrand days and by then minister of culture, appointed Bernard-Henri Lévy chairman of the Commission d'avance sur recettes (which decides, in the Centre national de la cinématographie, on the attribution of advances for film production): a post of some importance, since Bernard-Henri Lévy presided for two years (with the other commission members) over the feasibility of a large part of French cinema output, and also a gateway to a new sphere of cultural life that was to prove useful later, when he wanted to make a film of his own. On 19 June 1993, Jack Lang was a guest at the wedding of Bernard-Henri Lévy and Arielle Dombasle. Another guest was Alain Carignon, newly appointed to head the Culture and Communication ministry in Édouard Balladur's government. Two weeks after the wedding,[20] Carignon appointed Bernard-Henri Lévy to head the supervisory board of the TV station Sept-Arte, a chairmanship he still held in 2011.

It has to be said that Bernard-Henri Lévy is no mere fair-weather friend. In 1996, Carignon, then president of the conseil général d'Isère, was sent to prison for five years with one year's suspended sentence, fined 400,000 francs and excluded from public office for five years: the former minister of communication and mayor of Grenoble had been found guilty of corruption, complicity in and receiving the proceeds of theft of public property, and suborning witnesses. In *La Vendetta française*, the journalist Sophie Coignard recounts that when things became seriously sticky for Carignon, Bernard-Henri Lévy did his best to come to his aid.[21] First off, a petition of support written by Alain-Gérard Slama (a *Figaro* editorialist and diarist at France Culture) was rushed to Bernard-Henri Lévy to rustle up some celebrity signatures. Luc Ferry, then a 'philosopher', editorialist at *Le Point*, chairman of the National Education programming commission and a Grasset author, refused to sign the petition when lobbied by a friend of Bernard-Henri Lévy, and described the anxiety that followed his refusal: 'One way or another, they're going to make me pay.'[22] But it did not prevent him from becoming minister of national education in 2002, and the petition did get a signature from Gérard Depardieu, thanks to Bernard-Henri Lévy. When asked by Sophie Coignard, however, he could no longer recall soliciting those signatures.

When in 2007, after serving his sentence, Alain Carignon stood for election in his first constituency in Isère, voices were raised in protest, notably from within the centre-right UMP. Bernard-Henri Lévy took up his pen to defend him once again. He produced a long text in support that Carignon immediately made public. In substance, the argument rested on four points: 1) Carignon had paid his debt and had every right to hustle for office (perfectly true). 2) He had indeed committed a crime, but he was not the only one (so what?). 3) He at least had not enriched himself personally, what he had done he had done for political reasons (that was indeed the indictment); 4) and then, basically, he and BHL share the same ideas (it would have been worth mentioning that sooner).

The Carignon affair is not an isolated case. Friendship may have been the main factor there, but defending politicians against judges was a constant (also discernible in Bernard-Henri Lévy's relations with the business world, as we will see below). In the New Year wishes for 2004 given in his *Le Point* 'bloc-notes', he wrote of Alain Juppé: 'I form the wish that this man, from whom, as I know very well, everything or nearly everything would separate me the moment he re-entered the game, will not be prevented by judges from resuming his rightful place on the stage.'[23] In 2004, following the conviction of the former prime minister (for illegal use of employees of the City of Paris to do party work) and the subsequent declaration by Jean-Pierre Raffarin, he returned to the matter and gave his thinking in greater detail: 'And who threatens the principle of the separation of powers: a prime minister who says he is "surprised" – his right, after all – by what is effectively an abnormal court decision, or judges apparently drunk with the lust to write, in their own way, in the courts, the political – the institutional – history of their country?'[24]

Bernard-Henri Lévy is always more prompt to take up the defence of political leaders – right and left alike – than to wonder why they have come under attack (except when that useful standby 'populism' can be invoked). And when he opposes them himself (for that can happen), he does so in a way that stays within acceptable limits, as if he saw himself primarily as one of them.

BHL AGAINST, UP CLOSE AGAINST, NICOLAS SARKOZY

In this respect, his relations with President Nicolas Sarkozy, elected in May 2007, are revealing. How should they be read? How can it be that after his involvement in the French intervention in Libya in the spring of 2011, after the phone calls with Sarkozy, after being received by him at the Élysée (see below, chapter 6), he could say to the *Los Angeles Times* journalist who asked if he was playing the role of adviser: 'I'm a political opponent. I didn't vote for him. I won't vote for him.'[25] Here too, as so often, there is the story, and there are the facts.

'A KIND OF FRIENDSHIP'

The story as told by the writer is symptomatic in itself of a particular relation to power and to men of power. The link between Nicolas Sarkozy and Bernard-Henri Lévy is an old one. 'A kind of friendship,' the intellectual has called it.[26] He describes it in the opening pages of *Left in Dark Times*. In 1983, Sarkozy was twenty-seven and had just been elected mayor of the *haut-bourgeois* town of Neuilly. 'Due to family circumstances, I happened to be registered to vote in that suburb of Paris. He had a list drawn up of voters who might be useful to him. And he found that among them was the author of *Barbarism with a Human Face*' (p. xiii). 'Family circumstances' is a splendid euphemism for social determinism, but let that pass. The young mayor of Neuilly invited him to luncheon. 'I immediately took to the very young, incredibly peremptory kid, who during our first meeting was – already! – trying to understand how a man like me could possibly disagree with him' (p. xiii). A friendly relationship was born between the rising star of the

Rassemblement pour la République party and the left-wing intellectual then very close to Mitterrand's Élysée. 'Other lunches followed over the years. Dinners with our wives. Trips to the mountains.'

All very jolly, as recounted by *Paris Match* in March 2011:

> Early in the 1990s Bernard-Henri Lévy, Nicolas Sarkozy and their mutual friend Alain Carignon were skiing at L'Alpe d'Huez. They were at the top of the slope. 'Bernard, if you don't let Jérôme Clément go we'll shove you down the ravine.' The two RPR deputies were preparing their return to power and thinking about the future of the Arte channel. They ribbed the philosopher who was a fervent defender of the man who was then still boss of the Franco-German TV channel. They had a laugh …[27]

Did Jérôme Clément know that his fate was being played out on a chairlift? According to Bernard-Henri Lévy's own account, the friendship became more immediately political: 'I gave him ammunition for a debate with Tariq Ramadan.'[28] That was in 2003 when Sarkozy, then interior minister, agreed to a televised debate with Tariq Ramadan, the Muslim theologian and supposed defender of a fundamentalist Islam. So Bernard-Henri Lévy did perform, or so he boasts, the role of political adviser. But he was also a confidant: 'In a conversation during the Clearstream affair, in which he was accused of financial irregularities, with his face inches from my own, his voice trembling with rage and emotion: "Whoever did this to me, I'll hang him myself – do you hear? Personally hang him! From a butcher's hook!"'[29] Bernard-Henri Lévy seems to hint that he too had heard Sarkozy using the words 'butcher's hook' later to come to public notice as a presidential mannerism. 'A final meeting, in December 2006, in Marrakesh, with [film-maker] Claude Lanzmann, where I tried to explain to Sarkozy that you don't get to be president by spending too much time as France's top cop!' So Bernard-Henri Lévy did give strategic advice to the presidential candidate. A few weeks later came Nicolas Sarkozy's phone call to his friend (see below, chapter 3) soliciting his support for the presidential campaign: 'When are you going to join up with me? When are you going to write me a nice little article?'[30] But the intellectual turned him down and teamed up instead with Ségolène Royal, the Socialist candidate.

The story would have us believe that a break between the two men followed that phone call. But in reality contacts were maintained with the rightist candidate's campaign staff, in particular his diplomatic affairs advisers, Jean-David Levitte and David Martinon, lobbied by Bernard-

Henri Lévy and his entourage on Chechnya and Darfur. In March 2007, at a meeting organized by the collectives Urgence Darfour and SOS Darfour where the former 'New Philosopher' was a star speaker, Sarkozy was represented by a former minister, Nicole Guedj. With the other candidates, he signed the 'act of commitment' to Darfur promoted by the essayist.

After the presidential election the break between the two men seemed complete. In fact, between 2007 and 2010 Bernard-Henri Lévy regularly opposed policies applied by Sarkozy: he was against the notorious 'Dakar speech' of July 2007 (where Sarkozy referred to Africa having not yet walked onto the stage of History), against the proposal to impose DNA tests on would-be immigrants in September 2007, against the reception of Gaddafi at the Élysée in December 2007, against the ultra-security speech at Grenoble in August 2010, against the way the French government treated the Roma in the summer of 2010, and so on (see below, chapter 8). All this enabled Bernard-Henri Lévy to classify himself – and to be classified – as a political opponent. Nevertheless, the contacts continued. So that in 2008, during the Georgia crisis, when Bernard-Henri Lévy flew to the rescue of a small state partially invaded by Russian troops, he was in touch with the French foreign minister Bernard Kouchner and with Jean-David Levitte, who had become chief diplomatic adviser to the Élysée.

Others – mischievous tongues – found less immediately political reasons for the cooling of relations, such as Bernard-Henri Lévy's annoyance at no longer getting invited to the Élysée, after being a visitor since Giscard d'Estaing's presidency. Then there was the president's marriage to Carla Bruni who, it will be recalled, had replaced his daughter Justine Lévy in the affections of her husband Raphaël Enthoven. But those are motives unworthy of a great intellectual. Back to the script, then, which recounts that the two men were reconciled over Libya early in 2011, the urgency of the situation overriding the differences between those notorious political adversaries (see below, chapter 6). In reality it was a bit more complicated.

Firstly, although Bernard-Henri Lévy can say quite harsh things about the policies pursued by the president of the Republic, he usually manages to spare the president himself. The intellectual explained it himself when, some months after Sarkozy's election, a journalist asked why, if he was so critical of his policies, he had continued to see the president for so long. 'Three explanations. One: Sarkozy has changed, he's hardened, I'd never heard him say that before; two, he doesn't really think it completely; three, when what's at stake isn't intolerable – and it wasn't at the time – I have a tendency to separate ideas from personal relations. I'm made that way, it's my failing.'[31] He said it differently, and more clearly, in a long interview with *Marianne* in February 2010:

> Over Sarkozy, I'm prepared for every battle of ideas. I'm dead against his debate on national identity, the policy of his [ministers of the interior and immigration] Besson and Hortefeux, and yesterday that DNA tests business. But I reject attacks on his person or his behaviour. I reject – I find monstrous – the Le Pen side making fun of his grandson's name, Solal. I reject, I find sickening, the references to his so-called vulgarity, his nouveau-riche side, all that nonsense about 'bling'.[32]

As often, Bernard-Henri Lévy defends himself, or in this case Nicolas Sarkozy, by attacking 'anti-Sarkozism', when it takes an ad-hominem form, revives the slumbering spectre of anti-Semitism. A long article given by the writer to the *New York Times*, to mark the appearance of the president's book in English,[33] helps us to understand why nothing in Nicolas Sarkozy's behaviour can shock Bernard-Henri Lévy:

> Much has been said about his postelection escapade in Malta on the ostentatious yacht of the French billionaire Vincent Bolloré, which some have called Sarkozy's first political mistake. What if it was the other way around? What if the gesture was really in keeping with the part of his project that calls for *un*guilting us when it comes to luxury, success and money, even if it means going the whole hog into bad taste and kitsch? What if this young president wanted to reconcile France, if not with actual happiness, then with the signs of happiness that our puritanism, our depression and fear of glitter and success, have long discredited and suppressed?[34]

In fact, Bernard-Henri Lévy is even moved by what the man expresses in his book. 'In "Testimony" we discover the first president of the Republic who dares to write of love, true love, when discussing the tumultuous relationship he has had with Cécilia Sarkozy, the woman who left him, whom he re-conquered, who ended up coming back to him and is now our first lady in the Jackie Kennedy mold. Yes, a president who tells us about the storm and joys of love, about the woman of his life, about desire and suffering. Is it possible that this passion was more important to him in the end than his passion for power?'[35] In the rest of the article Bernard-Henri Lévy nevertheless spells out his differences with the newly-elected president: the wish to have done with May '68, a blinkered attitude to the darker pages of French history, the analysis of the 2005 *banlieue* disturbances ... but the fact of protecting the man himself, the decision to ignore aspects of his mode of action that could become problematic, are constants in his opposition to the president of the Republic.

'PERHAPS I AM TOO INDULGENT WITH NICOLAS SARKOZY'

Linked to this is the habit of attacking Nicolas Sarkozy's advisers, in particular Henri Guaino, instead of the man himself. Bernard-Henri Lévy does not like Guaino, and one can see why. An economist classified as a 'social Gaullist' and a long-time associate of Charles Pasqua, who inspired Chirac's successful 1995 presidential campaign (for which he revived the philosopher Marcel Gauchet's term 'social fracture', which caught on), Guaino wrote some of Sarkozy's most important campaign speeches in 2007. In addition to tapping the great traditional references of the French left (Léon Blum, Jean Jaurès), he had also infected the UMP candidate with notions such as the liquidation of the heritage of May '68, and an end to alleged calls for 'repentance' by critics of France's colonial past. Both themes are attacked explicitly by Bernard-Henri Lévy in the *New York Times* article quoted above. Once Sarkozy had been elected, Guaino became the new president's special adviser and an important figure in the political game. Above all, he was behind the 'Dakar speech' that the president of the Republic delivered on 26 July 2007 in the Senegalese capital, in which he suggested, among other widely-criticized absurdities, that 'the African has not fully entered into History'.

After that, Henri Guaino became Bernard-Henri Lévy's favourite Aunt Sally. On 9 October 2007, on radio France Inter to promote his book *Ce grand cadavre à la renverse*, he made a frontal attack on 'the guy who does Sarkozy's speeches'. After describing Guaino as being influenced by the nationalist thinker Charles Maurras, he went on: 'Guaino is a racist. He's the one, it appears, who wrote the Dakar speech which the president delivered, and he must have seen it for the first time on the plane, because Sarkozy isn't racist, he couldn't think things like that.' The words 'racism' or 'racist' are applied to the presidential adviser three times more in the minute that follows. Interviewed later that day by the news website *Rue89*, Guaino responded by calling Bernard-Henri Lévy a 'pretentious little twat' and added that he 'doesn't love France'.[36] The philosopher stood his ground.[37] Guaino flexed his biceps: 'Had this insult been pronounced in a TV studio, I might not have restricted myself to a verbal response.'[38] The altercation came briefly to public notice and earned Bernard-Henri Lévy some fresh credit as an opponent of note.

Two years later, in September 2009, he returned to the charge against Henri Guaino over the candidature of the Egyptian minister of culture, Farouk Hosni, for the job of UNESCO director general, which Bernard-Henri Lévy had opposed because of Hosni's alleged anti-Semitism. On learning that Guaino probably wrote Farouk Hosni's answer to his accusations,[39] he went back to the fray, flanked by Claude Lanzmann.[40] As usual, there was no mention of Nicolas Sarkozy. But why protect the president of the Republic to such an extent, when he must at least have had knowledge of the work done by his 'special adviser'? Why does one get the impression from reading or hearing Bernard-Henri Lévy that Nicolas Sarkozy had nothing whatever to do with the sadly notorious 'Dakar speech', when it was he who had given it? 'Well, perhaps I'm too indulgent, I don't know, yes, perhaps I'm too indulgent with Nicolas Sarkozy. In any case, I've never heard the Sarkozy I know say things like that and I can't imagine him even thinking them.'[41]

The two also have friends in common, like the businessman Alain Minc, an old crony of Bernard-Henri Lévy and an 'evening visitor' to the president of the Republic. And it was in a sphere where Alain Minc is deeply involved, the heavyweight media, that the real reconciliation took place. A meeting of the supervisory board of the Franco-German channel Arte (which Bernard-Henri Lévy had chaired since 1993, four consecutive mandates), held on 22 June 2009, was supposed to elect a new council. The writer wanted to have a fifth mandate. Jérôme Clément, chairman of the board of Arte France, agreed: the two men were old friends and their partnership at the top of Arte worked well, with Bernard-Henri Lévy leaving Clément a free hand to run the channel, but being able to buttonhole politicians of every stripe when necessary.

Nicolas Sarkozy was not so keen on that fifth term. But Bernard-Henri Lévy was very insistent, as was Jérôme Clément. A meeting was organized at the Élysée and reconciliation doubtless ensued, for Bernard-Henri Lévy ended by getting the president's support. He received a letter personally signed by Nicolas Sarkozy: 'At the end of your term, I would like to thank you for the work you have done and would favour its renewal.'[42] Was that interference by the president in Arte's affairs? The recipient thought not: 'It's a personal letter he addressed to someone he's known for twenty-five years.'[43]

As a matter of fact, during BHL's first mandate in 1993 the then president of the Republic, François Mitterrand, had intervened personally in his support. In any case, on 22 May 2009 Bernard-Henri Lévy was unanimously elected chairman of the council for the fifth time. An interesting side issue arose in March 2011, when Jérôme Clément reached the end of his mandate as chairman of the Arte board and expressed a wish to take over the chairmanship of the supervisory board, under the terms of a sort of private agreement with Bernard-Henri Lévy. The latter denied all knowledge of any such agreement, and Jérôme Clément's connection with Arte ceased to exist. Mutual support has its limits.

Bernard-Henri Lévy is the sort of intellectual politicians dream of. Of course, he will not join any party, and of course he would bridle and kick if harnessed. But let a nice little mission or an interesting post come up, and he will keep mum for a while. Or a dinner will soften him up, for at heart Bernard-Henri Lévy wants to be acknowledged by people whose power he admires; or whose power perhaps seems to him on a level with his own, which sometimes is not far from the truth. The idea of being at the centre of power, the idea of influencing, just a little, the political decision-making process – these are time-honoured fancies of the French-style intellectual. In Bernard-Henri Lévy this tradition takes the form of a taste for the company of government ministers and officials. With a romantic side – 'Bernard loves being the adviser of princes, even when the princes change', his former editor Françoise Verny explained in 1994[44] – and a more utilitarian one, the placing of pen and voice in the service perhaps of an idea, perhaps of his own interests, one can never really tell. As a result, for some people the acronym BHL has become synonymous with a particular mode of relating to government. The historian Emmanuel Le Roy Ladurie, who in 1978 was being fêted jointly by Mitterrand and Giscard, says today that he broke with both men because 'I was on the way to becoming these gentlemen's BHL.'[45]

BHL THE BUSINESSMAN

Bernard-Henri Lévy is rich, very rich, a euro multimillionaire. His books have earned a lot of money and he receives fees and emoluments for each of his jobs (publisher, diarist and the rest). But the bulk of his fortune is inherited.

A RICH HEIR

His father, André Lévy, formed in 1946, in Morocco, a company trading and distributing wood, Becob. In 1997 Becob employed nearly 2,000 staff and was the third biggest distributor in France of building materials, behind Pinault Bois et Matériaux, and the biggest trader in the specific sector of wood panels. André Lévy died on 8 November 1995. In that year, the group's turnover was three billion francs, and attracted covetous eyes. Mme Lévy, André's widow, was elected chairwoman of the board. Bernard-Henri Lévy, as vice-chairman, defended the company's independence: 'I've decided to retain the group's family identity. It's a way of being faithful to my father's memory,' he declared to *Les Échos*.[46]

African timber is exploited under conditions that are often harsh for local workers. While investigating the origins of the Lévy family's wealth, the journalists Nicolas Beau and Olivier Toscer tracked down a study whose findings are appalling.[47] Commissioned by Forest Monitor, a British NGO that seeks to prevent deforestation, the inter-association committee Jeunesse et Environnement examined sites in Gabon. One of them had been exploited for fourteen years (1983–1997) by one of Becob's subsidiaries. The report mentions the absence of drinking water for the workers, who had to walk several kilometres to get supplies from a river, at the risk of infection. It describes insalubrious lodgings, the semi-slave status of the workers and the absence of leisure time, as well as a school whose staff were so incompetent that the children were forced to go to school forty kilometres away. It is true that the study dates from 2000, three years after the Lévy family had sold Becob, but it seems unlikely that conditions would have deteriorated so much in just three years. Guy Carlier, who before becoming a diarist and humorist was finance director of Becob until 1982, put it differently: 'I've never hidden my regrets over having taken part in the deforestation and thus the impoverishment of the African continent, Cameroon and Ivory Coast in particular, while I was finance director of a company specializing in the import of tropical timber.'[48]

In 1997 the Lévy family changed its mind: selling to François Pinault, who already owned 12.5 per cent of Becob shares, now appeared as 'the most natural solution'.[49] It seems that flotation of Becob on the stock market had been considered, as well as a staff buy-out plan, by the minority shareholders (the business banking division of the Crédit agricole bank and the Institut de participation du bois et du meuble). 'But the majority shareholder (Mme Lévy) decided otherwise, probably because of the ties of friendship between André Lévy and François Pinault in their time.'[50] Friendship and interest combined, explicitly in a press release from the Pinault group: 'This acquisition enables the

Pinault-Printemps-Redoute group (PPR) to strengthen its positions in specialist markets closely complementary to those where its subsidiary, Pinault Distribution, is already present as the second largest French distributor of materials for the building trades and the largest importer of softwoods and hardwoods. Between them, Pinault Distribution and Becob achieved a total turnover of 6.5 billion francs in 1996.'[51]

The links between François Pinault and the Lévy family date from the 1970s, with the irresistible rise of the Breton entrepreneur in the timber trade. Links based on mutual respect and interest. André Lévy initially did some favours for Pinault who was embroiled in disputes with the Federation of northern timber importers, of which Bernard-Henri Lévy's father was an influential member. In 1985, when Becob got into difficulties in its turn, Pinault bought 12.6 per cent of the equity without seeking to gain control of the business. So the solution of selling Becob to Pinault might well have seemed 'natural' to the Lévy family. But the people employed by the firm had difficulty understanding the surrender to a direct competitor, and there was talk of 'sit-ins'.[52] The operation resulted in large-scale redundancies, with arbitration tacked on.

On 2 September 1997, Pinault-Printemps-Redoute announced an agreement with Mme André Lévy under which PPR would hold 89.5 per cent of the capital (having bought the 76.9 per cent of Becob owned by the Lévy family). We reckon that the deal would have given Bernard-Henri Lévy, his mother, his brother and his half-sister at least 50 million euros, and more probably something like 100 million euros.

Our calculations run as follows: in January 1998, PPR bought the 10.5 per cent remaining of Becob from IPBM for 28.5 million francs, putting the value of the whole company at about 280 million francs, 210 million for the 79.5 per cent bought from the Lévy family by PPR. With a small stamp premium of the order of 20 per cent for the former majority shareholder, the figure comes to 250 million francs (around 38 million euros). But this is a very low guess, based on the estimate that the transaction valued the company at twice its annual gross turnover, when in this sector a ratio of six or seven times turnover is more usual. So we would doubtless be closer to the truth if we assume the share going to the family was 700 or 800 million francs (more than 100 million euros). Moreover, in PPR's 1996 accounts the value attributed to 12.6 per cent of Becob was 79 million francs, corresponding to a valuation for the whole company of 624 million francs (around 95 million euros). So the estimated sale price of about 700 million francs is coherent and credible. The only flaw: it seems that Becob was carrying a debt of about

354 million francs (53 million euros), which may have been paid as part of the deal. That would reduce the amount received by the Lévy family by almost half. Nevertheless, in *Une imposture française*, Nicolas Beau and Olivier Toscer give the amount as 750 million francs, by virtue of a secret 1992 agreement between André Lévy and François Pinault. The weekly *VSD* suggested a 'value estimated at 120 million euros'[53] and the economic magazine *Challenges* wrote that 'the Lévy family is pocketing, according to our estimates, around 100 million euros.'[54]

It might be thought that here was an unexpected windfall for a man devoted to noble, pro bono activities. This was obviously not the case. In *Une imposture française*, Nicolas Beau and Olivier Toscer show that Bernard-Henri Lévy has been involved in the family firm for years. In his father's lifetime he looked after internal communications, acted as vice-chairman of the supervisory board, regularly took part in strategic meetings and used his political connections to obtain a public loan when the company was in trouble. In 1985–6, the business was close to bankruptcy. According to Beau and Toscer, the relations Bernard-Henri Lévy had at the time with Pierre Bérégovoy, minister of the economy and finance, then with his successor Édouard Balladur after the defeat of the left in the parliamentary elections, enabled Becob to obtain a public loan to keep itself afloat. Bernard-Henri Lévy confirmed it himself to *L'Express* on 10 January 2005: 'I threw in, at the time, not only Mitterrandian power but Chiraquian power! What's more, I admit it.'

A SHREWD COMPANY BOSS

Bernard-Henri Lévy's interest in economic matters seems to go back a long way. In the early 1970s, the employers' federation, the Conseil national du patronat français (CNPF) was trying to convert France to the market economy by targeting schoolchildren. While the minister of national education of the time introduced economics for the two senior school classes, the CNPF organized economic lectures for those classes, with the principals' consent. Referring to one of these, a lecture comparing the evolution of the Japanese and French economies, Michel Frois (then communication adviser for the CNPF president François Ceyrac) recalled in his memoirs 'one of those talented young lecturers who has made his way since, but in a domain other than economics, Bernard-Henri Lévy'.[55] It seems Bernard-Henri Lévy has never really stopped doing economics.

For an individual who claims to know nothing about financial matters, Bernard-Henri Lévy manages his money in a quite complex way. In fact, he runs several financial companies: BPL Finances (a 'business management' firm founded in February 2002), Finadeux (created in 1996), Finatrois (1998) and above all Finaquatre, the most important of these companies. It was set up in July 1999, with capital of 13 million euros,[56] ostensibly to manage Mme Lévy's affairs. Its activity is the 'acquisition, holding and management of transferable securities' (shares and other titles to invested capital). Its stated social purpose: 'All financial and transferable asset operations. Participation and financing of all activities in the artistic and cultural domains. All operations capable of developing the above activities.'[57]

More surprising still, Finaquatre is a limited partnership company. Most individuals who own fortunes of this sort choose less demanding and complex modes of management. For the limited partnership is a rather unusual form of company in the business world, quite complex and rigid (shares cannot be sold or exchanged without the unanimous agreement of all partners, for example), and even more unusual in the context of a family inheritance. 'The commonest current form is the family société à responsabilité limitée (in the UK, "company limited by shares", in the US, "corporation"),' explains a specialist in private asset management.

So Bernard-Henri Lévy is a company boss. The document listing the statutes of Finaquatre also says: 'Monsieur Bernard-Henri Lévy, general partner, undertakes to contribute, for the life of the company, his professional skills, his credit and his help in exploitation of the company. He undertakes to devote his time to the company, but only to the extent of 50 hours per month.'[58] Not enough, obviously, to keep an eye on his accounts …

In 2000, Judge Philippe Courroye opened an enquiry into insider trading, collusion and receiving in the context of a public takeover bid by Carrefour to acquire Promodès in September 1999. A report by the Bourse operations commission was submitted to the Paris public prosecutor's office, accusing the managements of Carrefour and the Société générale, along with several individuals including Bernard-Henri Lévy. Finaquatre had bought just over a thousand Promodès shares very shortly before the merger with Carrefour, an operation returning a paper profit of 164,235 euros.[59] Bernard-Henri Lévy denied having known in advance that the two companies were about to merge: having entrusted the Société générale with a discretionary mandate, he reportedly 'admitted having had knowledge of this financial return only a month after the transaction.'[60] Sometimes he is luckier. According to *VSD*, his lawyers enabled him to recover, in January 2004, '7.5 million euros entrusted to Etna Finances, a financial management company, which was prosecuted for fraud.'[61]

'MY FRIENDSHIP WITH FRANÇOIS PINAULT'

Bernard-Henri Lévy has a fairly unusual lifestyle for a French intellectual. Servants, a chauffeur, houses across the world. But he has acquaintanceships that are just as unusual, which prompt him sometimes to adopt incongruous positions.

In a *Le Point* 'bloc-notes', Bernard-Henri Lévy wrote in 1995:

> Questioned for the *n*th time – today by an American journal – on my friendship with François Pinault. It's funny how this friendship intrigues people and how that type of journalist has difficulty accepting that an intellectual and a boss, a writer and an empire-builder, might have, you know, things to say to each other … I try, in the event, to explain that the builder in question is above all an atypical character, pretty offbeat, of whom I am far from certain, for example, that he is driven by the taste for money or power. And I have the impression of surprising him greatly when I say that yes, of course, we've seen each other recently, that yes, it was perhaps the day, or the day before, or the day after, the famous 'raid on Suez' that seemed to interest him so much;[62] but that no, we didn't exchange a word about that, strange as it might seem, we had only talked, that morning, about the Venice Biennale, the eclipse of the avant-garde, the good quality of the Russian pavilion, and then about a writer, Salman Rushdie, of whom this man who is also, via FNAC, France's biggest bookseller, regularly asks me for news. How idle are the customs officers of culture. How hard it is to get them to accept, basically, that there are everywhere free men, capable at times of being foreign to themselves and their destiny.[63]

Why was 'that type of journalist' so interested in BHL's relations with François Pinault? Perhaps because he was surprised that an 'intellectual' in love with freedom could act with such eagerness and complacency as the relay for a big boss's PR agenda. Perhaps because when the writer describes the tycoon, in a flattering abbreviation, as 'France's biggest bookseller', he is dismissing with a disdainful sweep of the arm all the questions raised by the hegemonic position of FNAC in the French book market. For even if, on that particular morning, Bernard-Henri Lévy and François Pinault really did talk about nothing but 'the Venice

Biennale' and the 'eclipse of the avant-garde', it seems very unlikely that that is always the case. One does not have to be a 'customs officer of culture' to wonder whether the monthly breakfasts the two men took together in the 1990s[64] might not have had some other purpose than swapping news of Salman Rushdie. And was François Pinault thinking of their chats about the Russian pavilion when he said of Bernard-Henri Lévy: 'To me he's a confidant, often an adviser'?[65]

Everything plays out in the exchange of favours. In their biography of François Pinault, Pierre-Angel Gay and Caroline Monnot give an example:

> The Bangladeshi writer Taslima Nasreen was refused a visa by the minister of the interior Charles Pasqua, who said he could not guarantee her safety. BHL called François Pinault, who then decided to assure her protection personally. The affair was sorted out, but the billionaire asked FNAC to help hire the Mutualité auditorium and organize meetings with readers. When Salman Rushdie suffered from excessive restrictions around his visits to Paris, BHL sounded the alarm. The entrepreneur intervened to ensure a less rigid welcome for the writer. He made the bookseller mount a joint operation with the Centre Georges Pompidou and came to listen, in person, to the author of *The Satanic Verses* in the auditorium of the shop in the avenue des Ternes, in Paris.[66]

In 1997, when Bernard-Henri Lévy's film *Le Jour et la Nuit* (of which Pinault was a co-producer) came out, FNAC was mobilized again and organized the sort of promotion operation hitherto reserved for big concerts. On 15 February 1997, there was a reunion of the film crew in the forum of the FNAC-Étoile in Paris, with the event retransmitted to ten other shops, whose equipment was made available to the distributor.

'There is, I believe, a real intellectual complicity between us.'[67] Bernard-Henri Lévy plays the role of François Pinault's intellectual pretext with some application. 'It's undoubtedly François Pinault's little whim to surround himself with a few effervescent and sometimes quite leftist intellectuals,' explained Ambroise Roux, another big boss, to the businessman's biographers.[68] Roux had helped Pinault to join the very restricted club of which he was president, the Association française des entreprises privées, whose members are a few big shots of finance and industry and which campaigns for capitalism across the board, and had also until his death in April 1999 chaired the supervisory board of PPR. So, coming from him, the word 'leftist' pinpoints what Bernard-Henri

Lévy brings to François Pinault: connections in a circle that is not his own, and the official endorsement of the intellectual left in which the former New Philosopher has been one of the most fashionable figures since 1977. Bear in mind, though, that before becoming close to President Jacques Chirac, canny businessman Pinault protected his interests by associating with the socialists after 1981 and with the Giscardians before 1981, after inviting Jean-Marie Le Pen to his manor several times in the days of his youthful Breton ambition.[69]

'JEAN-LUC LAGARDÈRE IS A FRIEND'

But François Pinault is not the only French tycoon cultivated by Bernard-Henri Lévy, who met Jean-Luc Lagardère after the takeover of Hachette by Matra in 1981. Grasset, already owned by Hachette, and where Bernard-Henri Lévy was both an author and a publisher, became Lagardère's property; but relations of a completely different order were soon established between the two men. 'He's my friend. I don't have a lot of friends,' Lagardère said.[70] On his death in March 2003, Bernard-Henri Lévy delivered an emotional eulogy, reprinted in *Récidives*.[71]

Early in November 1996, Jean-Luc Lagardère was investigated for misuse of company property following a complaint from a small shareholder. Bernard-Henri Lévy naturally seized his pen to defend him.

> Jean-Luc Lagardère is a friend and, let's be clear, I have no special competence to assess the legality of the handover of Thomson to someone or other. With that proviso, perhaps I will be allowed an opinion on some features of the present time brought into prominence by this investigation. 1) The hysterical overheating of a discourse that, by gradual slippage resulting from semantic pleasure, transforms any chief executive questioned by a shareholder into a 'fraudster'. 2) The absurdity of a climate in which public opinion, or at best the press, presumes to understand the legitimacy and the value of the services provided by the head of the business in question. 3) The justification, lastly, of that public opinion playing a part, or thinking it does, in the prosecution of one of these 'big guys' whom it would like to use as scapegoats for the evils that it finds so shocking. I have no fears for Lagardère, whom I have seen prevailing over worse adversities than this. But I cannot help wondering about this massacre game for which we see, every week or nearly, a new chosen target. The Lagardère affair is a symptom. The 'destruction of the elites' continues apace.[72]

When, in 2000, Jean-Luc Lagardère was again in legal trouble, Bernard-Henri Lévy again hastened to his embrasure at *Le Point*:

> When we see a captain of industry led before the courts, when we see him required, like Jean-Luc Lagardère this week, to answer for a 'judicial abuse' as astonishing as it is incomprehensible since it seems not to have hampered the enrichment of his company or of the community, there are two possible types of reaction. One is populist clamour, the tarantulas' cry of joy – the relish of those in whom resentment substitutes for politics and who will anyway be satisfied, when the time comes, whatever happens in court, to have witnessed the humiliation of one of our 'high-profile' greats. The other is anxiety, instinctive rejection of show trials, a sort of unease with the idea of this France that, from Fabius with the contaminated blood affair to Strauss-Kahn and now Lagardère, has never stopped punishing its own elites. Circus games. Massacre games. There are, it goes without saying, other types of massacres, dramatic in other ways, that are the regular fare of this diary. But when all is said and done … Is it not on this terrain too that democracies are to be assessed? … Jean-Luc Lagardère is a friend. What I love about him is that great Condottiere, or Cyrano, leading his own life at the rhythm of one of those novels by Paul Féval to whom he might easily, after all, really owe his surname. However I do not believe, in these few lines, that I am yielding to our only passion in common, for the novelistic. The novel is not theatre: to defend the novel against theatre is to plead, Voltaire said, for republican culture …[73]

The 'tarantulas' cry of joy': with a slight effort of imagination, it's a metaphor to be savoured.

So, Lagardère is a 'great Condottiere', a 'Cyrano', a character from 'one of those novels by Paul Féval', is he? Being lettered seems to make proper insight unnecessary. So quick to talk of the need for a 'terrorism of the gaze' when he wants to force the public to look the world's evils in the face, Bernard-Henri Lévy can be a lot less demanding in other contexts.

When Vivendi decided in September 2002 to sell its publishing division (Vivendi Universal Publishing) and the Hachette group considered purchasing it, the world of publishing and culture in general, and on another level the Brussels Commission, were alarmed by the potential consequences of the dominant position in publishing that would result. The Lagardère group was present in EADS (European aeronautics and defence conglomerate and supplier notably of weapons and missiles) and owned Europe 1, but also Hachette, thus a quarter of the French magazine press (including *Elle*, *Télé 7 jours*, *Le Journal du dimanche*) and the management of the Nouvelles Messageries de la presse parisienne (NMPP) which distributes the press throughout France; and above all, through Hachette, a significant share of French publishing (with Calmann-Lévy, Fayard, Grasset, Hachette Éducation, Lattès, le Livre de poche, etc.), book distribution (with Hachette Distribution Services) and bookselling (with Virgin, Le Furet du Nord, etc.). It was feared that a merger of these two publishing giants, giving a single group control over *more than half* of the book market, might threaten creativity and diversity in publishing.

Bernard-Henri Lévy was not worried in the least. Quite the contrary:

> Finally, Hachette. It may seem odd to see Hachette in a bloc-notes mainly devoted to the week's bad trials. But still … what a storm of madness, once again, since Jean-Luc Lagardère declared himself a candidate for the purchase of Vivendi's publishing division! These are people who seem to find nothing amiss in the Larousse and the Robert falling into the hands of big Anglo-Saxon financiers … No one has the right to say that Hachette, which if successful would control one third of French publishing, would be in a position of 'monopoly'. No one has the right to claim that Hachette, which would then be less big than Mondadori in Italy, than Planeta in Spain, than Random House in the US, would establish a system so concentrated as to be 'unique in the world'. And speaking of a publisher who – it goes without saying, but bad faith is such that it is clearly better to say it, and in my own case, testify to it – a publisher who leaves his authors royally in peace, allows them to work as they please and naturally respects their freedom, no one has the right to insinuate that he represents a 'threat' [*sic*] to the freedom to write and to think. So stop it now, this trial by assumption. Stop the disinformation.[74]

Except that in the event, it was he who was spreading disinformation. As Frédéric Dupuis showed in January 2003 in *Enquête de personnalité*,[75] Bernard-Henri Lévy inserted into his plea an argument that had been distributed to Hachette staff, an argument that the author of *L'Éloge des intellectuels* and *Les Aventures de la liberté* used wholesale without checking the smallest of its claims. In an internal memo, the Hachette group had effectively asked its staff to tell anyone who might accuse the group of trying to impose a publishing monopoly that 'the whole of Hachette-VUP would represent a third of the total French-language book market'. And the memo gave some figures, to counter any idea that the conglomerate would constitute an exception: 'Mondadori: 31% in Italy; Random House: 27% in the US; Planeta: 38% in Spain.'

Bernard-Henri Lévy as Hachette's deluxe PR flack? Questioned by Frédéric Dupuis, he replied tersely: 'On that point, I went to see my friend Jean-Luc Lagardère and put to him the same questions that every writer or publisher on the French intellectual scene puts to himself. So since I asked questions and he gave answers, perhaps they were the same as the answers he gave to others. I wouldn't know.'[76] A rather brisk reply, from an 'independent intellectual' who prides himself on skewering the 'bad faith' of those who denounce the risks of publishing concentration, but is content with the unsupported word of a man who is its most prominent advocate.

Of course, friendship counts. But there is something else at work that greatly resembles a class instinct, as if respect for financial power and admiration for big capitalists – which characterize, week in week out, Bernard-Henri Lévy's 'bloc-notes' – were determined by a lifestyle and address book inconsistent with an awareness of the social issues and 'global misery' at our gates. More seriously, these attitudes determine in their turn positions that seem pretty incompatible with independence from the powers that be. Bernard-Henri Lévy goes along with things and, when it is useful to him, lends his voice to help them along.

BHL THE FILM PRODUCER

BHL long ago extended his influence to the film world. In 1991 and 1992, as we know, he ran the Commission d'avance sur recettes, a strategic element in the ecosystem of French cinema. And since 1993 Bernard-Henri Lévy has also been a film producer. 'Les Films du lendemain' is a company set up in August 1993 to produce *Bosna!*, a documentary on the war in Bosnia directed by Bernard-Henri Lévy and Alain Ferrari. A phone call from André Lévy apparently persuaded François Pinault to take half the shares in the company to finance the film. The association still survived in 2005, despite money worries and a fairly opaque style of management. In their investigation *Une imposture française*, Nicolas Beau and Olivier Toscer relate that in 2004 the company was on the verge of bankruptcy. They point out that from 1995 the CEO of Les Films du lendemain, Bernard-Henri Lévy, 'arranged to be reimbursed by the company and thus was paid, in hard cash, half what he claimed by his billionaire associate, for once little concerned with the established control procedures' (p. 118). Beau and Toscer add that the company's management was far from transparent, so far indeed that a statutory auditor's report on the accounts of Les Films du lendemain, dated 11 June 2004, refers to a paucity of detail in the 'information sent regarding the compilation and processing of accounts and financial information'.

Les Films du lendemain has more than twenty films to its credit since 1993. Two are films directly connected with Bernard-Henri Lévy: his first and only fiction feature *Le Jour et la Nuit* (1997) – an aesthetic and commercial disaster to which we will return – and *American Vertigo*, made by Michko Netchak and based on the eponymous book. The company has also made films featuring Arielle Dombasle, some of them very fine: Raoul Ruiz's *Le Temps retrouvé* (1999), *Les Âmes fortes* (2001) by the same director, John Lvoff's *Les Infortunes de la beauté* (1999), an adaptation co-authored by Frédéric Beigbeder, and Alain Robbe-Grillet's *Gradiva* (2006). But Les Films du lendemain has produced some very beautiful films without Arielle Dombasle: Christophe Honoré's *Ma mère* (2004), Pascale Ferran's *Lady Chatterley* (2006), Hou Hsiao-Hsien's *Le Voyage du ballon rouge* (2007), two films by Bertrand Bonello, *De la guerre* (2008) and *L'Apollonide (Souvenirs de la maison close)* (2011), Cédric Kahn's *Les Regrets* (2009) and *L'Arbre et la Forêt* (2010) by Olivier Ducastel and Jacques Martineau. This list, which includes young directors alongside established talents, does indicate an undeniable cinematic taste. Kristina Larsen, the company's director general, runs it day to day, but Bernard-Henri Lévy is never far off, the production company providing him with a lever to act.

Act, for example, to help his friends, as in the case of *Gradiva* by Robbe-Grillet. But also to use cinema to give another shape to his commitments, as he did when he produced *Terre et Cendres* (2005), by the Afghan writer and director Atiq Rahimi, shown at Cannes in the selection entitled 'Un certain regard'. 'I met BHL in Kabul in 2002,' Rahimi recalled, 'where he had been sent by Jospin and Chirac to report on the cultural reconstruction of Afghanistan' (see below, chapter 5). One day he heard that I was starting to make a film. He contacted me and said he absolutely wanted to produce my film.' Which he did: 'I was in talks with another producer. BHL bought the rights.' There were reasons for such imperative necessity. 'He wanted to make the first Franco-Afghan film,' Atiq Rahimi added. 'Through political commitment to this country. Besides, he likes my work. It was shortly after 11 September, and everyone wanted to do something for Afghanistan.'

In fact these films, like most French films, are co-productions. Ten of the Films du lendemain movies were co-produced by Arte France Cinéma among other producers (*Les Âmes fortes*, *Serbie année zéro*, *Ne fais pas ça*, *Ma mère*, *Après l'océan*, *Gradiva*, *Lady Chatterley*, *Le Voyage du ballon rouge*, *Yuki et Nina*, *Love and Bruises*), making Arte's film co-production subsidiary the main partner of Les Films du lendemain. The choice of films to be co-produced by Arte France Cinéma follows an established process, but the final decision falls to a selection committee with ten members, six of whom are permanent. Unsurprisingly, Bernard-Henri Lévy is one of those; and it will be recalled that he is also chairman of Arte's supervisory board. In other words, Bernard-Henri Lévy is one of the people who decide whether Arte – a public channel – puts money into films of which he is a (private, of course) co-producer. Looked at in one way, that could be called a strategic position from which to help ensure that important films are made; from another point of view, it could be called a conflict of interest.

BHL THE NEWSPAPERMAN

Bernard-Henri Lévy relates to the French press on several levels. Whether as a diarist, as we know, a sometime reporter, a shareholder, a supervisory board member, or a friend of the proprietor, he maintains very close relations with the majority of French newspapers.

The weekly *Le Point* has served as a central launch pad for years. Apart from his weekly diary there, his friend and Grasset colleague, Jean-Paul Enthoven, is the paper's literary critic, and another friend, François Pinault, has been its proprietor since 1998. One of the resulting anomalies was that *Le Point* published one of the very few reviews of a book published by Plon in September 2003, *Monsieur Lévy*. The book, a hagiography of Bernard-Henri Lévy, was the work of a young 'writer', Marc Villemain, who subsequently resurfaced as a member of the editorial committee of his master's review, *La Règle du jeu*.

The prestigious daily *Le Monde* has provided Bernard-Henri Lévy with a platform for many years. Until the middle of the last decade, in its literary supplement *Le Monde des livres* (and with the notable exception of a very cool review of *Comédie*), Josyane Savigneau was almost invariably positive in her coverage of Bernard-Henri Lévy's books. More importantly, *Le Monde* was very helpful in 're-legitimizing' Bernard-Henri Lévy after the failure of his film in 1997. The sociologist Erwan Poiraud noted: 'More in tune with the new management at the head of the paper since 1994, Bernard-Henri Lévy's byline appeared on no fewer than thirteen pieces between early January 1998 and early March 2000.'[77] At the top of the paper was one of Bernard-Henri Lévy's oldest friends, Alain Minc, who chaired the Society of readers of *Le Monde* from 1985 to 2003 and its supervisory board from 1994 to 2008, as well as Jean-Marie Colombani, the paper's director, who opened his columns to the writer's major works of reportage. Collaboration on that level lasted until August 2008, when a feature on Georgia – which turned out to be factually wrong in part – infuriated some editorial staff (see below, chapter 5). Since then there have been no big reports by Bernard-Henri Lévy in *Le Monde*. Nevertheless when, in June 2010, the journal was bought by the trio of Matthieu Pigasse, Xavier Niel and Pierre Bergé, Bernard-Henri Lévy was appointed, in all seriousness, to the supervisory board.

Meanwhile the weekly *Journal du dimanche*, owned by the Lagardère group, made itself the outlet for Bernard-Henri Lévy's big reportages (in Israel, in Libya) and the vehicle for his positions on issues of the day. In a different register, *Paris Match* also provides a regular and uniform mouthpiece. Another property of the Lagardère group, the weekly endlessly applauds 'BHL' the celeb, 'BHL' the hellraiser (in Ethiopia in 1986, where he was interviewed by his friend and travelling companion Gilles Hertzog,[78] more recently in Afghanistan,[79] Darfur, Libya ...), or 'BHL' the writer, the magazine systematically devoting an article or interview to the appearance of each book.

The left-wing daily *Libération* remained circumspect in its attitude to the intellectual for a long time. But from 2000 or so, *Libération* has reviewed Bernard-Henri Lévy's books quite positively and even published, fairly regularly, features, interviews and reportages that he has written. With all the ambiguity conferred on him by his numerous hats, he writes sometimes to champion a cause – the defence of Sakineh Mohammadi Ashtiani, the Iranian woman condemned to stoning, or the film director Roman Polanski (see below, chapter 7) – and sometimes as a journalist with a scoop (interview with Sakineh's son and lawyer). The frequent presence of Bernard-Henri Lévy in the newspaper of reference for part of the French left causes much grinding of editorial teeth, but as a number of journalists have said, senior editors are not consulted before publication, and Bernard-Henri Lévy's pieces arrive directly through the management. When he was *Libération*'s publication director, Laurent Joffrin confided one day to one of his journalists: 'Even when he's talking rubbish, BHL creates a buzz.'

And anyway, when, grappling with serious financial problems, the management decided in January 2007 to seek recapitalization to the tune of 15 million euros, Bernard-Henri Lévy became a shareholder. His financial participation is small – he is one of a dozen or so private investors who between them put up 1.2 million euros – but it gained him entry to the paper's supervisory board.

BHL THE NETWORKER

Alert readers will have noticed that many of the names mentioned in this chapter and the preceding one are those of individuals present at the twentieth anniversary party for *La Règle du jeu*: what is commonly called a 'network'. Publishing, the press, politics, finance: Bernard-Henri Lévy cultivates connections in each of these very different, very powerful circles. In addition, he has connections rooted in a specifically French social tradition.

One example is the preparatory classes for the 'grandes écoles' (École normale supérieure, École polytechnique, etc.). These classes are a 'place of memory' according to the historian Pierre Nora, where the French elites meet and get to know their peers in early youth. It was at Louis-le-Grand, a Paris lycée for high-flyers, that Bernard-Henri Lévy went through these classes ('hypokhâgne' and 'khâgne') between 1966 and 1968. His contemporaries there included Alexandre Adler (later an editorialist at *Le Figaro* and Europe 1), Olivier Cohen (founder, in 1991, of les Éditions de l'Olivier), Roger-Pol Droit (*Le Monde* journalist), Jean-Noël Pancrazi (writer), Jean-Marie Guéhenno (diplomat), Pierre Jacob (brother of Odile Jacob, who runs the eponymous publishing firm), Yann Moulier-Boutang (economist), and many more. At that lycée he also met Alain Minc, who was in 'upper maths', and to whom he has remained close. Old relationships, then, rather faded at times, but some of which can be reactivated when necessary.

Then there is the geographical question. France is a small country, centred on Paris. And in Paris, some districts count more than others. 'I live in an extremely enclosed, extremely limited space, a tiny village inside the village of Saint-Germain-des-Prés,' Bernard-Henri Lévy explained in 1977.[80] In fact, the space referred to is really a small world: small geographically, small in the sociological sense too. A world where publishers, authors, journalists, politicians, actors, directors and so on bump into one another daily. And in many cases they have been bumping into one another there for years, ever since school or university: École normale supérieure, Sciences Po Paris, the Sorbonne. Bernard-Henri Lévy has haunted the quartier for more than forty years now, from his flat in the boulevard Saint-Germain to the La Hune bookshop, from the Café de Flore to Éditions Grasset. Before he started to criss-cross the world, these were the streets he patrolled. How does all this really work?

For a partial answer, the case of BHL's film *Le Jour et la Nuit*, and its promotion early in 1997, is instructive in several ways. For a start, that cinematographic UFO benefited, even before it appeared, from an unusual level of media coverage. Then, once the film had bombed, the disproportionate nature of the advance eulogies cruelly showed up the feudal dependencies underlying them. The heavy advance promotion did nothing to deter, and may even help explain, the violence of the criticism that followed the film's public release, and, finally, the cinema-going public was largely unmoved by all the ballyhoo.

The aim of the campaign had been to cover all fronts.[81] In the written press alone, there appeared a number of articles and four cover stories in weeklies: *Paris Match*,[82] *Le Figaro Magazine*,[83] *Le Point*,[84] and *L'Évènement du jeudi*.[85] A few background details will help explain this list. Bernard-Henri Lévy was on good terms with the boss of *Paris Match* at the time, Roger Thérond, whom he had defended when Thérond was attacked for publishing photos of Mitterrand on his deathbed. He also had links with Jean-Luc Lagardère, who was then part-owner of *Paris Match*. As for *L'Évènement du jeudi*, the journal's management had apparently decided to 'go big' on the film,[86] in hopes that Bernard-Henri Lévy's ties with Lagardère might help the recapitalization of the magazine, which was seeking a buyer at the time (sure enough, *L'Évènement du jeudi* was bought in May 1998 by Jean-Luc Lagardère, with Georges-Marc Benamou, an old friend of Bernard-Henri Lévy, put in charge; but it is not certain that the connection was one of cause and effect).

For *L'Évènement du jeudi*, 'going big' meant the front cover, a shoot 'notebook', an interview with the director, a sidebar on Maurice Jarre who composed the music ('I was just reading one of his books when he phoned me'), and 'For and Against' opinions. The 'For' spokesman, incidentally, was Yann Moix who, as we recall, had his first text published by Bernard-Henri Lévy in *La Règle du jeu* and his first novel by Grasset (and who in 2003 published in *La Règle du jeu* a shoot feature on his own film *Podium* … a quid pro quo[87]). As for *Le Point*, Bernard-Henri Lévy has published his weekly 'bloc-notes' there since 1993, Jean-Paul Enthoven, his old friend and co-scriptwriter on the film, was adviser to the editorial management and Pierre Billard, its film critic, wrote the film's press pack …

An original aspect of this massive promotion effort was the publication of a whole series of shoot diaries: Françoise Giroud in *Le Nouvel Observateur* of 20 June 1996 (six months before the film's general release); Virginie Lewis in *L'Évènement du jeudi* of 13 February 1997, Daniel Toscan du Plantier in the *Figaro Magazine* of 1 February, and Karl Zéro in *Le Journal du dimanche* of 15 February. Bernard-Henri Lévy himself produced two, the first in *L'Express* of 13 February, the second in *Télé 7 jours* the following week (*Le Journal du dimanche* and *Télé 7 jours* belong to the Hachette group, which owns Bernard-Henri Lévy's publisher Grasset). A similarly intense summary can be given for radio and TV coverage.[88]

Until the film appeared, the critics were almost unanimously gushing. To quote a couple of pieces of studied bravura from *L'Évènement du jeudi* of 13 February, Virginie Lewis wrote in her shoot notebook:

> BHL knows [the scene] is important, decisive even. After mature reflection, he understands that it would be unthinkable to confide the shooting to the steady-cam operator, however brilliant he may be. So BHL shoulders the 40kg of equipment and starts on the takes. Once, twice … five times and more to get a feel for the shot, to frame it just right. When he finishes the last take he's streaming with sweat, exhausted, and still doesn't stop until he feels that it's 'in the can', crippled with aching muscles.

A success, according to Yann Moix in the same issue, praising *Le Jour et la Nuit* as a 'magnificent tribute to cinema itself'.

Soon after the film's release, some of the reviews were ferocious. Gérard Lefort wrote a hilarious piece in *Libération* on 'BHL pedalling through guacamole'. And several journals, including *Le Monde*, *Le Nouvel Observateur* and *Libération*, exposed the underside of a promotion campaign that excluded movie critics from the previews, apart from representatives of a few carefully chosen journals. The film was cold-shouldered by the public: eight weeks after its release, only 73,147 seats had been sold in France.[89] In a desperate rearguard effort, a few friends, Françoise Giroud among them, took up their pens to denounce a 'cabal' against Bernard-Henri Lévy.[90]

But enough of this banter. We must now examine methodically what is supposed to justify BHL's unarguable notoriety, over and above his multiple networks of influence: his 'oeuvre' as a writer.

3 IN SEARCH OF THE LOST OEUVRE

'You can write this down: I consider myself the best writer and most gifted essayist of my generation,' Bernard-Henri Lévy told Le Monde *in 1985.*[1] *Nearly twenty-five years later, the tone has changed but the message is the same, as modest as ever when, after listing his 'masters' – 'Malraux, Hemingway, Sartre, so many others …' – he adds: 'I have the feeling, nowadays, of not being completely unworthy of them.'*[2]

However, a closer reading of the catalogue of his personal output reveals that nothing much has endured, and over the years most of his texts have fallen into oblivion. Nevertheless, quite apart from the loud media clamour that accompanies each publication, there does exist a real demand for this type of output. In that context, the only form of criticism that hits home is ridicule: a custard pie in the face.

THE CATALOGUE

In a thirty-eight year career between 1973 and 2011, Bernard-Henri Lévy published more than thirty-five books. From this impressive total, however, we can subtract no fewer than eleven works consisting entirely of rehashed or reprinted articles, and texts already published elsewhere. With this padding eliminated, we can examine the 'essential' work, a most remarkable diversity of (usually) successful writings, in which it is nevertheless hard to identify the decisive contributions to thought.

ESSAYS

Bangla-Desh, nationalisme dans la révolution (Maspero, 1973), reprinted under the title *Les Indes rouges* (Livre de poche, 1985): aged twenty-five, just back from several months spent between India and the insurrectional East Bengal/Bangladesh of 1971, Bernard-Henri Lévy published his first book. The style is very different from his present one: austere, technical, infected with Maoist jargon and today unreadable, it is an essay that attempts to convey the reasons for the failure of the Bengali 'revolution'. Only the first three phrases give a hint of Bernard-Henri Lévy's stylistic future: 'Over there. Very far away. A lost corner of Asia.'[3] To the obvious question – why this book was reprinted twelve years later – the answer, as so often, has to do with the construction of his own legend.

La Barbarie à visage humain (Grasset, 1977; *Barbarism with a Human Face*, translated by George Holoch, Harper and Row, New York, 1979): Bernard-Henri Lévy attempting to do philosophy (see below, chapter 4).

Le Testament de Dieu (Grasset, 1979): an apologia for monotheism as sole guarantor of democracy and freedom. In it, Bernard-Henri Lévy bewails the end of democracy: 'I believe in the return of crude hatreds. A crisis? No, the word is too feeble to express the coming disorder … I believe in a proliferation of wars which will all be civil wars'. And he states the 'ten commandments of fundamentalism'. For Bernard-Henri Lévy is a prophet too.

'I live in a strange country, extraordinarily unknown, encircled by a high rampart of mists, fables and mirages,'[4] reads the opening sentence of *L'Idéologie française* (Grasset, 1981). No, Bernard-Henri Lévy is not posing as Bilbo the Hobbit: the sentence is an image and the country is France. In his fourth book, Bernard-Henri Lévy addresses 'French-style fascism' and questions – not unfairly – the somewhat sanitized reading of the behaviour of the French, intellectuals in particular, before and during the Second World War. But, carried away by enthusiasm, he denounces a France described as historically anti-Semitic, the crucible of a typically French fascism whose premises can be discerned in the discourse of André Gide, Charles Péguy, Paul Morand, Louis Aragon, Emmanuel Mounier (founder of *Esprit*), the Communist Party and the École des cadres at Uriage (founded by the Vichy regime to train administrators, and operating between 1940 and 1942), among plenty more.

Historians criticized the book violently for its crudely formulated accusations and sloppy research, but it made a big splash. It saw the inauguration of a technique that was to work perfectly for nearly thirty years: when presented with facts that invalidated his claims or allegations, Bernard-Henri Lévy – and his chorus of press admirers with him – would call that a 'polemic'. It also saw the first appearance of BHL the accuser, the nation's conscience. The historian of fascism Pierre Milza called it a book of 'extreme confusionism, governed exclusively by the law of strange combinations'.[5] The political scientist Raymond Aron savaged the over-simplification of its arguments and a number of hasty denunciations worthy of a 'literary-café Fouquier-Tinville'.[6] Ignoring the scholarly critiques that since that time have skewered the book with great exactness, BHL trumpeted eighteen years later, in the introduction to a reprint: 'I persist and I sign'.[7] And when pondering, in *La Guerre en philosophie* (Grasset, 2010), on the concepts that he will bequeath to History, he concludes that some of them are contained in *L'Idéologie française* (see below, chapter 9).

Éloge des intellectuels (Grasset, 1987): in this book Bernard-Henri Lévy complains, with a straight face, about the advance of flabby thinking, the lowbrow consensus, and culture as spectacle.

> Intellectuals have lived through dark periods. But they had never before experienced such a feeling of unreality. The most obvious sign of the malaise is, of course, the singular favour enjoyed simultaneously by the famous 'new stars' of enterprise, music or the world of show business ... Is it not somewhat ludicrous, in the France of Voltaire and Zola, to see the singer Renaud replacing Foucault, the businessman Tapie suggesting a meaning to life, or the generous but simple initiative of the 'restos du cœur'[8] becoming the prototype for future commitments?

Like something in a dream, Bernard-Henri Lévy denounces an evil of which he is himself the most blatant symptom, hand in hand with his pal Alain Finkielkraut – who noted virtually the same things in *La Défaite de la pensée*[9] – and then, with a characteristic embrace of self-sacrifice, proceeds to offer his services to reason, truth and complexity ...

La Pureté dangereuse (Grasset, 1994): secretly fearing perhaps that he may not be one himself, Bernard-Henri Lévy spends a great deal of time wondering what an intellectual is. According to this new essay, the intellectual ought to be 'a warlike man' committed to answering only these questions: 'Where is the enemy? Who is he? What forces does he have? How can he be vanquished?' Bernard-Henri Lévy knows where the enemy is: he resides in the idea of 'purity' at work in the nationalism of the new republics of the former USSR, in Islamist fundamentalism, in the Rwandan genocide, in former Yugoslavia, and so on (see below, chapter 5).

Ce grand cadavre à la renverse (Grasset, 2007; *Left in Dark Times: A Stand Against the New Barbarism*, Random House, 2008). Coming out a few months after the presidential campaign culminating in Nicolas

Sarkozy's victory, this book can be read (as so often) on two levels: as a reflection on the failures and dead ends of the French left (the 'great recumbent corpse' of the title, an expression lifted from Sartre's preface to Paul Nizan's *Aden Arabie*), and as an autobiography of Bernard-Henri Lévy as the covert director of the campaign by the unsuccessful Socialist Party candidate, Ségolène Royal (see above, chapter 2). The idea being put forward is that of a 'modern' – i.e., liberal – social democratic left (see below, chapter 8). But apart from a few staged debates, the thesis did not provoke much discussion. What small effect the book had was caused by its introduction, in which Bernard-Henri Lévy mentioned a telephone call from Nicolas Sarkozy, then still the candidate of the right in the presidential election: 'So, when are you going to write me a nice little article?' Bernard would not write it. For Bernard was 'left-wing' (see above, chapter 2).

De la guerre en philosophie (Grasset, 2010): Bernard-Henri Lévy's second attempt at doing philosophy. It was not a success (see below, chapters 4 and 8).

TWO TRAVEL BOOKS

Impressions d'Asie (Le Chêne/Grasset, 1985), or Bernard-Henri Lévy in the Lands of the Rising Sun. A text that contains one of his greatest aphorisms: 'The traveller of the future will be Kantian or will not be.' And photos: Bernard-Henri Lévy on a path in a Tokyo cemetery, Bernard-Henri Lévy in front of the railings of a Canton park, Bernard-Henri Lévy sitting in a rickshaw, Bernard-Henri Lévy in a 'secret garden' in Seoul ... the photographer's name, Guy Bouchet, does not appear on the cover. It seems he may have complained a bit too much about Bernard-Henri Lévy's insistence on being in every frame.[10]

American Vertigo: Traveling America in the Footsteps of Tocqueville (translated by Charlotte Mandell, Random House, 2006; Grasset, 2006). *The Atlantic Monthly* had the idea of sending Bernard-Henri Lévy across America in the footsteps of Alexis de Tocqueville. This produced a long reportage published in the magazine in May 2005, followed by this fat book. Bernard-Henri Lévy sees some country: Newport, New York, Los Angeles, Miami, Salt Lake City ... Bernard-Henri Lévy addresses the big issues: religion, democracy, justice, communities. Bernard-Henri Lévy meets some people: Barack Obama – presidential material;[11] Sharon Stone – 'she uncroses her legs', as is her wont; 'she recrosses them', phew! (p. 98); Hillary Clinton, Warren Beatty and others; but a miner's daughter in Colorado is just called 'Tracy', without the right to a surname. Bernard-Henri Lévy comes up with aperçus that are sometimes astonishingly perceptive. 'The truth is that this man is a child,' he says of George W. Bush, before adding, with even greater perspicacity: 'This child is a crafty child' (p. 52). We learn, too, that the neoconservatives are not imbeciles. The book consists of a long succession of very short chapters, each resembling a brand name, every one a cliché. Glyn Morgan, professor of political science at Harvard, puts it differently: 'His description of America has something to arouse admiration, in that the essence might be found in the pages of a travel magazine.'[12] Anatol Lieven, the journalist and historian, adds that 'one hopes however that no travel guide will ever be written in language as pretentious and boring as Mr Lévy's.'[13]

NOVELS

Bernard-Henri Lévy has written two novels, *Le Diable en tête* (Grasset, 1984) and *Les Derniers jours de Charles Baudelaire* (Grasset, 1988). The first tells the story of Benjamin, son of a French collaborator father condemned to death after the Liberation, who sinks into extreme-left terrorism before ending his life in Jerusalem, and is meant to be a generational fresco: the 1950s, May '68, bombings in Rome and Beirut … a bonsai *La Nausée* from Bernard-Henri Lévy as a baby Sartre.

The second is a long digression around the last lucid moments of Charles Baudelaire, exiled in Brussels.

The two texts apply the same narrative format to very different subjects: a succession of testimonies, private diary extracts, exchanges of letters … Bernard-Henri Lévy had found his 'schtick'. Why did he stop in such full spate? He could have written plenty more like that.

They were very well received by the press. Both novels won prizes (the Prix Médicis for the first, the Interallié for the second). *Vogue Hommes* wondered: 'Is Bernard-Henri Lévy a genius?'[14]

A STAGE PLAY

Le Jugement dernier (Grasset, 1992), was produced for the theatre by Jean-Louis Martinelli. The play, which aims to transform the history of the twentieth century into a show, breaks down into 'scenes' with metaphysical pretensions: Act I. On communism. Act II. On the Holocaust. Act III. On the apprenticeship of barbarism …

The piece is awfully heavy, partly because Bernard-Henri Lévy is trying so hard to be funny: 'Those Red Guards who wash whiter than white' is easily the best joke in the play.

INTERVIEWS AND DIALOGUES

Les Hommes et les femmes (Olivier Orban, 1993). Bernard-Henri Lévy also has things to say about love. A book of interviews with the journalist and former minister Françoise Giroud is devoted to this subject. Bernard-Henri Lévy's thought can be sampled here in all its infinite variety:

- aphoristic: 'There is always something a little sad about a pretty woman with dark-ringed eyes and greying hair' (p. 214);
- ethnological: 'A beauty is practised. She is wily, well versed in the game. She knows both the tricks and the rituals of seduction. And you know very quickly, in the end, whether it is going to happen or not. While a plain woman … She is so anxious, the plain one … So amazed by what is happening to her [being pulled by Bernard-Henri Lévy] … At first she's suspicious … Incredulous … She tells herself that there is something behind it, that one wants to make a fool of her … And then later, when she has understood, when she knows that you are serious and that the game is too, she discovers that she knows neither its rules nor its passwords …' (p. 48);
- visionary: 'Well, I say that the wheel has turned full circle and it's as if our societies, tired of sex and its new plagues, were in the process of falling back on the safe values of feelings' (p. 70);
- 'progressive': 'The woman who takes charge of herself and, as you were saying, takes charge of her life. The dynamic woman. The woman of power. The kind of woman you see in the morning, at crack of dawn, having a business breakfast in the dining room of a big hotel. The kind who smokes cigars. The kind who plays golf. The man-woman, in a word, who has copied from men their least attractive traits. I know, in a way, that that is 'progress'. … But it is not, in my view, the most becoming role for a pretty woman. And I feel a certain unease, to tell the truth, when I see them like that, half asleep, hastily made up, hair a bit awry, lipstick badly applied, talking business with a banker or media boss …' (p. 209).

Ennemis publics (Flammarion/Grasset, 2008; *Public Enemies*, trans. M. Frendo and F. Wynne, Random House, New York [paperback], 2011). Dining out together one evening, Michel Houellebecq and Bernard-Henri Lévy had a bright idea: 'Suppose we sent each other some emails, and then published them?' That produced this epistolary book, launched with much mysterious ballyhoo and turning out a flop (see below).

However, it starts well, with Houellebecq using the first message to say what he thought the two men had in common: 'We are both rather contemptible individuals.'[15] Somewhat taken aback by this opening, Bernard-Henri Lévy dithers between three possible positions. The first:

> Well done. You've said it all. You're mediocre, I'm a nonentity, and in our heads there's nothing but a resounding void. We both have a taste for play-acting, we could even be called impostors. For thirty years I've been wondering how I've managed to take people in. For thirty years, tired of waiting for the right reader to come along and unmask me, I've been stepping up my lame, dull, half-hearted self-criticisms. … You lay down your cards and I'll lay down mine. What a relief! (p. 5)

The second: 'I could go out of my way to explain that there are *also* happy beings, successful works, lives more harmonious than the killjoys who detest us appear to believe. I would take the villain's role' (p. 6). And the third:

> Why is there so much hatred? Where does it come from? And why, when the targets are writers, is it so extreme in its tone and virulence? Look at yourself. Look at me. And there are other, more serious cases: Sartre, who was spat on by his contemporaries; Cocteau, who could never watch a film to the end because there was always someone waiting to take a crack at him; Pound in his cage; Camus in his box; Baudelaire describing in a tremendous letter how the 'human race' is in league against him. And the list goes on. Indeed we would have to look at the whole history of literature (p. 6).

Of these three possible attitudes (lucid examination, defence of joyous liberty and inscription in the history of literature alongside Sartre, Cocteau, Pound, Camus and Baudelaire), it is not difficult to guess which will be chosen. In a way that is the problem with this book, each man pursuing the construction of his own legend: Houellebecq, more shrewdly, as a mediocrity with hidden depths, and Bernard-Henri Lévy as a misunderstood genius.

A DIARY

Le Lys et la Cendre: Journal d'un écrivain au temps de la guerre en Bosnie (Grasset, 1996): a chronicle of the author's commitment to the Bosnian cause. He set himself a rule for it: 'To avoid the personal; to erase, by design, everything that might have to do with other aspects of the world or of myself; to keep only, in a word, that which arose directly or indirectly from the Bosnian situation.'[16] This resolve soon flags, as in: 'I do not believe I am particularly "generous". But nor am I "envious", that is for sure. I do not "have it in for" my adversaries. Better than that: how many times have I not caught myself feeling admiration for my worst enemies, even to the point of admitting that they are right, against myself, in my heart of hearts? Masochism? No. Pride. I am one of those whom a *sin* (in this case, pride) protects against the ravages of a *vice* (in this case, vanity and envy)' (p. 79).

SOME FILMS

Les Aventures de la liberté. Une histoire subjective des intellectuels: a series of four films broadcast in March and April 1991 on Antenne 2.[17] As it is a subjective history, there is a great deal of Bernard-Henri Lévy in it, whether holding forth to camera on the history of ideas, or strolling through Leningrad, Berlin, Sigmaringen, the tunnels under the Chemin des Dames, and Nuremberg. The conclusion takes the form of a consecration. The voiceover commentary of the last episode – spoken by Bernard-Henri Lévy himself – ends with these words: 'Faced with the return of nations, faced with the rise of fundamentalisms, populisms and other tribalisms, who knows that we should not look forward to to one last metamorphosis that might give the intellectual a face and a voice.'[18] And whose face then appears on the screen? That of Bernard-Henri Lévy …

Nothing is wasted in a well-run small business, and Bernard-Henri Lévy brought out a book at the same time, entitled *Les Aventures de la liberté* (Grasset, 1991), in which all was explained: 'In the end, I would like the book to be read as an exploration of my own convictions as I survey the lives of other people. Equally, it is an attempt to sketch in the genealogies of those who have made me what I am, however unsavoury they may have been. It is unfortunate if my methodology offends those who champion a more "objective" approach to history.'[19] So in this history of ideas in the twentieth century there is nothing on Deleuze and not a line on Derrida; but a whole chapter devoted to Jean-Paul Enthoven (a friend, and also the father of the future ex-husband of BHL's daughter) and another to Philippe Sollers (a strategic friend in the occupation of fields).

Un jour dans la mort de Sarajevo (documentary broadcast on FR3 in December 1992), and *Bosna!* (1994): see below, chapter 6.

Le Jour et la Nuit (1997): this is Bernard-Henri Lévy's only fiction film to date, with a script co-written by Jean-Paul Enthoven. A movie producer (played by the TV presenter Karl Zéro) and his starlet (Arielle Dombasle) travel to the Mexican retreat of a famous writer at the end of his career (Alain Delon) to persuade him to adapt his early novels for the cinema. Against a background of peasant revolt, the household idles along in boredom and humidity. The writer's wife (Marianne Denicourt) spends her time having sex with a young vulcanologist who is helping the revolutionaries (the film-maker Xavier Beauvois), while the writer goes ballooning under the protective gaze of a mysterious woman (Lauren Bacall). An hour and a half later, the spectator regains consciousness. The starlet has been killed by unshaven Mexican rebels. This is a pity. She had restored the writer's will to live, by giving him back his taste for love (conveyed to us in an unforgettable scene in silhouette during which Arielle Dombasle, naked, with erect nipples, shakes her hair about in a conscientious simulation of ecstasy). Disheartened, the writer climbs back into his balloon, which rises very rapidly before exploding in a small fart.

The film was a mess. And it was a commercial failure, inspiring in Bernard-Henri Lévy the need to write another book, entitled *Comédie*.

A SATIRICAL INTROSPECTION

Comédie (Grasset, 1997) is meant to be an inquest on the failure of *Le Jour et la Nuit*, a sort of self-critical excursion through the wounded artist's ego. For 'in one word or a hundred, it is high time for me to talk about myself, really about myself.'[20] So, Bernard-Henri Lévy talks about himself. And his failure. At no time does he consider the possibility that the film might be bad. No, the problem is the 'cabal' (p. 53) which has set on him: 'All of them, on the same day, the word had been spread, the sniggers, the jeers, the fake agency reports from Berlin, the pack of photographers like a firing squad, the journalists saying they had been forbidden to see the film and trashing it on the same page, this business of newspaper editors, is it my fault if I have two friends – just two, gentlemen of the jury – who by dint of hard work, with some help from chance, have ended up running newspapers?' (pp. 51–2).

A 'PHILOSOPHICAL STUDY'

Le siècle de Sartre (Grasset, 2000; *Sartre, the Philosopher of the Twentieth Century*, Polity Press, Cambridge, 2003) represents a return to 'serious' work, in the form of an intellectual biography of Jean-Paul Sartre.

Setting aside the book's opportunist timing (the twentieth anniversary of the philosopher's death), the one or two moments when Bernard-Henri Lévy leans against the great man to justify himself ('That Sartre wasn't a writer any more, he was a label', p. 22), and the excursions into meaningless lyricism ('I like, not exactly this longing for recognition, but this astral relation to light', p. 26), this is undoubtedly the least bad of his books.

NOTES OF A WAR REPORTER

'What's the good of philosophy in the outskirts of Bogotá and Bujumbura?', wonders Bernard-Henri Lévy on the dust jacket of his *Réflexions sur la guerre, le mal et la fin de l'Histoire*, published at the end of 2001, after 11 September.[21] Well, clearly it's good for generating a 350-page book based on his feature articles for *Le Monde* on 'forgotten wars', adorned with innumerable 'reflections' on essential subjects: 'Autobiography: what I'm doing in this hell' (p. 132), 'Why I don't like myself liking Drieu' (p. 141), 'BH judges BHL' (p. 275), 'I remember Commander Massoud' (p. 318) … In the round, the book supplies a sort of *Trucker's Guide* to philosophy, punctuated with a few thoughts thrown in at random: 'The history of philosophy is dead in Burundi' (p. 252), 'What those in mourning bewail' (p. 270), 'Arendt, Sarajevo: what does it mean to be damned?' (p. 169), 'Debray, Kojève and the price of blood' (p. 174), 'What is a Wreck?' (p. 248) … And it makes a good export product, since this is the book that Bernard-Henri Lévy's US publisher, Melville House, first wanted to publish, before discovering the rich *Pearl* seam (see below, chapter 6). *War, Evil and the End of History* appeared in the US on 1 May 2004, with a handsome contemporary-retro dust jacket dotted with little Kalashnikovs.[22] As the author himself puts it so well: a philosophy is a 'style' before being a 'system'.[23]

COLLECTED ARTICLES

Under the title *Questions de principe*, Bernard-Henri Lévy published, between 1983 and 2010, eleven volumes containing pieces of all sorts: the 'bloc-notes' from *Le Point*, articles published in other French and foreign journals, interviews given to the press (sometimes called 'conversations'[24]), letters and emails. The prevailing 'principle' here is recycling, the goal being the publication of every word Bernard-Henri Lévy has written. Subjects of all kinds are addressed, haphazardly. When journalists from the women's magazine *Elle* asked him in May 2004: 'You touch on philosophy, Israel, large-scale reportage, literature, film ... Why this eclecticism?' he replied grandly: 'Because that's how I am. Free.'[25]

A REPORT

Rapport au président de la République et au Premier ministre sur la participation de la France à la reconstruction de l'Afghanistan (Grasset/La Documentation française, 2002): a botched contribution to French diplomacy and the resurrection of Afghanistan (see chapters 2 and 5).

A 'NOVELIZED INVESTIGATION'

Qui a tué Daniel Pearl? (Grasset, 2003; *Who Killed Daniel Pearl?*, Melville House, New York, 2003): a mixture of fiction and investigative journalism, following the tracks of the American journalist Daniel Pearl, kidnapped and murdered in Pakistan by terrorists linked to Al Qaeda in January 2002. As well as being crippled by errors and inaccuracies, the text is terribly complacent and Manichaean (see below, chapter 5).

Finally, let us mention some art books brought out by Éditions de la Différence: *Frank Stella* (1989), *César* (1990), *Piero della Francesca* (1992) and *Piet Mondrian* (1992).

USING 'BHL': SUPPLY AND DEMAND

His associations with men of power in politics or the media, his friendships, sincere or self-interested, his professional relationships, in short his 'network', are not sufficient to explain Bernard-Henri Lévy's role and standing in the French landscape. Alongside the energetic relational activity which is almost a profession in itself, Bernard-Henri Lévy offers a supply which meets a demand.

What BHL supplies is books that promote illusion, positions and commitments on issues of the day, projected through a 'multifaceted' communications strategy targeting fragmented audiences. For tabloid readers, the Hollywood fantasy of a star's lifestyle; for the readership of *Le Monde*, special reports (on Algeria, Massoud, Malraux, German reunification, human rights, Islam, etc.); for the chat-show audience, gossipy stuff about friendships with the great and good; for citizens horrified by the growth of the far-right vote in elections, anti-racist demos and anti-Le Pen platforms; for the female readers of *Elle*, a seductive and engaging dandyism.

Indeed one can hardly help seeing all of this, and in particular the coining of that heavy-duty, Teflon-coated acronym, hard-wearing as the ever-open shirt, as a particularly successful branding exercise. 'I can use his name without asking,' said the flamboyant luxury goods entrepreneur Pierre Bergé in 1993.[26] A sign of mutual trust and of brand recognition. 'BHL' is a trademark that can be declined like a noun, into different 'cases' that connect with varying discourses. 'Basically … *Le jour et la Nuit* is the sequel to *Diable en tête*, to *Baudelaire*, to *Le Jugement dernier*. Each work displays another way, different each time, of being myself.'[27] That is the supply side of 'BHL': himself declined. An almost industrial principle that enables him to talk about anything at all, with no legitimacy other than recognition by his peers in the 'village' of his unarguable and exceptional talent as a juggler, and of his name and face.

This declension exercise reached its climax between 1992 and 1994. In three years there appeared in quick succession the dramatist Bernard-Henri Lévy (*Le Jugement dernier*), the art critic Bernard-Henri Lévy (*Piero della Francesca*, *Piet Mondrian*), the diarist Bernard-Henri Lévy, and the militant pro-Bosnian Bernard-Henri Lévy, subdivided into the TV documentarist Bernard-Henri Lévy (*Un jour dans la mort de Sarajevo*), the documentary film-maker Bernard-Henri Lévy (*Bosna!*) and the politician Bernard-Henri Lévy (the 'Sarajevo list'). There was also the contemporary thinker Bernard-Henri Lévy (*La Pureté dangereuse*[28]) and the Bernard-Henri Lévy who analysed manners and morals (*Les Hommes et les femmes*[29]). Without forgetting the Bernard-Henri Lévy in love (and married to Arielle Dombasle on 19 June 1993). To which might be added Bernard-Henri Lévy the chairman of the Commission d'avance sur recettes, which part-finances French cinema, and Bernard-Henri Lévy the chairman of the council of the Franco-German TV channel Arte. All this in three years. Is Bernard-Henri Lévy Proteus?

Bernard-Henri Lévy can talk very well about all that, and does not mind doing it either. On a platform, he is a decent orator. In the newspapers, he cites authors. On the radio, he knows how to inflect his voice and keep to the allotted time. On television, he stays in the affective register (enthusiasm, indignation, narrative) appropriate to the medium as it is normally used today. In short, he is the prototype of the available, multi-purpose 'good client' (an important concept to radio and TV professionals, designating an individual who comes across well on screen, thus ensuring an audience and good advertising revenues).

The great talent of Bernard-Henri Lévy is that he learned very quickly to satisfy a demand. A political demand, as we have seen, but a media one too. Bernard-Henri Lévy is regularly used by information professionals and politicians on subjects touching on the Zeitgeist, the 'feel' of the time, owing to his undeniable talent for fastening onto the news of the moment – and sometimes for making the news (in 2000, for example, his biography of Sartre gave *Le Nouvel Observateur, L'Express, Le Point*, etc. the opportunity to proclaim a resurgence of Sartrean influence over French intellectual life). His books provide opinion makers pressed for time with a ready supply of accessible thoughts and opportunities to latch onto book trade events which they have no time to follow for themselves, thus giving the impression that they are up to speed with all the latest developments.

The sociologist Pierre Bourdieu complained about this trend in 1992: 'Producers connected to large cultural bureaucracies (press, radio, television) are increasingly obliged to accept and adopt standards and constraints linked to the requirements of the market. ... And they tend, more or less unconsciously, to measure all intellectual accomplishment by the forms of intellectual activity to which they are condemned by their working conditions (I am thinking for example of speed-writing and speed-reading, which often govern journalistic production and criticism).'[30]

On this basis – obviously he is not alone – Bernard-Henri Lévy has become an exemplary 'intellectual' among what might be called 'media intellectuals': newspaper editors and senior media staff who perform the ideological function of 'media intellectuals' by assuming the role of mediators, organizing the distribution of legitimate knowledge between the government and the general public, and exploiting the effect of symbolic consecration that can follow extensive media coverage of a book or a stage-managed public intervention on a subject of interest.

This is undoubtedly one of the keys to the incongruous but very durable audience for Bernard-Henri Lévy's discourse. The 'networks' and the 'BHL system' may be powerful and active, but they only work because market logic (in the sense of balancing supply against demand) has suffused the whole atmosphere of our time. The 'emptiness industry' denounced by Cornelius Castoriadis back in 1979 has since grown fat and prosperous.

STRATEGIES FOR FABRICATING THE SEMBLANCE OF AN OEUVRE

Despite the great variety of subjects discussed, genres adopted and inputs used, Bernard-Henri Lévy's output is astonishingly uniform. There is a 'BHL style', a way of putting a work together, discernible since the earliest texts.

SELF-QUOTATION

Quoting oneself is a way of being the agent of one's own legitimacy and creating the effect of a body of work. This is the performative side of self-quotation: acting as if one were the author of a work virtually produces the work in question. And Bernard-Henri Lévy has practised it since his very first book, something of an exploit. In *Bangla-Desh, nationalisme dans la révolution* – he was twenty-five – he found a way to quote his first article ... on Mexico.[31] Four years later, when he wrote his second book, *La Barbarie à visage humain*, he blandly quoted himself again (see below).

With the passage of time, Bernard-Henri Lévy had more and more books from which to quote himself. In the first 150 pages of *Qui a tué Daniel Pearl?* he found ways of mentioning his book on Bangladesh once (p. 19), the film *Un jour dans la mort de Sarajevo* once (p. 139), *Le Lys et la Cendre* twice (pp. 140 and 149), his other film *Bosna!* twice (pp. 139 and 153) and, best of all, hitched to a passing mention of the terrorist Carlos, his novel *Le Diable en tête* (p. 109).

REFERENCE

Bernard-Henri Lévy knows a lot of things, and he doesn't mind showing it. He collects ideas from here and there and assembles them into an astonishing hotchpotch. Thus the portrait he draws of the main character of his play *Le Jugement dernier*, in an interview given to *L'Infini*: 'Anatole, you see, has three convictions. "The world is made to culminate in a great work", that's Mallarmé. "*All the world's a stage*, the world is ruled by the spectacle", that's Debord. And then, "The adventure is over! History has ended! And the proof that it has is that I, Anatole, think it and represent it", and that's Hegel and Kojève. I'm very keen on these references.'[32]

At least on one occasion Bernard-Henri Lévy dropped the quote marks, and the words of others became his own. In *Le Monde* on 5 January 1979, during an interview with the journalist Gilbert Comte, he said: 'I believe the French language is both my most precious malady and my only possible fatherland. Refuge and den par excellence. Armour and weapon par excellence. One of the places, in any case, where I stand in this world.' Six months later, in an article that brusquely corrected the errors of *Le Testament de Dieu*, the historian Pierre Vidal-Naquet pointed out that these remarks are strangely reminiscent of parts of a letter sent by the poet St-John Perse to Archibald McLeish on 23 December 1941: 'Even if I were not an essentially French animal,

… the French language would still be my only imaginable fatherland, refuge and den par excellence, armour and weapon par excellence, the only "geometric spot" where I might place myself in this world without wanting to change anything.'[33]

In his defence, Bernard-Henri Lévy mentioned other authors: Borges and the treacherous memory of the 'reader' who quotes without knowing it, Michel Foucault who said he enjoyed slipping Marx into his texts without saying so.[34] Twenty-three years later, Pierre Vidal-Naquet recalled: 'He called *Le Monde* to add the sentence. He called Gilbert Comte, who told me so himself.'[35] But Bernard-Henri Lévy is not dishonest, he is facetious.

RECYCLING

The advantage of a good quotation is that it is reusable. Before the July 2001 G8 Summit held in Genoa, Italy, Bernard-Henri Lévy lambasted 'anti-globalists' in these terms: 'Nietzsche called them "*kaoten*", or "public hooligans". And he prophesied their appearance, proliferation and victory on the great European stages of the twenty-first century. Well, look: there they are.'[36] The image was striking enough to be reused the following year to talk about something quite different, the anti-Semitic attacks attributed to French youths of Maghrebi extraction: 'I find scandalous, for it tends to play down the phenomenon, the reasoning of people who tell us: "Look, it's nothing, these kids are penniless, without ideology, it's just petty delinquency" (the "*kaoten*" as Nietzsche called them, the "public hooligans" who Jew-bashed in 1930s Germany, were also after all brainless delinquents, and apparently without ideology …).'[37]

A more substantial example of recycling would be the circulation of a single text through several different outlets. Thus, for example, an article in *Le Monde*[38] which then became an editorial in *La Règle du jeu* (20 April 1993) and a chapter in *Le Lys et la Cendre*,[39] before being reproduced in *Récidives*.[40]

There is also 'copy/paste'. It is a little more time-consuming, because it calls for a small formatting effort. In one example, Bernard-Henri Lévy wrote in August 2002 the preface to the catalogue of the Andy Warhol exhibition at the Thaddeus Ropac gallery in Paris. In November of the same year he devoted the whole of a *Le Point* 'bloc-notes' to that exhibition.[41] The text was a perfect copy/paste job on the catalogue preface, minus a few paragraphs to reduce the length to suit, with a few small adjustments to cover up these cuts. There is no sentence in the 'bloc-notes' that is not taken directly from the preface.

Run at maximum pressure, this valiant recycling industry produces the bulk of *Questions de principe*. More than a quarter of the books published by Bernard-Henri Lévy are compilations of previously published texts.

WRITER'S SECRETS

Among the writer's manufacturing secrets is music: 'My manuscripts, in their primary state, are not written, but composed. They consist not of words, but of movements. They resemble not drafts, but scores.'[42] And: 'I write a page in the way a painter proceeds – a big splotch on the page – and like a musician: I can spend hours searching for the tune. I begin with the punctuation. I am probably the first writer to do that. I write music. To mark the rhythm of thought. I believe books should be composed, in the true sense of the term. That is what the French novel lacks.'[43]

Bernard-Henri Lévy can rely on journalists to pass on this cute mythology. Jean-Louis Ézine for example, who said in May 2004 in a broadcast of 'Le Masque et la Plume': 'I caught him one day when he was writing at home. The sentence stopped in the middle of the page and ended with: "The reason which is obvious." And there was nothing more, just a parenthesis a little further down, an exclamation mark, a semi-colon, a full stop. He punctuates before writing. He's a thinker who believes that an exact thought should be expressed in a rhythmic and punctuated sentence. He has a musical and musicianly way of working.'[44]

Another secret is the swimming pool. Bernard-Henri Lévy loves swimming pools, they inspire him. He explained to one of our well-informed 'honourable correspondents' that he had installed a voice recorder at the end of the pool in each of his houses. When he is swimming his daily lengths, sentences come to him. All he has to do is come out of the water, press the record button and capture the lucky find. He can then dive back in and splash up and down, awaiting new lightning-flashes: 'Some of my finest sentences have come to me like that.'

THE OMNIPRESENCE OF 'ME'

The claim to authorial subjectivity (see below, chapter 4) is a handy justification for an invasion of the word and idea 'me', which finds its way into every interstice of the text.

First and foremost, the strange verbal tic that consists of backing up the word 'I' with a 'me', in stock phrases of the type 'Me, I believe that …',

'Me, I think ...', 'I'd say, myself, that ...', 'As for me, I feel that ...'[45] The goal seems to be to help that poor, timid subjectivity to show that it really is there and has a right to be heard.

Next, the great difficulty of speaking about others without speaking of himself. Thus, when he interviews the historian Henri Lefebvre: 'When the conversation began, I couldn't help imagining myself in his place – at the age of ninety – recollecting for someone I didn't give two hoots about the ins and outs of a period of history which now seemed remote, time having moved on.'[46] For Bernard-Henri Lévy sees himself there already, white-haired, shirt a little less unbuttoned than in the past, under the respectful gaze of apprentice intellectuals come to sit at the feet of the old master ...

The procedure verges on the pathological when, for want of an interlocutor of equal stature, Bernard-Henri Lévy takes to holding a dialogue with himself. *Les Aventures de la liberté* includes a chapter entitled 'Berlin comes to Paris (dialogue with myself on the Cocteau question)'. Apart from the fact that the author is in two minds concerning Cocteau's attitude during the Second World War, it discloses that Bernard-Henri Lévy addresses himself formally as 'vous', and that he can be rather acerbic. 'No joking, if you don't mind,' he tells himself sternly.

In a chapter in *War, Evil and the End of History* entitled 'BH judges BHL', Bernard-Henri Lévy – in the mode of Jean-Jacques Rousseau, '*Rousseau juge de Jean-Jacques*' in his *Dialogues* – sends from Quebrada Naín, Colombia, his saddened thoughts on the inevitable misunderstanding that attends the reception of books by committed authors: 'In vain is he sincere when, in the bottom of his barge, he tells himself: "I am there for them, only for them, I have only one allegiance, to the mourners." He knows the tune too well, he is too used to the devilish tricks of self-forgetting, to create for himself the least illusion about the tainted, absurd quality of the system. When the chronicler shows horror, Paris looks at his pen; when he says, "Look at these conquered people," he is the one who emerges as conqueror.'

In *Comédie*, the book about the film-maker laid low by the 'cabal', there are a lot of mini-Bernard-Henri Lévys arguing drolly among themselves: BHL, L, the 'social me' and the 'inner me' (in reference to the Proustian distinction), but also the 'me of the film', the 'inner me of the film' and even 'the assembly of inner me's'.[47]

And stronger still, in *Récidives*: '4 June. Montaigne. *Essays*. Book II. Chapter 17. "Every man looks before him. I myself look within me." Reading these words, I realise, me, how little I think about myself.'[48]

WRITING THE LEGEND

In 1985, in his preface to the reprint of his book on Bangladesh (under the title *Les Indes rouges*), Bernard-Henri Lévy wrote: 'I would add, in order to be as complete, as sincere as possible, that all of this happened in 1971, a little over three years after the famous "May excitement" in which legend has it that I took part from my room, between a transistor radio and an ordnance survey map. There are many falsehoods, certainly, in legend.'[49] The repeated use of the word 'legend' in reference to what is at most an anecdote does seem a little exaggerated, especially as he is himself its inventor. In a *Playboy* interview dated May 1977, the question: 'Where were you in May '68?' got the reply: 'In my room, with a transistor radio and an ordnance survey map of Paris on which I followed, with impassioned but remote attention, the play and the stakes of the battles in the streets.'[50]

But all that arises from a desire for self-mythification that culminates a few lines further down: 'And that is why I can read this book now, absolutely not just as a "youthful effort" that I would refuse, out of bravado, to disavow, but as a primal stage rather, where there was once played out, in an incredibly ancient language, at times almost indecipherable, the birth of what I am.'[51]

WHENCE THE PIES (STATEMENT FROM LE GLOUPIER[52])

To some temperaments, the 'emptiness industry' begs for a direct, effective critical response in the form of satire or slapstick farce. The Belgian activist Noël Godin, who has 'pied' numerous personalities, considers Bernard-Henri Lévy to be his favourite target. Whatever one may think of the violence of these actions, they make their point on the appropriate level, which is that of a grotesque and ridiculous spectacle.

'BHL is the only running gag in the pie-throwers' epic, which began in 1969 against Marguerite Duras,' Noël Godin told us in 2003. 'To us, he absolutely personifies "look-at-me" smugness and arrogance. Every single time, he's reacted badly.'

> Bernard-Henri Lévy's pastry epic began on 3 November 1985 at the Palais des Congrès in Liège, on the occasion of a live TV debate, 'L'écran témoin'. In those days I acted only when transformed into 'Georges le Gloupier', dressed in a dinner jacket and complete with beard, spectacles and bow tie. BHL was late: I had to wait three quarters of an hour in the entrance hall where there were some other journalists. A big scare for me was

being welcomed by the RTBF press officer whom I knew well but who miraculously failed to recognize me. With me were my girlfriend Sylvie, her brother who had a small video camera and a Parisian woman friend, a photographer. Rudimentary kit. Bernard-Henri Lévy suddenly arrives, and I lunged straight at him with cries of: 'Gloup! Gloup! Gloup!' He instantly responded with punches. When I was on the floor, he bawled without realizing there was a video camera: 'Get up or I'll kick your head in!' Next day the pictures were shown on Canal Plus TV news, presented at that time by Coluche. BHL didn't sue. He'll never sue, it would be a disaster for his image.

The pie recipe is a classic: a nice soft pastry base, abundantly covered in layers of whipped cream. Care is taken not to add cherries or almonds or anything that might hurt the poor victim. We're skint, so we accept with joy the pies we are given. Great pâtissiers have sometimes offered their services, notably the famous Wittamer. We've always refused, not wanting to provide free publicity for big names.

On 3 October 1988, in a posh Brussels bookshop called Le Chapitre 12, BHL was giving a lecture to an audience of frightfully smart old ladies. Most treacherously, we had obtained permission to film the lecture: some friends had passed themselves off as producers of an RTBF magazine programme. Once the lecture was well under way, I popped up in the same gloup-gloup uniform. There being chairs in my path, some friends invited the ladies to stand up to provide a passage and I launched myself towards him, and which point he yelled: 'Not again! Enough already!' After pie had made contact with face, he reacted in the same brawny manner and upended me on the rostrum, raining blows on me. A protective friend said to him: 'You've got no right!' He replied: 'Oh haven't I, just watch me!' while I piped up with a war-cry in alexandrines: 'Entartons, entartons les pompeux cornichons!' [Let's pie, let's pie the pompous jerks!]

On 17 April 1991, at the Free University of Brussels, BHL was coming to give a lecture. Suspicion reigned. We waited for him near the car park. Volley of pies: his bodyguards formed a rampart with their bodies and stopped the lot. Completely untouched, he made a triumphal entry to the ULB campus. On the way into the lecture theatre, he stopped to give his autograph to a girl who innocently buttonholed him by the door to the toilets. While he was signing, a pie-thrower burst out of the lavatory and pied him point-blank. His bodyguards caught the pie-thrower, but he was freed by some journalists who were clustered around the door. BHL tried, for the first time, to get hold of the photographic film.

On 14 May 1994, BHL came to show his film *Bosna!* at the Cannes Festival. The minister of culture, Jacques Toubon, attended the screening as well as Jack Lang, Alain Carignon, Philippe Doute-Blazy and Michel Rocard. The security was huge. From early that morning Cannes had hummed with rumours that a pastry-based attack was imminent. At the entrance to the Palais, gents in very sharp dinner jackets offered us invitation cards: 'You'll make better use of them than us.' But soon after that we were spotted by security, which found pies concealed in our briefcases. We were swiftly evacuated. BHL arrived on stage and, by another miracle, one of us, Ivan the Ukrainian, had managed to slip through the net and reach the front of the stage as the cops patrolled the hall. No one took any notice of him. Like the discobolus, Ivan flung his pie and it landed on BHL's face. Arielle Dombasle rushed to his side and wiped him off. The pie-thrower was dragged into the nearest corridor by security and beaten up. He was bleeding and his clothes were torn. Our friend Jan Bucquoy, the director of La Vie sexuelle des Belges, was in the auditorium and ran towards the pie-thrower shouting: 'Stop it! Stop it! I'm the Belgian Ambassador!' And it worked …

On 22 May 1995, early in the morning, eight of us were at Nice airport waiting for BHL and Arielle Dombasle to depart after the Cannes Festival. My friend Zoé pied Arielle while I pied Bernard-Henri. It was totally synchronized. They both hurled themselves on us. Extras arrived with more pies. Following intervention by the airport police, BHL spotted me again – the cameras had been turned off – and they both went for me. He got me by the throat, Arielle flailed at me with her handbag and I went: 'Gloup! Gloup! Gloup!' Bernard-Henri and Arielle boarded their plane with no time to change their clothes. They entered that plane covered in whipped cream. I learned years later that Estelle Halliday was on board and had been surprised to encounter them in that state.

In 1997, the year of his film *Le Jour et la Nuit*, it was out of the question for us to mount the slightest pastry-based outrage against him: the film itself constituted a self-pieing on the grandest scale. But *Le Soir* relates that when passing through Brussels, BHL held a secret meeting with a journalist from the daily at a place unknown to her in advance, as an anti-pieing precaution. The Belgian daily also reported that when invited to the Mons film festival, BHL required that bodyguards be engaged by the organizers, and wanted me to agree a non-aggression pact with them.

27 February 2000: we were in Brussels, at the book fair. BHL was there to give a talk. The security was comprehensive and alert. Extras had been

planted in the lecture hall with pies, and others were posted along the route the philosopher was expected to take. Several big publishers had run the whipped-cream gauntlet earlier. BHL sneaks in through the garage. The first operation founders. Just before he's due to speak, as I arrive outside the hall, a lawyer friend introduces me to the directress of the fair, then walks me inside, arm in arm with me, amazing. BHL is introduced. Thirty seconds after his first words I get up, an accomplice slips me a great big pie and I advance down the gangway.

We hear BHL exclaim: 'Oh no!' The security jumps on me, other pie-throwers get up and are pulled over for questioning by the forces of law and order, but soon there are more pie-throwers than protectors, which enables four of them to jump onto the platform. BHL defends himself with a chair. He leaps down into the auditorium and, to general stupefaction, starts striking Jackie Chan-style postures: he must have been taking martial arts classes. He stops several pies, dashes along a gangway in the middle of the room and gets caught from behind by another team. It was like Hellzapoppin', the room was in uproar, some audience members came to his rescue. Scuffles broke out all over the room and cries of 'Gloup! Gloup! Gloup!' were heard everywhere. The conference resumed a few minutes later.

Bernard-Henri Lévy was 'pied' once more in March 2006, at the Salon du Livre in Paris, by imitators of Noël Godin. It could all start all over again ...

4 BIRTH OF AN IMPOSTURE

More than thirty years after the event, Bernard-Henri Lévy's standing as a 'philosopher' still rests on his participation in the ephemeral adventure of the 'New Philosophy'. To accept this is to forget that that so-called new current of thought was spawned by the media and for the media. After all, a quick reading of the book which established him as a 'New Philosopher' in 1977, Barbarism with a Human Face, *exposed its conceptual and ideological indigence even at the time. It should be borne in mind that the New Philosophy resembled a self-promotion effort, and that it provided a left-sounding justification for the conservative swerve then under way; that the self-proclaimed anti-totalitarian thinker Bernard-Henri Lévy had kicked off by denigrating Alexander Solzhenitsyn and that the 'philosopher' Bernard-Henri Lévy is a derivative product of the commodification of cultural life, in particular some of the new requirements of the publishing industry.*

Let us not forget, finally, that some intellectuals of renown saw immediately how noxious were the methods employed by the New Philosophers, and the danger they could pose to intellectual endeavour. This critique was confirmed and reformulated by Jacques Derrida at the end of his life.

THE FLOWERING OF NEW PHILOSOPHERS IN THE MEDIA

Before *Barbarism with a Human Face*, the best-seller published by Bernard-Henri Lévy in 1977, before he was thirty, philosophers on TV might sport the ascetic baldness of Raymond Aron, or at best the radiant smile of Michel Foucault, but they tended to look studious, austere and apparently afflicted by incipient divergent strabismus. Even the youngish ones looked old. After 27 May 1977 and the 'Apostrophes' programme that marked the media baptism of the New Philosophy, your standard

TV philosopher wore a white shirt unbuttoned to the midriff, held a cigarette – often up in the air as in portraits of Malraux – and had youthful features framed in the abundant locks of a rock star or playboy. They looked like 'BHL'. The day after that broadcast ('Are the new philosophers on the left or the right?') Bernard Pivot, the host of 'Apostrophes', heard his daughter say, 'I saw Rimbaud on the telly yesterday.'[1]

So the 'philosopher' Bernard-Henri Lévy was born on television, on the set of the leading literary programme on French public service television. Those images have circulated widely ever since, capital pieces in the young author's campaign to acquire notoriety. That TV epiphany has become, by dint of repeated retransmissions, a sort of televisual 'object of memory', providing the person concerned with an inexhaustible pretext for displays of modesty. 'Never, I've never watched it again, I promise you, never,' he told the journalist Daniel Schneidermann in 1996,[2] and in 2001 he told another interviewer: 'That "Apostrophes" programme, it's been mentioned to me ... I've never seen it.'[3] A false modesty perhaps tinged with retrospective lucidity, for the author of *Barbarism with a Human Face* cut a rather poor figure on the 'Apostrophes' set in comparison with his New Philosopher acolyte André Glucksmann, who came across as sharper, better informed and more charismatic, but had made the mistake of dressing in a voluminous, unbecoming pullover.

Important though they are on one level, these style footnotes should not be allowed to obscure the essential thing. Even before its author discovered that he was a TV natural, the book, despite its vaporous narcissism and conceptual vacuousness, had been taken very seriously by the critics. That was its real success. Hardly off the presses, it triggered a media avalanche, inaugurating a form of promotional blitzkrieg that over the years has become a trademark of the 'BHL system'. On 13 May, on the front page of *Le Monde des Livres*, Philippe Sollers (having already got over his own avant-garde ambitions) published a eulogistic piece on *Barbarism with a Human Face*, entitled 'The impossible revolution' and heaping praise on 'the first great romantic style since '68'. In the June 1977 issue of *Le Magazine Littéraire*, Dominique-Antoine Grisoni delivered himself of a piece entitled 'Twilight world; dawn of thought?' in which he announced baldly: 'A great book has been born, and joins the ranks of those, rarest of all, imbued with the flash of analysis and the thrill of genius.'

In *Le Figaro*'s view, Bernard-Henri Lévy had 'written a limpid and hard-edged book' one of whose 'strongest chapters ... deals with Marxism as a religion and the new opium of the people'. The paper went on: 'This anger is more than mere fashion. The "New Philosophers" may not always escape a certain conformism of thought, but they are keenly aware of its unacceptable, stifling, even disreputable aspects. All in all, their indignation is still worth more than the prevailing pieties.'[4] In *France-Soir*, Lucien Bodard saw Bernard-Henri Lévy as displaying 'the dynamism of a saint surmounting the neurasthenia of constricted times', and ended with a flattering sketch of him as a talented dandy: 'All he has left, deep down, is the art of living, the art of writing.'[5] Not all that wide of the mark, in fact.

The Catholic intellectual André Frossard, writing in *Le Point*, could hardly contain his delight: 'Wandering, enraptured, through the book by the very young philosopher Bernard-Henri Lévy, *Barbarism with a Human Face*, I pass through a number of spiritual glades filled with agreeable murmuring.'[6] The magazine *Elle* admired this 'left-wing, anti-Marxist philosopher, celebrated for his talent.'[7] The promising young television journalist Anne Sinclair, the future wife of Dominique Strauss-Kahn, invited him to debate on FR3.[8] And Maurice Clavel, writer, Resistance veteran, Gaullist commentator turned spiritual godfather to the Maoists post-May '68, and now the self-proclaimed 'uncle' of the New Philosophers,[9] wrote of Bernard-Henri Lévy in his *Nouvel Observateur* column: 'He is young, pretty, elegant, talented and famous … this tall young man, gifted by nature, also allows himself to succeed in culture.'[10]

And no less a figure than Roland Barthes expressed his admiration in a letter: 'I would like to say a word about what especially touched me in your book … What I found enchanting (read into that word pleasure, solidarity, fascination) was that your book is *written*. To important ideas – which will be seen to belong, for sure, in the political field – you have given that rare thing, the grain of a *writing*.'[11] A disconcerting accolade coming from that exact stylist, whose approach is so unlike the formal megalomania of *Barbarism with a Human Face*. Could the ageing semiologist have rushed into greeting the appearance of a new generation for fear of missing out? Might he have thought it expedient to go along with the vulgar critique of Marxism being pushed forward through the book's media and commercial success? Whatever the reason, his sponsorship played no small role in the accumulation of intellectual credit by Bernard-Henri Lévy and the New Philosophers.

In fact, outside the left and far-left press (an outspoken attack appeared in the Ligue Communiste Révolutionnaire's paper *Rouge*[12]) linked to the political organizations (Communist Party, Trotskyist groups) which had been Bernard-Henri Lévy's prime targets, overt debunkers were few and isolated. A mocking piece appeared in *L'Express* by Max Gallo[13] as well as a dull, condescending editorial in *Le Figaro* by the conservative Louis Pauwels.[14] A diary feature in *Libération* that attacked *Barbarism with a Human Face* for defeatism and social contempt was printed under the title 'La génération perdante/au vrai chic philosophique' (The generation losing out … to true philosophic chic): 'Moral: workers of all lands, submit. While you rot in your gulags, priority urban renewal zones and pensions at sixty, the intelligentsia will resist barbarism by cultivating art and metaphysics.'[15]

Thus, for good or ill, Bernard-Henri Lévy appeared on the scene as a New Philosopher. Indeed it was he who coined the term on 10 June 1976, on the front page of *Les Nouvelles littéraires*, to describe the handful of authors whose works he had started to publish at Grasset including *L'Ange*, by Guy Ladreau and Christian Jambet in 1976; André Glucksmann's *Les Maîtres Penseurs* in 1977, followed a month later by his own *Barbarism with a Human Face.* In his analysis piece in *Les Nouvelles littéraires*, he expanded the list to include Jean-Marie Benoist, Jean-Paul Dollé, Michel Guérin, Annie Leclerc, Françoise Lévy and Philippe Roger.

Although his own book would not appear for another year, he enrolled these authors as partisans of the same theoretical claim. In opposition to that '1960s cliché' holding philosophy to be 'dead, carried off bag and baggage in the shipwreck of humanism', he launched a 'slogan for the years to come' that on his lips had the ring of an advertising slogan: 'To make ourselves philosophers again'.

In reality, however, from the historical theoretical anti-Marxism articulated by Jean-Marie Benoist in 1970[16] to denunciations of the Gulag, Soviet totalitarianism and the blindness of Western lefty intellectuals,[17] from anti-materialist neo-spiritualism[18] to nostalgia for revolutionary feeling, the conceptual coherence offered by the self-appointed New Philosophers was only superficial, encompassing a rejection of Marxism, the State and the Enlightenment, and a condemnation of utopias. There were in any case already large numbers of militants and intellectuals who, drawing their own conclusions about the totalitarian excesses of Soviet Communism and the political deadlock afflicting leftism in the West, had not waited for the publication of *Barbarism with a Human Face.* Raymond Aron noted tersely in his memoirs: 'Neither *Marx est mort*, nor *La Cuisinière et le mangeur d'hommes*, nor *Barbarism with a Human Face* taught me anything at all about Marx, Marxism-Leninism or the Soviet Union.'[19]

So the New Philosophers were neither very new nor very philosophical. But the New Philosophy brand worked instantly as a media passkey, opening doors nationally and internationally. On 5 September 1977 they made the front cover of *Time* magazine – a first for French 'thinkers', not even Sartre had been granted the honour – with the headline 'Marx is dead: France's new philosophers speak out'. *Der Spiegel*, the *Observer* and *L'Espresso* published special feature articles; the Italian channel RAI made an hour-long film;[20] CBS was enthusiastic, and the Mexican TV corporation Televisa slaughtered the rest by inviting a heavyweight contingent (Bernard-Henri Lévy, Jean-Paul Dollé, Philippe Roger, Françoise Lévy and André Glucksmann) to travel around Mexico for a fortnight giving a series of seminars (which sometimes attracted a good pelting of turds, doing no harm to the spectacle).[21] It was nothing short of glory for everyone, but the greatest glory went to the most telegenic of the lot: Bernard-Henri Lévy.

CONFESSIONS OF THE CHILD OF A BARBARIC CENTURY

Politico-sentimental emphasis, historical navel-gazing, plaintive lyricism, flat-footed style, macabre romanticism and grandiloquent eschatology: it is hard not to smile when reading, more than thirty years later, Bernard-Henri Lévy's second book and first best-seller, *Barbarism with a Human Face*. It is introduced as a 'treatise on political philosophy for the use of new generations'.[22] The book's opening sentence, perhaps its most humble one – 'I am the bastard child of an unholy union between fascism and Stalinism'[23] – was thought striking at the time.

In five short sections, the work, a hybrid assembly of personal considerations, historical narratives and (very numerous) quotes from philosophers (Hegel, Marx, Nietzsche, Bentham, etc.), announces the death of socialism, judged essentially totalitarian, as an alternative to capitalism, and prophesies the imminent advent of an age of tyranny, for the 'Prince', in other words the 'administration', in other words the state, 'is an inevitability' (p. 2). He concludes: 'Life is a lost cause, and happiness an outmoded idea.'

Written in cod romantic-poetry style overlaid with eager contrition, *Barbarism with a Human Face* is stuffed with epigrammatical dicta. 'What is the Gulag? The Enlightenment minus tolerance' (p. 119); 'The world is a disaster with man at its summit' (p. 67). There are some vapid generalizations: 'No, the world is not in a good state, and it will probably get no better' (p. 2); 'Man, even in revolt, is never anything but a failed God and an aborted species' (p. 67); 'politics is a sham and the Greater

Good is inaccessible' (ibid.). Some historical short cuts: 'it goes without saying that Leon Trotsky was *in reality* a pure product of Stalinism' (p. 200). And a score or two being settled. A footnote, for example, tells us that in Bernard-Henri Lévy's opinion the obscure work *Singe d'or* by the equally obscure Guy Lardreau (a future New Philosopher, though) 'disqualifies' Jacques Derrida's reading of Rousseau in *De la grammatologie*.[24] But how does it do so? Does Bernard-Henri Lévy even know?

With a similar paucity of argument he also lays into Gilles Deleuze, whose theory of desire, dismissively described as an 'ideology', is expounded as follows: 'From the ideology of desire to the apology of rottenness on the dungheap of decadence, from "libidinal economy" to the innocent welcome extended to raw and unmediated violence, from "schizo-analysis" itself to the death wish on a foundation of powerful drugs and forbidden pleasures, the sequence is not only clear, it is indeed necessary' (p. 116). In other words, there is a causal connection between Deleuze's philosophy and putrefaction, gratuitous violence and the suicidal impulses of junkies. And that is not all.

> Go and see *The Night Porter*, *Sex O'Clock*, *Clockwork Orange* or, more recently, *L'Ombre des anges*. Listen to the poor wretches on the road to death, killing themselves with a final 'fix'. Read the open racism that used to be displayed in the productions of the Centre d'Études et de Recherches sur la Formation Institutionelle [where Félix Guattari was a senior staff member] … You will know almost everything about the effects and the principles of the 'ideology of desire' (pp. 116–17).

A sideswipe containing an unsupported accusation of racism against Félix Guattari, the close philosophical colleague of Gilles Deleuze …

Artworks and social data, cultural criticism and personal abuse: everything gets scrambled in the moralizing gaze of the author of *Barbarism with a Human Face*, with total disregard for the most basic prudence in attempting analysis. To give substance to this travesty of an argument an orotund phrase, or better still a striking image, can do wonders: 'Winter has done its work. A dark and faded sky hangs over the bare trees. A gloomy, frozen wind sweeps the world and turns it to stone. A wind from the East or a wind from the West? I have no idea, after all, for I have lost my compass and my charts' (p. 191). Interviewed by *Playboy* magazine when the book came out, Bernard-Henri Lévy explained the approach of the New Philosophers, and by extension his own, in similarly vivid and pointillist terms: 'Our task is to wear out our eyeballs staring at the horror, to shout ourselves hoarse denouncing the crimes of red tsars and white princes.'[25]

But metaphor – be it agricultural, corporeal or maritime – does not a philosophy make. Nor can egotistic agitation on its own pass for subjectivity. In the notes published at the end of *Barbarism with a Human Face*, Bernard-Henri Lévy edges himself constantly onto the stage: 'I am well aware that for a Deleuzian ...' (p. 199); 'I will often return to this notion of naturalism ...' (ibid.); 'On this point, I can do no better than to refer to the great book by ...' (ibid.); 'I will sometimes have occasion in the course of this book ...' (p. 200); 'It would be ungracious not to recognize my debt here to ...' (p. 201). He refers to his own articles on three occasions – and he was just twenty-nine at the time. 'Michel Foucault was kind enough to explain himself on this in an interview with me' (p. 203); 'Merely developing here what I said on this in *Le Nouvel Observateur* ...' (p. 215); 'See my article ...' (p. 204). He even alludes to texts still unwritten: 'This work will one day have to be pursued' (p. 204); 'We need a debate about fundamentals, which I have neither the space nor the means to undertake here' (p. 205). But Bernard-Henri Lévy does manage to find the space for historical rectifications of the first importance: 'I emphasize, for the sake of historical truth, that I myself was never directly involved in the Maoist adventure ...' (p. 205). But all this smugness still fails to mask a general inconsistency of form and some fundamental lacunae.

Cack-handed self-admiration, a discourse whose arrogance is proportional to its conceptual poverty: the failings of *Barbarism with a Human Face* are those of a very young author avid for recognition and (preferably intellectual) authority. From the lugubrious blast of mounting evil to the psychotropic effects of Marxism, from the hellishness of modern times to the advance of barbarian hordes, there is a lot, a hell of a lot, about past and future catastrophes in Bernard-Henri Lévy's book. But of concepts, theoretical systems, analytical arguments or problematic statements, there is not the slightest hint, not a trace.

How does one seriously discuss a text so manifestly devoid of meaning, how does one discuss philosophically a work so lacking in abstraction? From his first and brilliant publishing coup, Bernard-Henri Lévy has managed the considerable feat of producing work that gives no purchase to criticism. It is not coherent enough, not sufficiently composed as a philosophical essay, to be dealt with as such. Nevertheless, Bernard-Henri Lévy's stentorian confession that he was the child of a barbaric century blazed like a bush fire through the politico-mediatic landscape of the late 1970s.

ME, MYSELF, I

In France at the end of the 1970s, when the fashion for punchy, epigrammatic phrases or 'sound bites' was spreading among politicians, those pioneers of media clever-dickery the New Philosophers were inventing a rough equivalent for intellectual use: a way of being understood, a vocabulary, an implicit mode of discourse based essentially on placing the speaker at centre stage. As a post-neo-Kantian form of 'thought' positing a return to the subject, in counterpoint to the thematics of the 'death of the author' carried by structuralism and Derridean deconstruction, the New Philosophy succeeded in embodying its ideological postulate by exploiting, through the agency of television, a narcissistic foregrounding of its authors that also served as a promotional lever. Such was the complaint of François Aubral and Xavier Delcourt, two observers infuriated by the intellectual con-trick, in a pamphlet that missed its mark, doubtless through excess of seriousness.[26]

Le Nouvel Observateur (a journal to which Bernard-Henri Lévy was then a contributor) was not too wide of the mark when, noting in January 1981 that the 'BHL' acronym was all the rage, it described the young author as the 'Liz Taylor of the intelligentsia'.[27] Two years later, Bernard-Henri Lévy was to loop the loop by giving his communicational egotism a theoretical gloss: 'Philosophers had unlearned how to speak in the first person … but I chose to "bring the *I* back into play" in philosophy', a decision which reflected his 'philosophical bias'.[28]

SMASHING '68

Jacques Derrida opened the conference entitled 'Les États généraux de la philosophie', held at the Sorbonne in June 1979 at the instigation of twenty-one professors including François Châtelet, Gilles Deleuze, Jean-Toussaint Desanti, Vladimir Jankélévitch, Jean-Luc Nancy and Paul Ricœur, with a warning:

> There lies, in the techno-politics of telecommunications, a challenge that cannot be dodged, a challenge that is also philosophical, and very new in some of its forms, its operations, its evaluation, its market and its technology … No one today, neither the more wide-awake philosophers nor people who are even minimally aware and trained in discernment in those domains (publishing, press, television), would ever point to the

vitality or rigour of philosophy with reference to much, or to most, one might say, of what has lately been exhibited on the most prominent platform; to what noisily calls itself philosophy in all sorts of studios where, since a relatively recent and clearly determined date, the loudest speakers have had the loudspeakers handed to them without wondering (even in the best of cases) why columns and channels were being turned over to them to talk *thus* and to say exactly *that*.[29]

Those 'loudest speakers' who had been handed the 'loudspeakers' were obviously those philosophers who played television's game more persistently than their colleagues, first and foremost the New Philosophers. Bernard-Henri Lévy later caused a minor fracas during the conference, taking the microphone to complain about the lexical proximity between 'anti-media vigilance' and 'anti-fascist vigilance', and nearly coming to blows with his old teacher at the École normale, Jacques Derrida. A press photo of the dramatic altercation between the two men was among the first pictures of Derrida to appear in the press.

The New Philosophers experienced their entry into the arena as a replay of the quarrel between the Moderns and the Ancients. They had chosen the televisual agora over the university, media legitimation over academic credibility. Natural heirs of '68 through their association with leftism (genuine in the case of André Glucksmann, who had been a Maoist, more distant and partially reconstructed in Bernard-Henri Lévy's case), the New Philosophers emerged as very well placed to criticize the alleged excesses of that period. More or less consciously, more or less deliberately, they delivered a ready-made, spiritualist-inflected political and intellectual subterfuge – a sort of soul supplement to sweeten the collective reconversion to capitalism and the social norm.

One modernity was coming to prop up the other, generating a staggering level of arrogance. During the Estates General of Philosophy conference, the young Bernard-Henri Lévy, carried away by the fit between his own discourse and the spirit of the times, demanded unblushingly: 'Do you think professors of philosophy were the first to denounce the Gulag? It was television and it was the media.'[30] The assertion naively confuses the media with mediatized commentators, ignores the fact that there would have been no 'Solzhenitsyn effect' in France without the publisher Claude Durand and the publishing house Le Seuil, and forgets that there would have been no André Glucksmann without people like Cornelius Castoriadis and Claude Lefort (and, before them, Boris Souvarine and other anti-Stalinist skirmishers driven by their own convictions and wholly indifferent to the imperatives of the 'media stage'.[31]

In 1974 Claude Durand, future managing director of Fayard, published at Le Seuil the French translation of Alexander Solzhenitsyn's first book, *The Gulag Archipelago*; and it was essentially the review *Esprit*, then edited by Jean-Marie Domenach, that in the 1970s opened the debate on 'anti-totalitarianism' and 'real socialism' in Eastern Europe, whose history and contemporary reality were largely unknown to the left-wing vulgate of the time. The most serious criticisms of Soviet totalitarianism, which came from the extreme left – among them Robert Linhart's book *Lénine, les paysans, Taylor*, published by Seuil in 1976, and those published in the review *L'Alternative*, set up in 1979 by the publisher François Maspero – were a good deal less influential than writings coming from the left-Christian circles of *Esprit* and, a fortiori, than the mediatized exploits of the New Philosophers.

The philosophers who participated in the Estates General found themselves relegated to the role of academic authorities. These were acclaimed heavyweights, whom the New Philosophers did all they could to disparage by making them out to be backward in their practices, corporatist, uninterested in great world causes and withdrawn from real life.

Nevertheless, the sensation caused by the New Philosophy, resounding but ephemeral, was symptomatic of a phenomenon that ran deep. For French society, whose 'fundamentals' had remained essentially unchanged since 1945, the turning point of 1977–1978 constituted a major break with the past (undoubtedly greater than 1968), and shook up many established economic, political and intellectual parameters. September 1977 saw the collapse of the Union de la gauche, the electoral alliance between the Socialist and Communist Parties, which then lost the legislative elections of March 1978; in January-February 1978, the number of unemployed in France passed the million mark; the 'leftist' nebula imploded for good, destroyed by the dogmatism in which it had frozen the promises of May '68; and the founding myths of the left and extreme left, rattled by the 1974 publication of Solzhenitsyn's *Gulag Archipelago*, were shaken to the core by revelations of mass murder by the Khmer rouge in Cambodia and the exodus of boat people escaping from Vietnam.

The 'ideological left' lost the foundations of its identity, as the sociologist Jean-Pierre Le Goff explains:

> The second half of the 1970s saw the collapse of the revolutionary hopes carried by the far left. Since the end of the 1960s, the development of struggles in Europe and the wider world seemed to have made the idea of revolution credible once more, but history seemed to be going through a great reversal, as if a U-turn had begun … The revolutionary rank and file fell apart, to be supplanted by a concern for ethics and the aesthetic dimension of life, broadly repressed by revolutionary militants. These factors emerged as contrary to politics which now became synonymous with ideology, illusion and lies. The new values which were now being openly asserted went hand in hand with a process of depoliticization.[32]

The process is being accelerated by the New Philosophers:

> The confession of their errors has to be made in public and displayed in the media, as if one had at all costs to be forgiven for one's wild oats, without necessarily understanding what that might have stood for beyond one's own subjectivity. With them, historical analogy is going to be pushed as far as it will go and ethics will turn to imprecation. Overflowing the personal field, it is going to turn back on society and history, set itself up as judge and develop a logic of guilt on the scale of society.[33]

The great achievement of the New Philosophers was to have caught a whiff of this reversal in the air of the time. Their young, rebellious image made them the perfect heroes for a restoration of political and social order. So that, after the great terror May '68 had struck into the hearts of conservative and business circles, business as usual might resume. Everything must change in order for everything to stay the same …

HOW BHL MISSED THE SOLZHENITSYN EVENT

When Alexander Solzhenitsyn died in 2008, the French media wanted to know what Bernard-Henri Lévy had to say. What could be more natural than to ask the 'philosopher' of human rights about the author who had denounced the horrors of the Gulag? As usual on such great occasions, he saw things in large format. 'In the first place he was a colossus, a giant of literature,' he declared on TV.[34]

But, as the journalist Philippe Cohen reveals,[35] he had not always had such a high opinion of the Russian writer. When *The Gulag Archipelago* appeared in 1974, the young Parisian seemed very doubtful of the work's importance. At that time, Bernard-Henri Lévy was editing the 'Ideas' section of the Quotidien de Paris, a recently launched opinion journal.

In May the young author ran a series of his own articles on the opposition in the USSR. They contained a paean to the new dissidents, 'nothing like the clowns who turn up from time to time, nineteenth-century novelists lost in the twentieth, of the Solzhenitsyn type'. A few weeks earlier he had written that 'there has been much talk of Solzhenitsyn, who is not a great writer, but who would be well suited to our purposes'. The Soviet author was also referred to as a 'fantasist', a 'blunderer' and a 'showbiz man' in the journal's brief notes.

It is true that these are minor, disobliging jabs rather than a real attack, and even less a dispute with the Russian writer over the nature of the Gulag. But the tone is scornful, and any assessment of Solzhenitsyn is reduced to the sole issue of his literary style – a somewhat tenuous approach, given the political scope of the work. The importance of the book just published by the survivor of Soviet concentration camps totally escaped the young BHL, who clearly failed to grasp that the recipient of the Nobel Prize for Literature (in 1970) was changing for ever the way the world saw the Soviet Union. Thirty-four years later, when the dissident writer died, BHL was to assert unhesitatingly that Solzhenitsyn was the 'Dante of our time' and *The Gulag Archipelago* the 'Divine Comedy of our time'.[36] How opinions can change over the years!

What was the reason for the astonishing blindness of 1974? Philippe Cohen thinks it came from contact with the Marxist intellectual Louis Althusser, his professor at the École normale. Solzhenitsyn's voice was surely still too disturbing to the world of French books and journals – still heavily weighted to the left, six years after May '68 – for an ambitious young intellectual to dare stand up as its defender. It was just a matter of media tempo, and a good nose for the way the wind was blowing. Three years later BHL 'did a Solzhenitsyn' (but without saying so) in his first best-seller, *Barbarism with a Human Face*: 'Stalin did not die in Moscow or at the Twentieth Congress. He is here among us, a stowaway in the History that he still haunts and bends to his demented will.'[37] The overwrought style, so absurd to a modern ear, was no more perhaps than the fruit of unconscious remorse – unless the success of *The Gulag Archipelago* and the aura it bestowed on Alexander Solzhenitsyn had incited him to fly the colours of anti-totalitarianism from then on.

TELEVISION AND THE 'MARKET ENVIRONMENT'

It is a story that plays out at the rhythm of the Fifth Republic. After 1958, the presidentialization of the regime was accompanied by the increasing use of television by General de Gaulle, who sometimes embellished his press conferences with the short, memorable utterances, known today as 'sound bites', that suit television news perfectly. The head of state had been quick to understand the value of the new medium, which provided a fabulously propitious setting for the events that would punctuate his political trajectory (for example the speech against the 'quarteron de généraux' – the obsolescent word 'quarteron' meaning both a small number of people and 'quadroon' – in Algiers, who attempted a putsch in May 1961).

May '68 came during a period when commercial offshore radio stations ('radios périphériques' in France) were proliferating, owing to the existing legal monopoly of public broadcasting. It also marked a new stage in the 'politicization' of public television, both through the growing presence of political subjects and discourses on air and through giving a platform to student leaders such as Daniel Cohn-Bendit and Alain Geismar. From the 1970s onward, TV became the dominant outlet for political material, in a dynamic that accompanied the deterioration of the historic structures of the public domain: a collapse of attendance at public meetings, a weakening of the power of parliament.

Alongside these institutional developments, arrangements were being put in place to project culture as a spectacle, binding its destinies ever closer to the evolution of communications. Early in the presidency of Valéry Giscard d'Estaing (1974–1981), in March 1974, the first secretary of state for culture, Michel Guy, was appointed, and on 31 January 1977 the Georges Pompidou Centre was inaugurated in Paris. It was the laboratory of a new type of institutional theatre which many in the post-'68 ambiance of the time – deeply suspicious of any involvement of the political authorities in cultural life – regarded as a sign that artists and intellectuals were to be subjected to the will of the state.

The process gathered momentum during the Mitterrand era with the cultural promotion policy led by the minister Jack Lang, insatiably keen on music festivals, film festivals and the showbiz side of things in general. The appearance of commercial television channels in the 1980s completed the overturning of this cultural space, importing marketing methods and imposing the logic of audience ratings on the artistic and cultural domains undergoing a media-friendly overhaul. The ambitions of television to generate popular culture were blunted and impoverished, authors and artists were forced to compete, in a growing culture of self-promotion and narcissistic inflation ... In Jacques Derrida's baleful expression, a 'market environment'[38] was being established.

Where do the New Philosophers fit in? The televisual domain was acquiring an intellectual credibility it had previously lacked. Television, in the form of literary programmes like 'Apostrophes', was opened up to 'intellectuals' who were invited to speak about their works to far bigger audiences than they could ever have dreamed of. By letting themselves be 'televisualized', prestigious intellectuals such as Barthes or Foucault, authentic men of learning, played a role in the intellectual legitimization of television which others, among them Deleuze, Lyotard and Derrida, refused to support. Following the death of Barthes in 1980, and Foucault in 1984, the erstwhile New Philosophers would find themselves de facto virtually alone in the role of television 'intellectuals'.

PUBLISHING AND THE LOGIC OF THE 'COUP'

But the flowering of the New Philosophers and the notoriety that quickly surrounded them were also directly linked to developments in the publishing field around 1975–1978.[39] The mid 1970s saw the beginning of a transformation in reading habits, which occurred in tandem with changes in book production. A dynamic of concentration had seized the publishing world, led notably by the Hachette group, which had owned Grasset – launch pad of the New Philosophers – since 1954. The aim everywhere was to rationalize management structures and modernize management practices. Éditions Grasset et Fasquelle suffered the consequences, along with all other French publishing houses. Apart from covering their backs with pocket-sized reprints, publishers became steadily more cautious and risk-averse. The new ideal was to publish texts that would generate an instant response on the widest possible scale. The policy of the 'publishing coup' was becoming the norm.

As a matter of fact, Éditions Grasset was somewhat ahead of the game. Its founder, Bernard Grasset, had been a precursor of modern publishing attitudes between the wars ('Don't say Radiguet's a genius, say he's only fifteen!'). And from the mid 1960s Bernard Privat, who was running the firm, had gathered a young team around him, its members including Jean-Claude Fasquelle, Yves Berger, Françoise Verny and François Nourissier. It was apparent to them that in a context of rising book production, they would need to win literary prizes to obtain good sales. And to ensure such prizes, they would need backing from the press and the ability to seduce prize juries. The obvious solution was to cultivate retainers in the press, assets whose loyalty the publishing house would sometimes purchase by offering to make it worth their while. Nobbling the juries was equally essential. Yves Berger, a literary director whose manner exudes artless southern bonhomie, is a master practitioner: take them to lunch, become their friend, and when it comes to it dangle the prospect of a connection with the house (here again the size of any honorarium carries a certain clout), thus securing their vote. 'Whether it's morally reprehensible or not, that's a different kettle of fish,' the same Yves Berger concludes.[40]

At the same time a structural evolution was taking place in publishing production. As Rémy Rieffel notes in *L'Édition française depuis 1945*, 'In the human sciences, the division between "specialized" and "popularizing" works saw the appearance of a third category, the "essay"'.[41] A new format emerged, which was shorter, less subject to academic prescrutiny, and addressing current events directly.

This is the context in which Bernard-Henri Lévy's arrival at Grasset should be seen. It ticked every box: recruitment of a writer-journalist, media-savviness, policy of the 'coup' and promotion of the essay form. Bernard-Henri Lévy and *Barbarism with a Human Face* were products of the 'literary marketing' imposed on the publishing houses by the market, as well as of an internal logic specific to Grasset. The firm's knowhow and Bernard-Henri Lévy's knack for making each book a new focus of debate were an alliance made in heaven.

There are competing versions of Bernard-Henri Lévy's original arrival at Grasset. The man himself, as is his custom, gives several more or less consistent accounts. In 1973, aged twenty-five, he came back from Bangladesh with a manuscript under his arm. He contacted two very different publishers: François Maspero, who published left-leaning works of social science and politics, and Grasset. Maspero answered first and agreed to publish the text.[42] According to one of the author's versions,[43] he was then seen by Françoise Verny who ran the 'Essays' division at Grasset and who said that she too wanted to publish the manuscript. But Bernard-Henri Lévy had already given his word. The text would stay at Maspero. By now very set on getting him for Grasset, Verny suggested that he edit a series. He refused. She suggested another one, and he refused again. When she offered him three series, he gave way and accepted. That is one of the versions.

Verny has another version, supported up to a point by some of the author's other accounts.[44] Her story is that Bernard-Henri Lévy came to Grasset to offer her a book on worker self-management. 'I waited for Bernard at the top of the stairs. He had just published *Les Indes rouges* at Maspero.' (In 1985 Bernard-Henri Lévy republished his book on Bangladesh with Livre de poche, under that title.) 'He was superb, interested in everything. There was a sort of freedom about him, of having had it up to here with Marxist dogmatism. You could say it was the boy that interested me rather than Bangladesh or self-management.' So it was the 'boy', more than the author, that got to her. But what on earth was Bernard-Henri Lévy doing at Grasset with a book on self-management?

The fact is that at that time he was one of a 'group of experts' working for François Mitterrand, the leader of the Socialist Party. When the topics were allotted to the different advisers, he was landed with self-management. He knew nothing about it, but 'to start educating myself',[45] as he put it, he proposed a book on the subject to Grasset. He was willing to work at it, so long as the product of study would not be of use only to Mitterrand. The book never saw the light of day, but the young man's profile – handsome, clever, doing a little philosophy, a little journalism and a little politics – fitted the firm's new image to perfection. Françoise Verny had brought off a 'coup'.

NEW PHILOSOPHY: PHILOSOPHER-PROOF

Did the New Philosophy ever have any connection with actual philosophy? Twenty years or so after the media splash of the New Philosophers, Françoise Verny set the record straight on her former protégés in an interview with the trade weekly *Livres Hebdo* (30 January 1998). To the question 'What's left of the New Philosophers?' she replied, 'Nothing.' She went on: 'I had understood that this handful of authors, André Glucksmann, Bernard-Henri Lévy, Guy Lardreau and Christian Jambet, had in common a horror of Marxism and of French universities that, having cultivated Kant for two centuries, no longer cultivated anything but Marx … Basically, it was a cleansing operation. All scholasticisms are bad and Marxism had become a scholasticism. It enabled people to clean out their minds. And it sold books, which was, after all, the object of the exercise. But behind all the fuss there was no real spark of new thought and, inevitably, the New Philosophy hasn't stood the test of time.'

So was the New Philosophy nothing but an exercise in product labelling, mere philosophical parody? One person who never doubted it was Gilles Deleuze. Initially reluctant to attack something that did not seem to merit even that much attention, he finally took up his pen to denounce the appearance of 'literary or philosophical marketing' in a text dated 5 June 1977, copies of which were distributed free in bookshops at his request. Entitled *À propos des nouveaux philosophes et d'un problème plus général*, the pamphlet said notably:

> I believe their thought is worthless. I see two possible reasons for that worthlessness. Firstly, they proceed by using big concepts, as big as hollow teeth, The Law, Power, The Master, The World, Rebellion, Faith, and so on. They can thus come up with grotesque intermixtures, summary dualisms: the law and the rebel, the power and the angel. At the same time, the weaker the content of the thought, the more important the thinker seems to become, the more importance the enunciating subject acquires in relation to the empty statements ('as a lucid and courageous individual, I say unto you ..., as a soldier of Christ ..., as one of the lost generation ..., we, as the people who did May '68 ..., as people who are no longer taken in by appearances ...'). With these two procedures, they are undermining work. Because for some time past, in all sorts of areas, people have been working to avoid those very dangers. They have tried to form concepts that are articulated finely, or in a very differentiated way, to escape from such grossly dualistic notions. And to identify creative functions that would no longer emerge through the author(ial) function (in music, painting, audiovisual, cinema, even in philosophy). This massive return to an author or an empty and very conceited subject, and to stereotyped summary concepts, represents a vexatious force of reaction.[46]

In this context of commodification of the publishing project, Deleuze added, each New Philosopher had his own role to play: Clavel as '[Doctor] Mabuse', Jambet and Lardreau as 'Mabuse's henchmen' Spöri and Pesch, Benoist as 'runner', and Bernard-Henri Lévy – with his innate genius for multi-tasking – doubling as 'impresario', 'script girl', 'cheery animator' and 'disc-jockey.' His are functions that are subsidiary only in appearance, being in reality crucial in establishing the new set-up. 'The multitude of newspaper articles, interviews, seminars, radio and TV broadcasts,' the text continued, 'are meant to replace the book, which might as well not exist at all ... They amount to a whole body of activity which, on that scale and with that level of organization, seemed excluded from philosophy, or to exclude philosophy.'[47]

For, in the absence of philosophy, there is still plenty of novelty about the New Philosophers, residing principally in their 'very adapted analysis of the landscape and the market'.

> [Print] journalism, in liaison with radio and TV, has become increasingly aware of its ability to create news (controlled leaks, Watergate, surveys of behaviour and opinion). And just as it had less need to refer to external events, since it was creating a large part of the news, it also had

> less need to resort to analyses from outside journalism, or to characters of the 'intellectual' or 'writer' type: journalism was discovering within itself an autonomous and sufficient form of thought. That is why, when it comes to it, a book is worth less than the newspaper article written about it or the interview it gives rise to. Intellectuals, writers, even artists, are incited to become journalists if they want to conform to prevailing standards. It is a new type of thought, interview-thought, conversation thought, one-minute thought. One can almost imagine a book about a newspaper article, instead of the other way round. The balance of forces between journalists and intellectuals has changed completely.[48]

There followed a polemic in the columns of *Le Monde* (with Jean-Marie Benoist in the role of the New-Philosopher Modern), and a lasting grudge against Deleuze on the part of Bernard-Henri Lévy.

Two years later, in 1979, it was the turn of another proper philosopher, Cornelius Castoriadis, this time taking Bernard-Henri Lévy to task in a directly personal way on the appearance of his third book, *Le Testament de Dieu*,[49] which eulogizes monotheism as the sole bulwark of freedom. As founder in the late 1940s of the radical libertarian group 'Socialisme ou Barbarie', and an impartial historical critic of the totalitarian Soviet system, Castoriadis appeared politically close to the 'New Philosophers'. But the apparent ideological compatibility was blown sky-high by a long and detailed diatribe, 'L'Industrie du vide' ("The emptiness industry"), which he published in *Le Nouvel Observateur*. 'Under what sociological and anthropological conditions,' it thundered, 'in a country of old and great culture, can an "author" let himself write any old rubbish, the "critics" praise him to the skies, the public meekly fall into line and those who expose the fraud, while not being silenced or imprisoned, get no effective hearing?'[50] A few weeks earlier, in fact, the appearance of *Le Testament de Dieu* had given rise to a violent polemic between Bernard-Henri Lévy and the historian Pierre Vidal-Naquet, a renowned Hellenist and figure of great moral standing on the left.

In a text sent to several papers and journals and published by *Le Nouvel Observateur* on 18 June 1979, Vidal-Naquet points out with mordant irony the gross errors littering Bernard-Henri Lévy's book. Historical howlers abound. Robespierre is accused of 'putting the one and sovereign God to death', when he had devised a cult of the Supreme Being. Stalin is alleged to have organized a mass demonstration in Red Square in 1928 'in an assault on the party that had put him in a minority', a demonstration that never took place, any more than the Soviet leader was ever in a minority). It is full of anachronisms. Sophocles' Antigone is presented as being set in Thebes at the end of the fifth century BC when really the play, first performed in Athens in 442 BC, is set in the Thebes of the second millennium BC. Texts written between the first century BC and the first century AD are presented as contemporary with 'the last breaths of Rome.' An 1818 text by Benjamin Constant is said to 'echo spectacularly' one by Fustel de Coulanges, dated ... 1864. A theological absurdity is found in original sin being placed on the seventh day of Creation. And there is invention pure and simple: Himmler's 'deposition' at the Nuremberg trials, when the Nazi interior minister had committed suicide after his arrest by British troops on May 23 1945, six months before the trials opened (they ran from 20 November 1945 to 10 October 1946).

Precise, severe and blunt, Vidal-Naquet's correction nevertheless gave Bernard-Henri Lévy the opportunity for what seemed at the time a formidable riposte. Turning the very basis of the historian's scientific legitimacy against him, he accused him of using 'police' methods, 'public pillorying', 'learned thuggery' and organizing a 'grand academic tribunal'. Behind the ostensible attack on a fussy, meddling academe, he could pose as the heroic victim of a critique which, while appearing formally just, was fundamentally unfair being authoritarian, technically pedantic and trivial when set against the sweep of history and the nobility of the ideas he claimed to embody.[51]

It was a brilliant parry. Pierre Vidal-Naquet's response – again published in *Le Nouvel Observateur*, which was delighted by such a long-running story[52] – and a counter-offensive from Castoriadis had little effect. Bernard-Henri Lévy would henceforth perform in a space where accurate references, historical truth and serious analysis were no longer real criteria. By rejecting early on the rules of a democracy of learning in which one talks nonsense at one's peril, he had excluded himself from the world in which that learning is constructed and developed. But on media terrain, increasingly autonomous from the late 1970s onward, the New Philosopher won the battle hands down. Questioned in 2004 on Bernard-Henri Lévy's intellectual impunity, Pierre Vidal-Naquet replied: 'We've moved on from the Republic of Letters to the Non-Republic of the Media. I thought I'd "killed" BHL, but I hadn't. I consider that I was beaten. To me, it's a defeat.'[53]

What was at stake in the battle was more important for Bernard-Henri Lévy than it might have appeared: continuing to pass himself off as a philosopher. In 1977, during his first big media offensive, he could have chosen to appear as what he was: a professor (briefly), a journalist and an adviser to Mitterrand. In his aspiration to call himself a philosopher lay the ambition to 'do' scholarship or, more precisely, to lay claim to the intellectual kudos attached to an academic practice well beyond his abilities. Bernard-Henri Lévy played the 'philosopher' card entirely deliberately. And the credit he gained from it was immense: intimidating prestige (what mere journalist would dare try to square up to a philosopher?), legitimization of his own, classical, culture little acquainted with more contemporary forms of academic endeavour (it's easier to claim authority with a Hegel or Nietzsche quotation than by reference to the work of scholars unknown to the mass of the public), and presenting himself as the heir to a lineage of great thinkers.

At the end of his text denouncing the 'emptiness industry' at work in Bernard-Henri Lévy's books, Cornelius Castoriadis called in 1979 for a collective civic response: 'We have to fight for the preservation of an authentic public space for thought in opposition to state power, but also against bluff, demagogy and prostitution of the mind'; 'trafficking in general ideas – at the intersection of the human sciences, philosophy and political thought – is starting to pay off handsomely, especially in France. This is where the function of criticism could and should be crucial, not because it is easy but precisely because it is difficult.' On the new, mass public that has come into being without giving a thought to its responsibility as an actor in the public space, Castoriadis added: 'The more people read, the less they are reading. They read books presented to them as "philosophical" in the same way they read crime thrillers … They are unlearning how to read, to think and criticize. They are simply keeping up to speed … on the "latest hot topic".'[54]

By the grace of a striking phenomenon of collective amnesia, there remains after more than thirty years no active trace of that stint on the battlements by a great intellectual figure anxious to re-establish an ethical form of discourse. On the contrary, soon afterward, the intellectual con-trick from which Bernard-Henri Lévy still benefits today (although decreasingly, see below, chapter 8) was in place. A funny sort of philosopher he was, to be sure, without an oeuvre, without lectures, without students, without a place of work other than the wholly private space in which his own books and articles are gestated. One consequence of this fraudulent appropriation of a philosopher's identity was the blunting of the image of the philosopher in the media, particularly television. When still a small girl Justine Lévy, Bernard-Henri Lévy's daughter, used to give her father's profession when filling in forms as 'philosopher'. 'What is a philosopher?' a teacher asked her one day. She answered: 'Someone who goes on the telly.'

THE CRITICISM OF JACQUES DERRIDA

We spoke to Jacques Derrida in June 2004, a few months before his death. We questioned him at length on the notion of the 'media intellectual', on the genesis of that figure and the political, cultural and media context of its violent irruption in French intellectual life. A lot of the things he told us that day were very useful to us in planning this chapter. As we talked, Derrida opened up with some thoughts of a more personal kind, among memories which he recounted with a mixture of gravity and amusement.

> Another example, typical of the media intellectual in action. I remember taking part in a meeting to protest against the murder of Algerian writers and intellectuals. The room was packed. There were four or five of us on the platform to speak about our indignation over these killings. Everyone said what he had to say. There was consensus. And all of a sudden, there was Bernard-Henri Lévy, who wasn't invited, elbowing his way in, crossing the room, and sitting down at the table – he hadn't been invited, remember – and taking the microphone, to say pretty much the same as the rest of us. He had come with photographers, who took photos of him. He was hissed by the people in the room. And as soon as he finished talking, he left. Walked out of the room. That's typical of the way the media intellectual operates. They have to be there, for good causes, obviously. But in this case, Bernard-Henri Lévy came solely so that it would be known publicly that he had come, with pictures to prove it. And that was all. He didn't stay, even to be polite, for the rest of the meeting which continued without him for quite a while. It's typical … But here we're talking about a strictly mediatized intellectuality. I mean representation of the self, narcissistic and promotional, which makes use of a cause rather than serving it. That to me is the definition of the media intellectual: using a cause rather than serving it. That's what makes the difference. It's sometimes a subtle difference, but real, I believe.
>
> Question: On the subject of Bernard-Henri Lévy's real work, was there ever a time when you regarded him as a peer? Was he at any time, in your opinion, a philosopher?
>
> Answer: For me, no. I regard Bernard-Henri Lévy as an intelligent man, very intelligent. Who understands philosophy. He wasn't a bad student … But what he produces philosophically, in my view, isn't very

interesting. What he does from a purely journalistic point of view, the 'bloc-notes' for example, that's not bad. I find it very annoying, for a lot of reasons. But it isn't criticizable for what it is. It's intelligent, often sound. But that isn't what, from my own point of view, I call philosophy.

Q: What about the impunity of some of these media intellectuals? Over the years, Bernard-Henri Lévy has said and written things that turned out to be wrong, but despite that, even when his errors are exposed and denounced, it doesn't damage him.

A: Firstly, to tell the truth, this impunity isn't reserved for media intellectuals, it works for politicians as well, or for journalists … And secondly, there isn't as much impunity as you think. Because they noticed themselves, at a given moment, that their media visibility discredited them. They know it. That's the ambiguity of media intellectuality, the auto-immunity of the thing. They're all clever. They know that the more media credit they have, the less credit they have in certain circles which are in the position to create standards of evaluation … Bernard-Henri Lévy knows it very well. He knows he's got a bad reputation. A few years ago now, I read somewhere that he wanted to pull back a little, because he could see it was counterproductive. It's true, it's counterproductive. So it's equivocal. The gain can become a loss. And the reason he hates people like me so much, for example, is that he knows what I think about it, that I have anyway a little credit and that, even though I've never written anything or said anything publicly, he knows me well enough to know what I think about all that and to know that there are quite a few people like me, or around me, who think the same and dismiss him as a media intellectual, in the bad sense …[55] And that's the punishment. Not in the sense that a lie or manipulation is being penalized. But in the sense that their image becomes devalued as the audience level goes up. The more books you sell that are forgotten in six months, the more your image declines. It's terrible, but that's the way it is. They know it … They don't want to be regarded as media showbiz people. But they know that's what they are, that they do everything to be that while denying it. That's where there's punishment, I think, where there's chastisement. In any case, a price to pay.

Q: Which is also the price of posterity. Because their intellectual and political posterity is questionable, and by no means assured.

A: You're right. There are no disciples of Bernard-Henri Lévy, or of Sollers or Glucksmann. At the same time, because they feel – they're intelligent enough for that – the critical and severe judgement of them in their own milieu by people like me and others, they hate them. They hate me.

Q: Really?

A: Lévy at first was a friend. Until 1975. He'd been my pupil to start with. And when he left the École, he used to come back to see me. He even wrote a very favourable article about me. He used to give me advice. One day he said: 'You know, you ought to get rid of all those little disciples who are damaging you.' Then he named some people I won't name, but who weren't actually so little. And he added: 'Look, whenever you want, I'll get them to give you an article in Paris Match.' So yes, they're on their own. But because they feel that all the same they have adversaries, in the shadows, who criticize them, they team up. They form leagues, constellations. All of a sudden you notice that Sollers is defending Lévy, why? That Lévy is defending Sollers, why? That suddenly Finkielkraut, who has every reason not to agree with Bernard-Henri Lévy, is allying with Lévy … There's a configuration of all those intellectuals, an assembly, a mechanism. And I think they close ranks because they are both combative and cornered. And they feel indicted, in a way. It's a strategic alliance. They're alone, and they congregate so as not to be alone …

I believe that this age of the media intellectual, which began some decades ago now, will have to end sooner or later. And in the media, too – this is both a hope and a prediction – there will have to be a transformation and a diversification, enabling intellectuals to speak in different modes and rhythms, with different aims. Without an eye on commercial promotion, I mean, and taking the time to say things properly. … I do think – I hope – that little by little, television and the papers will change the conditions and impose on intellectuals – or intellectuals will impose on the media – other standards, other tastes, other rhythms, other requirements; and when that time comes, there will be no more talk of media intellectuals. There will be intellectuals doing their work, each in their own way, intellectuals who will be able to speak publicly, which I believe actually is an intellectual's responsibility. Once you publish anything, you become a media intellectual. I'm a media figure myself, since films have been made about me, two at least. In one of those two films, I say that even now, at my great age, and having published a lot, I still wonder whether it's right; whether I've published because I'm too exhibitionist, whether I've published just to seem interesting. Anyway, that's a question I ask myself. If the intellectual feels it's his responsibility, essentially as a citizen, to speak out in public, there will always be media intellectuals in the broad sense. And there's nothing wrong with that. But on both sides, there ought to be contracts which will make the quality of things improve. I believe that, little by little, there will be moves in that direction.

5 THE WORLD IS MY SPECTACLE

Bernard-Henri Lévy has been the most media-savvy of the 'politically committed' French intellectuals since the late 1970s. But committed to what, to what vision of the world? His convictions follow one another without any obvious coherence. But he excels at producing and directing a show of himself striding the world stage. In book after book, he makes his own person the lead character, influenced by mythical figures he aspires to emulate. This role-playing leads him to contradict himself and change his mind when he crosses a frontier, for example on the American war in Iraq.

The real problem is that this permanent self-staging is accompanied by egregious errors on the subjects he addresses. He distorts the reality of the 1990s Algerian civil war by absolving the generals of any involvement in the massacres. He invents a meeting with commander Massoud of the Northern Alliance in 1981 to perfect his image as an Afghan warrior. And when he goes to report on the war in Georgia in 2008, he describes a scene of pillage that exists only in his imagination.

THE SHOWMAN OF COMMITMENT

Is Bernard-Henri Lévy a committed intellectual? One might doubt it, judging by what he says himself. In 1977, when *Barbarism with a Human Face* came out, he took the attitude of a dandy, scornful of the sweat and tears of political struggle. Commitment? 'The very word repels me. I much prefer to think in terms of "testimony".'[1] In the absence of commitment, what remains? Morality, the same interview goes on to tell us. 'The essence of the problem is that I no longer believe in politics, that I no longer have the slightest yardstick for choosing sides in politics, and the remaining criteria are of a different order: I'd say they were ethical, at the risk of being misunderstood.'[2] In the same year, the left-wing daily *Le Matin* asked Bernard-Henri Lévy, 'Does that mean that you reduce the question of government to moral terms?' and received the reply, 'Absolutely. The real problem is a return to morality. For my part, if ever I write another book, if I have the courage and boldness to do it, I'll write a treatise on morality.'[3]

Contrary to the model of a Sartre-style universal intellectual (a learned man who in keeping with his oeuvre, in the name of the prestige it has brought him, makes the choice of public commitment to a cause he believes to be just), the New Philosopher adopts a moralistic posture from the start. In the name of his rejection of ideology, he dismisses all political and social theory and sinks back into a much more abstract view of the world, governed by the polarization between Good and Evil. This conception is supposed to apply to everyone and its main principles, envisaged as absolutes, are supposed to guide all the rules of human conduct in society. It meant a fundamental U-turn in harmony with the more general withdrawal from politics that was becoming noticeable on the threshold of the 1980s, the 'grey years' described by Gilles Deleuze. The individualism set free after years of collective commitment would now cheerfully put up with an economic liberalism decked in all the virtues, by way of a gratifying celebration of ethical values too general to impose any real constraints.

So fifteen years later, when Bernard-Henri Lévy embraced the cause of Alija Izetbegovic's Bosnia following the break-up of the former Yugoslavia, he could say blithely: 'Anyhow, the truth is known. It is neither technical nor, strictly speaking, political. It is moral.'[4] Telling words, that in three sharp strokes justify all the failings, errors of analysis, errors of fact and approximations that (as we shall see) litter his interventions on the war in former Yugoslavia. And that sound resonates, most of all, like an injunction to fall into line with him. If Bernard-Henri Lévy is on the side of righteousness and justice, who would dare to suggest a couple of adjustments, at the risk of tipping over into the evil camp?

Nevertheless, in 2004 – ten years after Bosnia – he was able to say the exact opposite without even blinking: 'I always distrust, you see, discourses that exhort political leaders to be more moral. And for a long time now, I've preferred politicians to act like proper politicians, rather than aping moralists.'[5] He said the same thing elsewhere even more clearly at more or less the same moment: 'I myself am a philosopher. A militant.'[6]

So, Bernard-Henri Lévy is a militant grown weary of commitment, and at the same time a moralist who has always distrusted discourses advocating morality … Subtle dialectic or mental confusion? The latter perhaps, judging by some of the questions on the dust jacket of the French edition of *War, Evil and the End of History*. 'Who describes, most closely, the reality of our time: Nietzsche or Spinoza, Hegel or Andy Warhol? … Why did Hegel and Kojève believe that Evil no longer has a future?' And so on and so forth.

In June 1993, in civil-war-torn Algeria, several intellectuals were murdered and the killings claimed by Islamist groups. On 27 June there was a meeting in Paris where intellectuals protested about these crimes, in particular the murder of Tahar Djaout, a French-speaking Algerian writer. As Jacques Derrida told us in 2004 (see above, chapter 4), Bernard-Henri Lévy, who had not been invited to speak, arrived at the Maison des écrivains in the middle of the meeting, grabbed the microphone, spoke, had himself photographed, and left without staying to hear anyone else. Mohammed Harbi, a respected Algerian historian who had been invited onto the platform that day, recalled the 'popping of flashbulbs' and added: 'Bernard-Henri Lévy stayed on his feet and said: "As they've got it in for a French-speaker, I'm off to the ministry of Culture tomorrow to organize a big seminar in Algiers." I remember being scandalized by this jaw-dropping display of cultural nationalism. After that Bernard-Henri Lévy left, without waiting for the end of the meeting.'[7]

A committed intellectual … committed above all to himself, perhaps. The accusation does follow Bernard-Henri Lévy around. He never espouses a cause without a camera present to film him in action; he has never engaged with a subject without getting a book, film or even stage play (see above, chapter 3) out of it, or at least an article or two. His public commitments are endlessly recycled and privatized. He has staked everything on his voluntarist ability to embody the causes he sets out to defend; he personalizes to excess the issues he appropriates. One result is that any criticism of what he says or does can be interpreted as a personal attack: 'I've survived low blows and the unfair indictments that go with them';[8] 'What have I done to make some people even now, at *Esprit* for example, reach for their revolvers when they hear the name Lévy? I have a strong feeling that it isn't over, it's a battle that will outlive us.'[9]

Récidives, a retrospective collection of articles and diaries published in 2004 (see above, chapter 3), offers a striking cross-section of this egotistical commitment. The great majority of the texts gathered in the 'Bosnia' chapter, one of the longest in the book, open with a stentorian 'I'. 'I was in Sarajevo again yesterday' (p. 556); 'I remember Bosnia' (p. 628); 'I left him in Sarajevo' (p. 624); 'Izetbegovic was my friend' (p. 659); 'A war? A real one? Faced with these first images, faced ... with the incongruity of those scenes of carnage in the middle of the Maastricht epoch, my first reflex was like everyone's: "No, come on, it's impossible"' (p. 647); 'At last the tone has changed. France, then Britain, seem to have made the leap. And for those who, like me ...' (p. 617). Bosnia is him. He is Bosnia. To criticize him is to have it in for Bosnia. To criticize Bosnia is to have it in for him.

SELF-INVENTION

'Suppose the true heroes, in life, had always been actors, all of them? Malraux an actor ... Hemingway an actor ... Real members of the brigade, artillerymen of the "España" squadron, actors ... George Orwell, an actor... Dos Passos, an actor ... Actors, actors, actors... *All the world's a stage* ... Life is a slightly less inconstant dream ... All mixed up, all confused.... I must urgently return, alone, to Bosnia.'[10] As Bernard-Henri Lévy wishes to be a 'true hero', he will be an actor. Indeed in 1977, before becoming a New Philosopher, he had a go on the boards in a televised adaptation of Aragon's *Aurélien* (co-written by the publisher Françoise Verny), playing the character of Paul Denis, a sincere and rather ridiculous poet. He was excellent in the part. And Bernard-Henri Lévy has played many roles since.

BERNARD-HENRI LÉVY AS SARTRE AND MALRAUX

'I belong to a generation that had a choice between two clichés.'[11] Bernard-Henri Lévy chose both.

Malraux has been the more consistently-played role. At thirty there was the perpetual cigarette, brandished more than smoked, and the departure for Bangladesh; these days there is the effort to make the voice tremble a bit during public utterances. Then there was Bosnia: 'Hard to deny in fact that in Bosnia, for example, the image and example of Malraux were constantly in my mind. What would he have said? What would he have done?'[12] 'On every one of my journeys, there's been no day when I haven't wondered, before acting or while acting, how he would have reasoned, and what he might have concluded.'[13] Best of all is the recognition that dawns when he sees himself on television, bawling during a demonstration: 'Have I ever looked so old, so out of sync, as I do in that image? Malraux, when he saw himself in his famous photo, fist raised, convulsed between Peyrefitte and Debré during the great Gaullist demonstration of 30 May 1968 in the Champs-Élysées, must have felt something similar'.[14]

Sartre is a later role.

> He is like Camus, they used to say of me … A defender of human rights, and thus like Camus. And then again like Malraux, obviously, in his nostalgia for heroism and adventure, for the author's ability to be a character larger than life, living out his work to the full … I allowed them to have their say … Even if I personally knew that the 'larger than life' character, the model of the total writer, the figure of the intellectual which was going to be so cruelly missing from the new era, was incarnated first and foremost by Sartre.[15]

So Bernard-Henri Lévy tricks himself out as a Sartre of the 'new era'. He's another philosopher who writes novels and does theatre, of course, but he also copies tiny details. In *Sartre*, he describes a 'man reputed to see nothing', an 'absolute conceptual who pretended, flirtatiously, to wait for Simone de Beauvoir to tell him about things before seeing them'.[16] A foible he attributes to himself in *Comédie*: 'It even became a joke with A. [Arielle Dombasle]. "What's the weather like today?" Or: "What do I think, already, of this view?" Or: "This landscape, my eyes are closed, describe this landscape for me"'.[17] Incapable of having Sartre's oeuvre, Bernard-Henri Lévy can at least borrow his blindness.

BERNARD-HENRI LÉVY AS LEN DEIGHTON

When he is in a country at war, Bernard-Henri Lévy becomes an airport paperback hero.

> I am so intensely afraid in Tenga, Burundi, during the gunfire, then on the road back, with the wounded soldier who is dying next to me, under the effect of this fear, in the whiff of horrible life it breathes into me, it's other fragments of memory, with no connection to the situation, obscene, intrusive, that rush into my mind: a caress, a sigh, a Mexican sunset, A.'s hair in the light of a Mediterranean landscape, a word from her, a gesture that's familiar about which I understand, for the first time, that it was hers alone, a snow-covered landscape, a cup of tea, a sunset on the Positano bay, a childhood treasure-hunt, a film shot that I didn't realize had impressed me so much.[18]

BERNARD-HENRI LÉVY AS FREDERICK FORSYTH

And like other airport paperback heroes, Bernard-Henri Lévy, when at rest, chases tail. '"Oh my God! My God!" The blonde seems more upset than anything. She has reclosed her purse. Crouching like that, bottom on heels, blouse half undone, she looks even more beautiful; I imagine her round belly, her white lace panties, the way she must have of refusing herself, or of acquiescing, or perhaps both at once; I imagine her boldness, her modesty, her scent of freshly fucked woman ...'[19]

IRAQ WAR, 2003: HOW BERNARD-HENRI LÉVY CHANGES HIS MIND WHEN HE GOES THROUGH IMMIGRATION CONTROL

Sometimes Bernard-Henri Lévy assumes positions that fall into a sweet mixture of ethics and politics. In 2003 and 2004, unlike his film-maker pal Romain Goupil, he was against the war in Iraq, wrote as much and said so in interviews. But he also thought that 'from the moral point of view' it was 'pretty just'.[20] The Americans in Iraq were 'angels playing at ogres'.[21] But the withdrawal of his country's troops by the new Spanish prime minister, José Luis Zapatero, looked like a 'new avatar of Munichism'[22] (a reference to the Munich accords in 1938, endorsing the inaction of the European democracies in the face of Hitler's expansionism). Against the war in practice, but for it in principle, he condemned the country that had pulled out with even greater vehemence ... one must confess this is hard to follow.

Just as baffling were the remarks he made in 2002 on the US public TV network PBS. 'I was against the Bush administration when it decided to go to war against Iraq. I thought it was a mistake, a serious and historic mistake. But today, there we are: we're in Iraq. And I think of the ordinary Iraqis, the raped women, the orphans, the children, all the ruined men of that country. We should now finish the job. It's our duty to be over there. It's our duty...' The interviewer interrupts: 'To send troops to Iraq?' Bernard-Henri Lévy resumes: 'It's our duty to send people to Iraq. I don't know whether they should be troops as such, everyone has their own knowhow and knowledge. You Americans know how to win a war. We French know how to do nation-building. Perhaps you are good cops. Perhaps we are good nursemaids. Perhaps we ought to bring the cops and the nursemaids together in Iraq.'[23]

So, while resolutely opposed to American intervention in Iraq in the French media, Bernard-Henri Lévy in the end falls a little short of that position on the US airwaves. Mind you, he was speaking at the moment when his book *Who Killed Daniel Pearl?* was being launched in the

US, and his promotion campaign was partially organized around the notion of 'anti-anti-Americanism', which he was supposed to represent in France (see below, chapter 9).

THE MAN WHO 'CANNOT QUITE BELIEVE' IN THE MASSACRES ORDERED BY ALGERIAN GENERALS IN THE 1990S

Interviewed in 2004 by *Libération* when a selection of his old reportages was coming out in *Récidives*, Bernard-Henri Lévy justified his choice of texts as follows: 'There's the risk of being wrong. There's the risk, when you republish texts like these reportages from 1992, in Algeria, of retrospective refutation. Fine. That's how it is. I withdraw nothing, today, of my basic analysis that the Islamists were responsible for the massacres. Even if I have a tendency, with hindsight, to think that perhaps I underestimated the possible instrumentalization of those Islamists by the military government.'[24] An impressive self-justification: insisting on 'withdrawing nothing', while thinking it possible that he may have written the opposite of what might have happened. 'Fine. That's how it is.' The confession of incompetence, rare in itself, is transformed miraculously into a eulogy. As if republishing texts one suspects of having a tenuous connection with reality were evidence, not of an immense idleness, but of courage. A fundamental matrix of the 'committed' Bernard-Henri Lévy's self-legitimization equipment is revealed: bad faith.

The pieces published by *Le Monde* in 1998 (not 1992, he got the date wrong) were entitled 'Choses vues en Algérie' (Things seen in Algeria).[25] This 'low-key' title makes implicit reference to the writings of the great French novelist Victor Hugo (1802–1885) collected and published in 1887, two years after his death, under the title *Choses vues*. Bernard-Henri Lévy was later to use this 'find' again, as we shall see, as a title for his astonishing 'reportages' from other zones, like Darfur and Georgia. But what did the Algeria pieces say?

Based on interviews with (among others) the governor of Algiers and the head of security for the production zone of the country's six gas pipelines, accounts of the massacres that had just occurred in the Mitidja triangle, a colourful description of the Algiers Casbah as a 'cut-throat quarter' and other descriptions mentioning 'paths of the Evil One', where the narrator is subjected to hostile treatment outside an Algiers mosque (an incident described in strikingly similar, but less violent terms as one outside a Karachi madrassa in *Who Killed Daniel Pearl?*), the articles are consistently critical of the Algerian army for being more inclined to protect wealth-generating zones than villages, and blames the sluggishness of the military hierarchy for the failure to mobilize its men quickly enough to protect the civilian victims of massacres.

In the week following its publication, this reportage was the target of a volley of brickbats from *Le Canard enchaîné*, summed up by the satirical weekly as follows: 'The Algiers dailies have just saluted his performance, four pages in *Le Monde*. But without mentioning that they are riddled with errors, approximations and omissions.'[26] Given the right to reply, Bernard-Henri Lévy quibbled over the *Canard*'s own errors of detail but did not answer the main charge.

A little prior research might have helped to make his articles more rigorous. A year earlier, on 19 November 1996, Amnesty International had revealed that Algerian security forces engaged in anti-terrorist operations were carrying out extra-judicial executions, that the families of victims were forced to sign declarations that their relatives had been killed by terrorists, and that hundreds of individuals had been reported missing after being arrested by men from the DRS (Département du renseignement et de la sécurité, formerly Sécurité militaire, the political police that had controlled the country since 1962, strongly influenced by the Soviet KGB and its avatars like the East German Stasi or Romanian Securitate).

In the spring of 1997 – six months before Bernard-Henri Lévy's visit to Algeria – Pierre Sané, secretary general of Amnesty International, wondered: 'Why is a state that has shown such confidence in its security strategy unable to protect its population twenty minutes outside the capital?'[27] Between 1 and 25 August 1997, more than thirty massacres of civilians took place, essentially in the Algérois, resulting in nearly 500 deaths. On the evening of 28 August a particularly bloody raid on the village of Raïs, in an Islamist suburb of Algiers, left more than 300 dead and 200 injured.

The circumstances of that massacre point starkly at the army. Situated in an area 'bristling with barracks', Raïs had to wait five hours for the requested reinforcements to arrive, after the killing was over.[28] In September, it was learned that at the beginning of August the army chief of staff had sent a note to all the country's unit commanders asking them not to undertake anti-terrorist operations without express orders from the top of the hierarchy.[29] Later it emerged that for having tried, despite the absence of orders, to help some Raïs villagers who were being massacred, the lieutenant responsible for protecting the sector had been incarcerated at the military prison in Blida for 'disobeying orders'; his detachment had already been cut by four fifths before the atrocities.

In the summer of 1997 (four months before Bernard-Henri Lévy's report), some US papers – Roger Cohen in the *New York Times* of 2 August, Flora Lewis in the *International Herald Tribune* of 5 September – raised the possibility that an army 'clan' could have been involved in organizing the massacres. At the end of August, the Islam specialist Bruno Étienne was wondering how such small terrorist groups (no more than 1,000 combatants) were managing to defy security forces numbering 400,000 and massacre civilians on such a huge scale without ever getting caught. 'The Algerian government is telling us stories. The generals say they are fighting Islamists, but it seems more likely that they are fighting each other.'[30] After the massacre at Bentalha (22 September 1997, more than 400 victims), the few survivors said the same sort of things as those of the other massacres: 'We had rusty old weapons and the terrorists had "Kalashes" and grenades. Who are they, these terrorists? Islamists, or military?'[31]

Nevertheless, despite this bundle of coherent pointers from diverse sources, Bernard-Henri Lévy chose to whitewash the army in his piece published in January 1998. 'Military incompetence, assuredly; indifference, perhaps; the thought, why not, at the back of certain minds, that the life of a good soldier is worth more than that of some peasant who yesterday was still playing footsie with the FIS; but a "staff" or a "clan" or even a "special service" fomenting massacres, or arming the killers, or disguising – it has been alleged! – their men as Islamists: that is a hypothesis I cannot quite bring myself to believe.'[32]

The hypothesis that Bernard-Henri Lévy cannot quite bring himself to believe – the involvement of army and DRS special forces in the massacres[33] – was confirmed two days after his reportage appeared by the testimony of two policemen from Algerian anti-terrorist units, printed in the British weekly the *Observer*.[34] Since that time the revelations have multiplied, establishing in incontrovertible fashion the context and form taken by the Algerian generals' 'dirty war'.[35] Over ten years, they organized operations attributed to the Islamists and shaped the army and security forces into a terrible 'killing machine', based on torture, forced disappearances and extra-judicial executions on a large scale, a machine responsible for tens of thousands of deaths.[36]

The facts have since been clearly established, as the journalists Lounis Aggoun and Jean-Baptiste Rivoire wrote in 2004:

> Since 1992, and especially since 1994, the [Algerian] generals have made savage violence their main political management tool: whether using

> special forces and police units, DRS death squads, the GIA (Groupes Islamiques Armés) or militias to batter the civilian population, their underlying strategy throughout has been to shed blood and maintain a climate of terror to consolidate their power. And, whenever that power appeared under threat, they intensified the violence, used both as a 'message' aimed at their adversaries (and at the international community) and as a means to smash any thought of revolt on the part of the population, and especially its Islamist fringe.[37]

In October 2000, following the publication of the sensational book by a survivor of the hideous Bentalha massacre,[38] Bernard-Henri Lévy seemed flustered for a moment. He wrote in his *Le Point* bloc-notes: 'Who did the killing at Bentalha, the village on the outskirts of Algiers where in a single night, on 22 September 1997, 417 men, women and children had their throats cut? Islamists, some affirmed, and that is the conclusion I had reached myself in the series of articles I gave *Le Monde* some months later. The army, replies a survivor, Nesroulah Yous, at the end of a meticulous counter-investigation published by Éditions La Découverte with a preface by François Gèze. Worrying. But not convincing. I shall come back to it.'[39] Eleven years on, his readers in *Le Point* are still waiting for him to do so.

How could Bernard-Henri Lévy, who on several previous occasions had publicly stood up for the right of Algerian Islamists to a defence in court,[40] have found himself thus propelled into the camp of the Algerian 'eradicators'? He remains there to this day, for lack of critical reconsideration … 'Fine. That's how it is.' How can he be on the side of those who maintain that the 'Islamists' alone are responsible for the massacres, to the point of being blind to the exactions of an 'army of corrupt torturers who have chosen to seat their power on the generalized use of the rubber hose and napalm?'[41] Lounis Aggoun and Jean-Baptiste Rivoire have given an edifying account of the propaganda campaign directed abroad, orchestrated from November 1997 onward by the Algerian regime to 'correct the image that is being spread of Algeria'.[42] It included visits to Paris by Algerian personalities to rally French political leaders to their discourse; the organization of a solidarity meeting at La Mutualité, on 21 January 1998 ('Algeria: silence kills'), addressed notably by Bernard-Henri Lévy and Khalida Messaoudi, a feminist militant, long-standing member of parliament for the RCD (Rassemblement pour la culture et la démocratie, close to the regime) and future spokeswoman for the Algerian government; and a visit to France (arranged by the DRS) of two woman 'victims of the GIA', to bear witness to Islamist atrocities in the studios of the Franco-German TV channel Arte, broadcast on the same day, 21 January.

The special permits granted to Bernard-Henri Lévy and to André Glucksmann (author of a 'travel diary' broadcast by France 3 in the same period[43]), were evidently part of this PR strategy by the Algerian government, at a time when the journalists who normally covered the country for *Libération*, *Le Monde*, Capa or Canal Plus were being confronted with innumerable administrative hassles, and as often as not the suspension pure and simple of their authorization to work on Algerian territory. It is difficult to understand why this difference of treatment, and clearly of favour, did not alert the two Frenchmen at the time. When asked in 2004 by the weekly *VSD*, 'How come you could get into Algeria in late 1997 when journalists couldn't?' –, Bernard-Henri Lévy replied, 'Perhaps because I didn't introduce myself as a journalist, but as a film-maker researching this film, for which incidentally the permit was refused by the generals I'm supposed to have "whitewashed".'[44]

Was it naivety? A strong wish to assess the Algerian terrain for himself despite everything, despite the very restrictive conditions placed on his visit, including permanent surveillance, vetting of interlocutors, and strictly controlled and supervised travel? Understandable vertigo caused by the absolute horror of the massacres? Bad faith graven in the stone of his obsession with the Islamist menace? More than one of these perhaps, but Bernard-Henri Lévy went along, consciously or not, willingly or not, with a strategic expedient perfectly controlled by the military ... and which achieved its purpose. The reporter-writer paid them unambiguous homage in a press conference before leaving Algeria. 'I shall leave Algiers with the feeling that you are going to win thanks to the patriots, the communal guards, and to the army, but also thanks to the resistance of the people and to the courage of the journalists who have chosen to stay in Algiers.'[45] Before, once again, largely absolving those same military of involvement, he stated, 'Today, I obviously wouldn't exclude the possibility that there might here or there have been cases where the military security has pulled something nasty. What army hasn't? ... But I have the feeling, primarily, that the bulk of the crimes are being committed by the very people who are claiming them: the GIA.'[46] Pulling 'something nasty' ['*faire des cochonneries*'], in the context of the tens of thousands cruelly murdered in Algeria's dirty war, is an expression that makes the blood run cold.

As do the words of praise lavished not long afterwards on Bernard-Henri Lévy and André Glucksmann by General Khaled Nezzar, one of those mainly resposible for Algerian state terrorism in the 1990s (and who will go down in history as the butcher of Algerian youth in the October 1988 riots, when more than 500 died). Nezzar declared in the Algerian daily *El-Watan* that the two men 'by their courage have made known the truth', before assuring 'these men of courage and conviction' of his 'greatest respect' and 'highest regard'.[47]

The really amazing thing, undoubtedly, and one that speaks volumes on the dereliction of the French media, is that all of this passed pretty much unremarked, give or take the reactions of a few intellectuals, who were able to get published all right, but who were absolutely ignored. In 1996, the sociologist Pierre Bourdieu had written that 'it is not worthy of a sociologist to talk about Bernard-Henri Lévy. ... People should see that he is only a sort of epiphenomenon of a structure.'[48] But he emerged from his reserve after the publication of the two-part feature in *Le Monde*, in his only text devoted directly to Bernard-Henri Lévy (whom he refrained from naming, but who is plainly identifiable).[49]

In his view, Bernard-Henri Lévy had acted as a 'negative intellectual', executing 'a base operation of symbolic policing, the absolute antithesis of everything that defines an intellectual: freedom vis-à-vis authority, criticism of received ideas, demolition of simplistic alternatives, restitution of complexity to problems', by means of two articles 'written at the end of a visit under escort, programmed, supervised, and invigilated by the Algerian authorities or army, to be published in the greatest French daily newspaper although filled with platitudes and errors and as a whole oriented towards a simplistic conclusion, pitched to give satisfaction to superficial compassion and racist hatred dressed up as humanist indignation.'[50]

The historian Pierre Vidal-Naquet and the publisher François Gèze reacted vigorously to the above-mentioned TV broadcast on the Arte channel and to Bernard-Henri Lévy's articles, with their strange conflations and blinkered bias favourable to the Algerian government.[51] In his reply, Bernard-Henri Lévy warned them against the 'Timisoara syndrome', raised the 'frightful spectre of a new type of negationism' (a surreal accusation, given Vidal-Naquet's role in denouncing a Holocaust revisionist, an authentic one this time, Robert Faurisson) and wrote scoldingly:

> By going back too far, by being too bound up in the game of the bad origin and the ultimate explanation, we set a terrible trap that always blunts, in the end, what was horrible about the crime, what was inaccessible to all reason. Was Auschwitz in the Versailles Treaty? Stalin in Brest-Litovsk? And will the women of Relizane be advanced when they understand that the murderers of their sons and husbands are the remote descendants of the Bey of Algiers and of Bugeaud? Excuse by explaining … normalize the crime by diluting it … tie murder into a chain of reasons so tight that it becomes, from one to the next, first necessary and then natural …[52]

In the new-style anti-fascist struggle that Bernard-Henri Lévy believes he is waging by denouncing 'God's lunatics', anything goes. A complex reality can be sacrificed in favour of a grossly oversimplified discourse, and worse still, investigation and clarification are disqualified to the profit of moral judgement alone. In any case, by placing himself, as he claims, on the victims' side he serves no cause but his own, and that of the powers that be.

THE ALLEGED MEETING WITH MAJOR MASSOUD IN 1981

'If there is one underlying intention that haunts the work I have undertaken from one end to the other, it is precisely the refusal to lie, the rejection of the "sham" of dialectical skills. It is entirely ordered by an ethic of truth and lucidity.'[53] That's the principle, anyway. In practice, slippages can occur.

There are the small bits of trumpery, like the reinvention of anecdotes to suit the interlocutor and context, for example, Malraux's call for the constitution of International Brigades for Bangladesh. 'I shall always remember that autumn afternoon as I dawdled on the terrace of the Closerie des Lilas and heard on the radio that voice, breaking as much with age as with emotion, that feverish and painful declaration: Malraux was offering his services to drive an assault vehicle and proposing the constitution of new international brigades,' he told the glamour magazine *Playboy* in 1977,[54] before launching into the narrative of his own Bengali epic. By 2001, on Michel Drucker's show, the version had changed: 'It's a story that began on television,' he confided to the presenter with a collusive air, before recalling in misty-eyed fashion the feverish, grandiose and pathetic Malraux who had appeared before him on the small screen.[55]

And there are the lies, knowingly constructed over the years. In his

War, Evil and the End of History, Bernard-Henri Lévy published a fragment dated 10–11 September 2001, two days after the murder of Major Ahmad Shah Massoud, the leader of the Afghan Northern Alliance who had fought the Soviet occupation and later fought the Taliban. The fragment was a sad, bitter farewell to a man 'met … for the first time, in 1980, right after the Soviet occupation of Afghanistan.'[56] A few months later, on a mission to Afghanistan on behalf of the president of the Republic, Jacques Chirac, and the then prime minister Lionel Jospin, with his long-time travelling companion Gilles Herzog and Dr Frédéric Tissot, representing the 'French Doctors', he placed a small plaque on the tomb of the Tajik chieftain at Bazarak, in the Panjshir: 'To Major Massoud, to the fighter for liberty, to the resistance leader, to the friend of France, the homage of his friends of twenty years' standing.'[57]

In December 1979, at the 'request' of the pro-Soviet Afghan government, Soviet troops invaded Afghanistan. There ensued an unprecedentedly violent war of occupation. In 1981 a French photographer, Alain Guillo[58] (a member of the association 'Les Amis de l'Afghanistan', founded by Jean José Puig and his late wife Marie-Berthe), had the idea of clandestinely delivering some radio transmitters to the Afghan resistance. But the small group lacked the financial means to get the transmitters to the Afghan frontier. Guillo then made contact with Bernard-Henri Lévy and the Jewish writer Marek Halter in the hope that 'they could find financial backing to cover the purchase of the material and the transport costs. They said OK straight away.'[59]

On 29 June 1981 there appeared in *Le Nouvel Observateur* a first appeal for 'a free radio in Kabul'. The short piece, signed by Bernard-Henri Lévy, announced the scheme's launch at a press conference in Paris on 30 June. The campaign was successful, the money was collected and a few weeks later a handful of radio links was established on the heights of the mountains encircling Kabul. 'The use of these radio broadcasts was primarily psychological,' Guillo recalled. 'The whole radio business spread incredible panic in the Soviet services, although the transmitters had a range of less than 50 kilometres. The Soviets tried everything to capture these radios because of all the clamour made in France. Very few people in Kabul could say they had really heard the broadcasts, but if you ask now, everyone remembers hearing them.'[60] Six years later, Alain Guillo paid dearly for his audacity. Accused of espionage by the KGB, he was arrested and detained for nine months.

Since that time Bernard-Henri Lévy has milked for all it's worth his support for the Radio Kabul operation, never missing a chance to recall his role in that first small victory over the Soviet empire. The episode became a recurrent reference in his articles and interviews: 'My first visit to Afghanistan dates from 1982 [a self-contradiction: in reality it was 1981 – in 2001, as we have seen, he claimed it was in 1980] when, clandestinely, I was carrying the transmitters for Radio Free Kabul to Massoud's people';[61] 'It is another way of keeping the promise to Massoud I made twenty years ago, when I brought to his combatants the first transmitters for Radio Free Kabul';[62] and 'I admired him very much, and for a long time too, since the time twenty years ago when he was still just a very young major in the resistance against the Red Army in the Panjshir.'[63]

He ran through the episode again on Michel Drucker's show in November 2001.

> I met Massoud a very, very long time ago. He and I were both very young. He was thirty, I was a little older perhaps. It was just after the Soviet intervention in Afghanistan. Some of us decided to make these small radios and take them to the Panjshir, the place where Massoud was fighting ... And since I'm in the habit of trying to square my actions with my thoughts, I went myself to take the first transmitters to Massoud. I understood on that day in 1981 that he was the incarnation of that democratic Islam, democratic and enlightened ... He was already so brave, that young commander who waged war without enjoying it.[64]

On his return, he published in *Le Nouvel Observateur* (12 September 1981) an article that put everything in place to establish the action of the European radio smugglers as a heroic feat. He used a title echoing the history of the French resistance ('This Is Radio Free Kabul'), a lyrical tone, and photos of himself and Marek Halter in Afghan dress, their hair bound in elaborate turbans in wild landscapes, surrounded by combatants. Later the French media began gradually to take more interest in the Afghan conflict, and in 1998, thanks to Christophe de Ponfilly's film *Massoud l'Afghan*, the public at large discovered the existence of the 'Lion of Panjshir', one of the few Afghan leaders to have stood up consistently against the Soviets. In 1981, however, in the piece of reportage by the author of *Barbarism with a Human Face*, the major who is mentioned – and whom the reporter compares to an 'Afghan double of Antonin Artaud' – is identified in somewhat evasive fashion: 'His name? His name doesn't matter much. For narrative convenience, we will call him Amin.' That 'Major Amin' was Amîn Wardak, a French-speaking Pashtun major from Wardak province, who had been seeking French contacts in Pakistan. In this article Bernard-Henri Lévy had made no mention of Ahmad Shah Massoud, or of the distant enclave of Panjshir. But the stage had been set for a mystification by passing off one for the other, leading eventually to the constructed legend of the meeting with Massoud.

Back in France, as a guest of the TF1 news show presented by Yves Mourousi, Bernard-Henri Lévy came up with a new anecdote: 'We met a major from the Afghan resistance who knew that shortly before his election to the presidency, François Mitterrand had said he saw no reason not to recognize the Afghan resistance. The major in question, whom we will call major Amin for convenience, asked us to remember, when we returned to France, to remind President Mitterrand of his promise.'

Had Bernard-Henri Lévy and Marek Halter met Ahmad Shah Massoud, or Amîn Wardak? It was not easy for Westerners unfamiliar with the Afghan terrain to distinguish among rebel soldiers who had in common a resolute opposition to the Soviets, a rejection of Islamist fundamentalism and great personal charisma. 'Bernard-Henri Lévy and Marek Halter didn't meet Massoud at that time,' Alain Guillo explains.

> They were 400 kilometres from the Panjshir as the crow flies. They met his representatives in Peshawar, including one of his brothers. A promotion operation was needed. I took them to the Pakistan–Afghan frontier. I took photos of Marek Halter and Bernard-Henri Lévy in the mountains of Pakistan, at the border with Afghanistan, which certain captions, not of my making, might have rendered misleading. I put them in touch with some participants in the operation, belonging to mujahideen groups. I organized the photo session, and they took the rolls away with them. They stayed on for ten days or a fortnight and then they left.

So Bernard-Henri Lévy and Marek Halter were not even, strictly speaking, in Afghanistan. They could just about glimpse its mountainous landscapes. A number of observers recall in private conversation that at the time, it had been common knowledge that the two French intellectuals had not set foot on Afghan soil. 'Bernard-Henri Lévy went for a walk one day in 1981 in the Pakistani-Afghan borderlands, like Lord Byron at Missolonghi, turban, fine moustache and all,' according to the American historian Michael Barry, a leading Afghanistan specialist.[65] 'Pakistani-Afghan borderlands', not 'Afghanistan'. It would not have been news to Gilles Deronsoro, professor at the Institut d'études politiques in Rennes and author of an acerbic critique of Bernard-Henri Lévy's reportage on Massoud (published in *Le Monde* on 13 October 1998):[66] 'In the absence of any knowledge of Afghanistan (apart from a short visit to the Pakistan frontier) …'[67]

Laurence Laumonier-Ickx is a doctor who went to Afghanistan six months after the Soviet intervention to train local health workers under the aegis of Medical Aid International. While not involved in the Radio Kabul operation, she was the first Westerner to have met Major Massoud in the Panjshir in 1981, and remained close to him until his death on 9 September 2001. Without hesitation, she confirmed that

> Bernard-Henri Lévy and Marek Halter were at the Pakistan-Afghan frontier, thirteen days' march from the Panjshir where Massoud was. To my knowledge they didn't meet him at that time. When during his mission to Afghanistan, in 2002, BHL had that plaque put up 'to our friend of twenty years', adding 'on behalf of the French Doctors', on Massoud's tomb, I asked the Afghan authorities to remove it. We had never been 'French doctors' in Afghanistan but '*doctor-e-Francawi*'. People shouldn't be dishonest. I have a lot of respect for guys who throw themselves into causes like that, with courage, but it does demand a certain level of humility and honesty.[68]

In his September 1981 article in *Le Nouvel Observateur*, Bernard-Henri Lévy is very precise about his feelings and doings. He describes in detail the people he meets, the landscapes he discovers, the excitement that grips everyone before the first radio broadcast. The longest expedition he claims to have accompanied lasted no more than a day – nothing like enough time to reach the Panjshir, a territory that 'Massoud never left' according to the CERI (Centre for the Study of International Relations) researcher Mariam Abou Zahab.[69] Memories fogged by time perhaps, or genuine hesitation … the fact is that in the big portrait he devoted to Massoud in *Le Monde* in 1998, after an expedition to Afghanistan, Bernard-Henri Lévy wrote, 'So here he is, this legendary commander, at war for nearly twenty years … He is smaller than I imagined him.'[70] As if they had never met before! In 2002, in his *Report to the President of the Republic and the Prime Minister*, he gave a quite different version: 'I remember Major Massoud from our first meeting, twenty years ago.' In the meantime Massoud, murdered by an Al Qaeda squad, had become a symbol of resistance to Islamist fundamentalism, a celebrated hero after nearly twenty years of neglect by Western governments and heads of state, and a very isolated figure for all that time. He was all too easy to co-opt as a 'friend' of long standing.

AUGUST 2008: MARCHING THROUGH GEORGIA

In his armoury as a showman of commitment, Bernard-Henri Lévy's heaviest weapon is his war reporting. For years his reports were published in *Le Monde*, the paper read by France's elites, a major customer for the epic BHLian style, providing the essayist with a powerful outlet and a prestigious endorsement – until war broke out between Russia and Georgia in 2008.

On 8 August of that year the small Georgian republic, led by the young president Mikheil Saakashvili, elected following the 'Rose Revolution' of 2003, attacked the separatist province of South Ossetia and took its capital, Tskhinvali. Russia in reprisal shelled Gori, in Georgia. The conflict, at midsummer, took the world by surprise, and outside observers found it difficult to apportion responsibilities. The war only lasted three or four days, a ceasefire being signed on 12 August. The peace plan went a long way towards satisfying Russia's demands, leaving Europe uneasy over a poorly resolved conflict.

It was against this complex, shifting background, difficult to decipher even for seasoned Caucasus-watchers, that Bernard-Henri Lévy turned up in Georgia. He got an article out of the trip, published by *Le Monde* on 19 August 2008 and next day by the US website the Huffington Post: 'Choses vues dans la Géorgie en guerre', or 'Georgia at War: What I Saw', the title again echoing Victor Hugo. The author is prominently featured, travelling the Ossetian roads, observing Russian troops, interrogating a peasant, meeting Saakashvili, sharing a nightcap with the US diplomat Richard Holbrooke, architect of the Dayton accords of 1995 that ended the war in Bosnia. The text is littered with clichés: Russians smell of vodka, a wounded man is 'dazed and terrified', there is a 'slight odor of putrefaction and death', and tanks 'rumble'. Satirical comment started to appear almost immediately. A cruel parody appeared on the French news website *Rue89*: 'I run my hand through my wild three-day beard. I've left my razor in Istanbul, where I had read Atatürk's memoirs on the shores of the Bosphorus.' A pro-Russian version appeared on the opinion site Causeur.fr.

In the piece, Bernard-Henri Lévy paints an apocalyptic portrait of Gori. The Russians have 'burned it down, pillaged it, reduced it to a ghost town. Emptied.' The essayist goes on to say that 'in their wake, Ossetian and Cossack bands pillaged, raped and murdered', that 'fathers were killed in front of their sons. Sons in front of their fathers'; that in one family 'the adults were made to kneel before being executed with a bullet through the head.' Based on the testimony of a single individual, with no indication of location or the number of victims, these are allegations of war crimes at least, meriting more serious treatment than this somewhat throwaway approach. The situation in Georgia is twice compared to that of Chechnya.

The real problem was that the Russians had not actually burned Gori. A *Le Monde* journalist and specialist in the former Soviet zone, Piotr Smolar, managed to get into the Georgian town a few days after the signature of the peace agreement (12 August 2008). 'The inhabitants were frightened, you could feel a huge collective anxiety,' he told us. 'But the town was in no way destroyed. There were bullet marks on the walls. I only saw one building severely damaged by artillery fire at the entrance to the town, but apart from that there was no destruction. The town had been looted in places, but not burned down, or emptied, or reduced to the state of a ghost town.'[71]

Tara Bahrampour, a *Washington Post* journalist, was one of the group of Western observers that included Bernard-Henri Lévy. And she too visited Gori, a few weeks after his article was published. 'When I went to Gori the town hadn't been burned, although I saw traces of fire on two or three buildings, and some broken windows in the main square. The Georgian government was cleaning the place up, and it must have been in a worse state before I arrived there, but real damage was restricted to a few places.'[72]

In reality, Bernard-Henri Lévy never set foot in Gori. So we were told by a former member of the European parliament for the French Green party, Marie-Anne Isler-Béguin, who had unexpectedly become his travelling companion.[73] On 13 August 2008, as chairwoman of the observer group in Georgia for the European Parliament, she was trying to get to Gori in the convoy organized by the Estonian ambassador to Tbilisi. During one stop at a Russian checkpoint she became aware of a 'rabble of journalists' with, at its centre, a man 'who wasn't dressed like a journalist': white shirt, black jacket and 'velvet shoes that were picking up the dust'.

The man was Bernard-Henri Lévy, who, seeing that only cars belonging to the diplomatic convoy were going to be let through, was asking to be taken along too. The Estonian diplomat, believing that he was dealing with the French ambassador, gave his permission. On the back seat of the car, Isler-Béguin moved over to make room for him. 'But the person accompanying him, the publisher Gilles Hertzog, climbed in too, and I asked him to get out. It was an official delegation after all,' the former parliamentarian recalled. 'But then someone opened the car boot and two other young fellows with BHL got in there: one was André Glucksmann's son, the documentary maker, the other a journalist from a French public radio station.' Another roadblock was negotiated. 'It was then that I noticed that in the front of our car was seated a scarred heavy who hadn't been there at the beginning of the trip. Turned out he was BHL's bodyguard,' the Euro-MP recalled, by then thoroughly disconcerted. He too had muscled his way into the car.

The car was halted again by Russian troops a few kilometres from Gori. The passengers got out. No one was going to be allowed any closer, with the sole exception of the secretary of the Georgian National Security Council, Alexander Lomaia, who was let in to recover some injured people from Gori. The French were stuck at the side of the road, blocked by Russian tanks, a kilometre or so from Gori. A very long wait ensued. The heavy took some photos of BHL beside a Russian tank. 'We stayed there for hours and didn't do anything else,' the former European member of parliament went on. 'The Russian military engineers came past and we tried not to get run over.' Around them, she remembered, 'the fields were burning, it was impressive. But it wasn't the town that was on fire. There's no need to exaggerate things, the situation was quite bad enough as it was.'

The *Washington Post* journalist, Tara Bahrampour, told us, 'We approached the town of Gori, but we were stopped before reaching any sort of urban or residential area. Where we were, there was no housing at all, not a dwelling to be seen. Like the rest of us, BHL spent those few hours on that country road.' After a long wait, the convoy turned round and started back towards Tbilisi, going through all the checkpoints again. At one of these roadblocks some journalists were waiting. Bernard-Henri Lévy got out and improvised a press conference. Minutes later a reporter recognized Marie-Anne Isler-Béguin and said, 'So, sounds like you had a pretty hair-raising time in Gori!' The parliamentarian was furious. 'I protested: "But we weren't in Gori! We did absolutely nothing, nothing at all. [BHL] says anything that comes into his head".' In the days that followed, Isler-Béguin would see BHL at the Tbilisi Marriott hotel, where most of the international press were staying. Wearing shades and his 'stage costume', the Green member of parliament recalled, he was calmly holding press conferences and giving interviews.

Bernard-Henri Lévy's 'things seen' in Georgia, then, are unsound from the factual point of view; and they are also extremely biased. His article sings the praises of the Georgian president, Mikheil Saakashvili, compared to the 'great resistance fighters', yet a man 'unfamiliar with war, its rites, its emblems, its culture'. When according to the chronology that has now been established, it is Saakashvili who began the hostilities by launching a military offensive in South Ossetia, probably provoked into it by Moscow's manoeuvres, to his great cost. When in 2009 the European Union published its report on the causes of the 2008 conflict, Tbilisi was indeed judged the responsible party.

'We were all treading on eggshells,' remembered the *Le Monde* reporter Piotr Smolar. 'There was a real information war going on and both sides were lying, drowning us in press releases, pictures and reports. What figures for victims and refugees should we believe? What words should we use to define the conflict or to describe South Ossetia and Abkhazia? The most important issue concerned the beginning of the conflict, to know who had started it. That would determine who was the aggressor and who was the injured party.'[74] No such prudence restrains Bernard-Henri Lévy's text. Putin 'must be told to stop', 'or the man who went, in his own words, "down into the toilets" to kill the civilians in Chechnya will feel he has the right to do the same thing to any one of his neighbors.'

Does the end really justify the means? Will any argument do, however biased and trumped-up, when it comes to alerting public opinion to the fate of civilians in a country at war, and of a fragile democracy threatened by Russian power? 'I don't regret having let him come along in our convoy because what's done is done; but if the circumstance arose now, I wouldn't do it again,' Marie-Anne Isler-Béguin told us three years after the event. Since then Bernard-Henri Lévy has moved on to other causes: denouncing Iran, defending Israel and the film director Roman Polanski. No real trace remains of his ephemeral commitment to the service of Georgia in his writings or statements. But one of his travelling companions – Raphaël Glucksmann, son of Bernard-Henri Lévy's old New Philosopher comrade from the late 1970s, André Glucksmann – went the whole hog. Following the appearance in November 2008 of a book of interviews with Mikheil Saakashvili,[75] he became his adviser on communication and international affairs.

Those 'Choses vues' in Georgia marked a turning point in Bernard-Henri Lévy's adventures in the land of journalism. For the first time in his career since the late 1970s, an article was immediately and repeatedly refuted. Significantly, this took place on the Web, where online journalists and commentators jostled gleefully to contradict him. The most ruthless salvo was fired by the French news site *Rue89*, in the form of a detailed counter-investigation of the errors and lies in the essayist's piece.[76] In the age of the Internet, of 'crowd sourcing' and online journalism, partially emancipated from the 'culture', sociology and professional customs of print media reporters, Bernard-Henri Lévy's ring-fenced impunity appears a quaint anachronism. On the Web, every mistake is a thousand times more visible and a thousand times shot down. The aura of his old persona as the dishevelled writer-traveller had taken a severe knock.

So severe indeed that Alain Minc, valued adviser to members of the French economic and political elites, and careful to maintain good relations with them, used *Libération* as a platform to contest Bernard-Henri Lévy's reportage.[77] And *Le Monde* was forced into the supreme humiliation of publishing an article explaining why they ran the controversial piece.[78] In the prestigious daily's offices and newsrooms there was no shortage of outrage. 'That double spread was a slap in the face for us,' grumbled one *Le Monde* hack. Bernard-Henri Lévy was quoted in the article, breezily owning up to the possibility of humbug: 'Perhaps my pen, in that instance, did allow itself to get carried away.' That was the last piece of 'war reporting' by BHL to appear in the great French daily. It had been comprehensively outflanked by the energetic punctiliousness of the web-surfing hordes.

6 THE MURDER OF DANIEL PEARL: HOW IT WAS COMMANDEERED BY BHL

'Who Killed Daniel Pearl? *appeared in April 2003. Part enquiry, part fiction, it went on the trail of the American journalist who was kidnapped in Pakistan in January 2002 by terrorists linked to Al Qaeda and beheaded on film by his captors. The book was very well received, and it established Bernard-Henri Lévy as an enlightened observer of the contemporary world.*

The book, described as an investigation that took up a whole year of the author's life, is shot through with half-truths and errors, few of which were picked up by the French press at the time, enthused as it was by the marvellous new genre of 'faction' that the book embodied. Bernard-Henri Lévy gave dramatic accounts of scoops that were nothing of the sort, and interpreted them in slapdash fashion. He commandeered for his own purposes the atrocious conditions under which Daniel Pearl died, gave a false version of the story that had taken Pearl to Pakistan, and identified the wrong man as his murderer. The central thesis of the book – that the Pakistani state is directly involved in Al Qaeda terrorism – is utterly absurd, but fits perfectly into the dangerously simplistic discourse of the mainstream media on radical Islam and Islamist terrorism.

A WHOLE YEAR?

According to his 'bloc-notes' in *Le Point*, Bernard-Henri Lévy was much concerned, between the spring of 2002 and the spring of 2003, with giving his opinions on events of the day. During the electoral campaign for the presidential election of April 2002, he denounced the Lutte Ouvrière candidate Arlette Laguiller, the tolerance shown by her party for revisionist ideas,[1] and the 'sympathy vote' for the far left. After

Lionel Jospin's defeat in the first phase of the presidential election, he appealed to the electorate to 'drown Chirac in votes'.[2] He denounced[3] the racist pamphlet published by the Italian journalist Oriana Fallaci[4] in May 2002, and in August stigmatized[5] – quite rightly – the 'racial' conception of nationality that the writer Renaud Camus was defending on his website. He made his contribution[6] to the 'Lindenberg affair' (named after the author of the pamphlet on French intellectuals *Le Rappel à l'ordre*[7] which appeared in November and monopolized that week's chronicle). He alerted readers, for its opening night, to *Hysteria*, the play being produced by the actor John Malkovitch at the Marigny theatre.[8] He recounted his role in the September launch of *Les Nouvelles de Kaboul*, a multilingual newspaper published in Dari, Pashto and French.[9]

He also watched some TV: TF1, movies on the Arte channel. He criticized the excessively baggy suit worn by François Hollande, national secretary of the Socialist Party, at the European Social Forum in Florence,[10] and mentioned the Poivre d'Arvor brothers' latest book,[11] published in November 2002;[12] paid tribute to his deceased friend Paul Guilbert, a journalist at *Le Figaro*,[13] then in January 2003 to Françoise Giroud,[14] who had died a few months later; denounced the call from the University of Paris-VI for non-renewal of the cooperation agreement between the European Union and Israel,[15] and praised the 'dashing style' of Dominique Strauss-Kahn on France 2.[16] In February 2003, he eulogized[17] a book by Marie-Claire Pauwels[18] on her father, and stated his admiration for Eric Marty's text 'Genet à Chatila', published in *Les Temps modernes*.[19]

In short, a weekly diary, covering with gleeful avidity the latest scuttlebutt on Parisian life. Unblinking attention and continuous work, with the exception of nine weeks scattered between February 2002 and January 2003, and a further six weeks' interruption between February and April 2003.[20]

Nevertheless, when he published *Who Killed Daniel Pearl?* on 23 April 2003, Bernard-Henri Lévy repeated endlessly that he had devoted twelve months of effort to it: 'The enquiry took a year';[21] 'I decided to put a year into following his trail';[22] 'that bizarre, slightly crazy adventure, that I lived through for a year'.[23]

And the book advances some 'terrifying conclusions'. The American journalist Daniel Pearl, kidnapped and later murdered in Karachi in January 2002, could have been the victim of a 'state crime', killed by, or with the complicity of, agents of Inter-Services Intelligence (ISI), the

Pakistani military intelligence organization. Daniel Pearl – according to the author – could have been on the point of exposing complicities from inside the Pakistani state apparatus with Al Qaeda, involving the intention of certain ISI officials to transfer nuclear technologies to Osama Bin Laden's terrorist network.

A year is quite a long time to spend on a story. Certainly a great deal longer than newspapers usually give their reporters to complete their investigations. To Bernard-Henri Lévy it is a weighty argument, a gauge of credibility even, a guarantee of work properly carried out. But it is an assertion that is hardly compatible with his schedule over the preceding year. How can the time, energy and physical presence required to occupy the social and media spaces indicated by his chronicles in *Le Point* be reconciled with the rigour, concentration, effort and commitment demanded by such a long, wide-ranging enquiry, tracking one of the world's most redoubtable terrorist networks over the murder of a Western journalist in distant Karachi?

The fact is that Bernard-Henri Lévy had pulled off a chronological conjuring trick by making people believe in a year of research without having had the time, or anything like it, to spend a year on the work. Even a year-long enquiry need not mean a year spent enquiring, still less can it mean the few weeks during which his 'bloc-notes' did not appear. In the chorus of praise, virtually unanimous, that greeted the appearance of his book, not a single journalist could be found to raise the question of this anomalous agenda in apparent contradiction with his activities as an editorialist. This was the first of the 'myths' the author would promote to generate media attention.

AGENT BENNETT'S DOUBTS

In February 2002, as Bernard-Henri Lévy began his mission to Afghanistan on behalf of the French government, and a few weeks before he decided to follow the trail of Daniel Pearl, US security in the provinces of Sindh and Baluchistan was being run by Randall Bennett, a special agent who had already served four years in the US Consulate in Karachi. Backed by a team of Pakistani police officers, he was leading nightly sweeps through the city in the hope of finding, before it was too late, the thirty-eight-year-old Daniel Pearl, South-East Asia bureau chief of the *Wall Street Journal*.

The journalist had been kidnapped on 23 January 2002, when a false intermediary offered to set up a meeting with Sheikh Mubarak Ali Shah Gilani, leader of the radical Islamist movement Jamaat ul-Fuqra. But Bennett's efforts to find him were fruitless. On 27 January, Pearl's captors sent a message demanding the repatriation of Pakistanis detained at Guantanamo Bay and of the former Taliban ambassador to Islamabad, Mullah Abdul Salam Zaeef. On the 30th they issued a threat to kill Pearl within twenty-four hours, and (rather oddly) demanded delivery of the F-16 fighter aircraft ordered, and paid for, by Islamabad from Washington several years earlier.

Emailed to several US newspapers, four photographs of Daniel Pearl in captivity were reproduced all over the world (one, with a firearm pointed at the captive's bowed head, was chosen by Bernard-Henri Lévy as the cover picture for his book). The affair caused considerable embarrassment to Pakistan's president, General Pervez Musharraf, who was just beginning a visit to the US.

In their messages, the kidnappers described Pearl as an agent of the CIA, then of the Israeli Mossad secret service. Denials from the *Wall Street Journal* and the CIA were followed by appeals for clemency from the association Reporters sans frontières, the boxer Muhammad Ali, the Rev. Jesse Jackson and Sheikh Yassin, spiritual leader of the Palestinian movement Hamas, and the luminous interventions of Pearl's French journalist wife, Marianne, seven months pregnant at the time. All fell on deaf ears. After a final message on 31 January, offering a twenty-four-hour stay of execution, the kidnappers lapsed into silence. The tragedy ended on 21 February with the transmission to the US Consulate in Karachi and the Pakistani press agency Online of a macabre video cassette, shot by his murderers, of the journalist's execution. Pearl was dead.

Not until 16 May, nearly three months later, were his remains found in a desert area on the northern fringes of Karachi. Bennett was the first to be informed, and he supervised the exhumation. In her book *A Mighty Heart*, Marianne Pearl gives a heartrending account of those days of searching, of anguished, futile waiting … when in reality, Pearl had been murdered after just a few days in captivity.[24]

Two months after the discovery of Pearl's body, on 22 July 2002, Bennett left Pakistan. After five years' service his departure, so discreet as to be almost clandestine, had been decided in some haste in light of the new death threats that Al Qaeda was uttering against him. A few weeks earlier a car bomb had exploded under his office windows, killing twelve people. In Madrid, where he was now posted, Bennett (who does not speak French) read large extracts of the English translation of *Qui a tué Daniel Pearl?* (published in September 2003[25]) of which he had first learned from journalist friends. As he explained to us when we met him in Madrid in July 2004, he quickly came to doubt the authenticity of the writer's account:

> I don't believe Lévy ever went to the places he claimed. If he had, he'd be dead. In my opinion, it's unlikely that he really talked to people in possession of that sort of information on the inside of the Pearl business. I'm an intelligence professional. None of us could have done what he says he did without getting killed. What's more, it would have been impossible for him to pursue that enquiry, on his own, too, in Karachi without everyone knowing about it, including the bad guys.
>
> I had an arrangement with the Pakistani authorities: whenever a foreigner showed up in a potentially dangerous place – anywhere outside the south side of the city, the residential quarters of Clifton and Defense – and was spotted by their services, they called me. If Lévy had gone where he claims, their intelligence would have called me and told me about it. It happened a number of times with other people.[26]

Bennett's comments, authoritative by definition, nevertheless cannot carry the same weight after his departure from Pakistan, partway through the 'year' Bernard-Henri Lévy says he devoted to his investigation. In the visits he made after Bennett's departure, might the investigative writer have succeeded in achieving what the American agent doubts so strongly? In theory, he certainly could have. In the book, at least, he gives a lot of detail on his actions and movements. His account is sufficiently focused on the progress of his investigation (and on his own person) to enable the reader to follow his trail fairly closely: the visits to Karachi, the hideout where Daniel Pearl was confined, the restaurant where he was kidnapped, Aurangzeb Park, the drug-addicts' quarter, the small guest houses remote from the big hotels and the Binori Town Mosque. Randall Bennett actually recalled meeting Bernard-Henri Lévy in Karachi at the beginning of his 'investigation' in 2002, and giving him the same security briefing that he had given Daniel Pearl a few months earlier. 'The briefing I gave him told him to do the opposite of what he claims to have done. So either he's lying or he didn't understand a word of it. I told him specifically not to go where he says he went.'[27]

In his office, the American keeps a photo of the team that joined Daniel's wife Marianne in starting the search for Pearl at the beginning of 2002: Jamel Youssouf, head of the Karachi police liaison committee; Dost Ali Baloch, from military intelligence; 'Captain', the police officer who first found the trail of the journalist's kidnappers; Asra Q. Nomani, a journalist and Pearl's colleague; Steve LeVine, a reporter for the *Wall Street Journal*, and Randall himself. He has remained on close terms with Marianne Pearl, has retained close friendships in Pakistan and is still resolutely (and patriotically) committed to the struggle against terrorism. He is also an intelligence professional, a man who knows the value of precision.

In other words Randall Bennett is a stickler for detail. And it was in just that area of detail – a multitude of small inaccuracies – that he came to suspect Bernard-Henri Lévy's narrative, especially in the long passage devoted to the description of the American reporter's place of captivity. Captured on 23 January 2002, Daniel Pearl was murdered just a few days later; the timing only became clear to investigators a long time after the event. During that short period he was hidden in the north of the city. Bernard-Henri Lévy refers to this place several times in his book: the 'house of the crime' (a chapter title in the book refers to it), the 'farmhouse',[28] the 'house where Pearl was detained'.[29] The description elicited Bennett's first objection: 'There was no house! Really it was a garden, planted with vines and young olive trees and full of weeds, with a wall around it. Pearl was kept in a breezeblock lean-to. Twenty feet away there was another small shed made of bricks, that was used as a toilet.'[30]

No house? Perhaps in his haste the narrator used a slightly misleading definition that need not cast doubt on the general validity of his observations. The problem is that over ten pages or so, Bernard-Henri Lévy describes visiting a place that bears less and less resemblance, as the chapter advances, to the one found by Randall Bennett when he came to recover Pearl's remains (photographs of the site still hang in his office).

Bernard-Henri Lévy thus describes, 'in the heart of the neighbourhood of Gulzar e-Hijri',[31] a 'lowly place, a disreputable and dangerous area, propitious for all sorts of trafficking and full of the same sort of houses as this one, and where the industry of kidnapping, which flourishes in Karachi, has always had its hideouts.'[32] He notes in passing that to get there by car 'one does not quite leave the town'. Once there, he mentions the existence of two other houses, a *madrassa* and two buildings still in construction 'curtained by acacias with white plastic bags hanging from their branches. 'Hidden from sight by another dense row of green acacias', is Pearl's place of detention: 'the concrete block building, a narrow rectangle with its two rooms and no electricity (although the rest of the neighborhood is electrified), low ceilinged (I had to lower my head, I imagine he did too)', surrounded by a small 'abandoned garden, full of insects, and the odors of jasmine mixed with those of the pestilent trench'. Pearl is imagined trying to escape 'among the trees'.[33]

Later in his account, he mentions having visited this place in May 2002, perhaps at the time that Pearl's body was being disinterred by Randall Bennett. With his characteristic concern for precision – he accompanied his own account with a sketch – Bennett himself recalled 'a desert, scattered with a dozen houses, a mosque and dirt roads. Not a single tree. No sign of local organization, still less on the district level, no activity, no shop. The place is lost in the sand and there's nothing there.' He added:

> There's no kidnapping industry and the police had never had to go there before. No one bothered with the place, so far from everything, desert-like and desolate. Vines and a few olive trees were planted on the plot where Danny's remains were found. The room where he was held prisoner was of normal height. No need to stoop to go in. He tried to escape twice. But there was nowhere to go: he would have had to walk miles to find anyone.[34]

'FACTION': AN OBJECT OF (ALMOST) UNANIMOUS ADMIRATION

There are two possible explanations for these contradictory versions. Either Bernard-Henri Lévy did not go to the place in person – which would explain the inexactness of his description – and used the accounts of one or more witnesses. If so, why does he place himself at the scene with such insistence? Or, perhaps he did actually go there, but has 'enriched' what he saw with imaginary elements, to the extent of imposing repeated twists on reality. All the evidence suggests that what he describes is completely false. But why the effort to provide telling details for a readership that knows no better either way?

What makes everything more complicated is that this mixture of genres, this inextricable tangle of real and invented details, important or trivial, swerving back and forth between verified and imagined facts, is the main innovation in a book identifying itself with a new literary genre: 'faction' ['*romanquête*']. 'The facts, nothing but the facts; and when the real was too elusive, a forced share of the imaginary; in sum, a faction,' he wrote in his introduction. A genre which he attributed, after the book had appeared, to an illustrious creator: 'The inventor of the faction? Hugo in his essay on Walter Scott. "Few historians," he says, "are as faithful as this novelist". Lévy also says: 'I would rather believe in a novel than in history', for 'I prefer moral truth to historical truth.'[35] In the absence of professional credit, nothing beats an illustrious predecessor to impart a little literary credibility.

So although it calls itself an 'investigation' into a world described in airport spy-novel terms (a 'world of bloodthirsty fanaticisms and passions, interminable trails, perilous manipulations and state lies'[36]), *Who Killed Daniel Pearl?* admits that it is part fiction, in absolute contradiction with the usual ground rules of journalistic investigation: narrative integrity, respect for observed fact, and the honesty of the narrator concerning his own deeds and movements.

More than a little surprisingly, this is where the book enjoyed its greatest success. Despite everything, it was much appreciated by journalists, at least the great majority of those who reviewed it. Consecrated, in particular by way of a distinctly eulogistic interview,[37] by the respected Jean Hatzfeld, chief reporter for *Libération* during the wars in former Yugoslavia and author of two important books on the Rwanda genocide;[38] defended by Robert Ménard[39] – then a moral authority, all the more so for being violently criticized over his reporting in Algeria in January 1988 by the general secretary of Reporters sans frontières – Bernard-Henri Lévy was also lauded by *Le Monde* ('damnably convincing'[40]), *Libération* ('Bernard-Henri Lévy's book could only be vertiginous'[41]), *Marianne* (a 'shattering book'[42]) and *Le Point* (a 'splendid and terrifying book'[43]).

Of course, Bernard-Henri Lévy made a whistle-stop tour of the TV and radio stations. On 28 April 2003 he was the guest of France 2's 'Mots croisés'[44] in the evening, after spending the day on France Culture taking part in a 'special Daniel Pearl day' to coincide with the book's appearance ('Les matins' from 7 to 8.30 a.m., 'Tout arrive' from 12.45 to 1.30 and a special broadcast from 7.30 to 10 p.m.). He had already broadcast for France Culture on 26 April, as Jean-Marie Colombani's guest on 'La rumeur du *Monde*' from 12.45 p.m. to 1.30. At 5.10 p.m. on the same day he had been on LCI as the guest of another *Le Monde* figurehead, Edwy Plenel.[45] Later that evening, at about 11 p.m., he was also on France 2 in 'Tout le monde en parle', a programme presented by Thierry Ardisson. The next day he appeared on Canal Plus at lunchtime in Karl Zéro's 'Le Vrai Journal' from 12.30 to 1.30. Not forgetting Patrick Poivre d'Arvor's 'Vol de nuit' on TF1 at 11 p.m. on the 29th and Franz-Olivier Giesbert's 'Culture et dépendance' on France 3 at 10.30 the following evening. Back to France 2 on 8 May at 10 p.m. for Guillaume Durand's programme 'Campus' ... and there were further appearances on La Chaîne Sénat, Europe 1 and so on.[46]

A few, a very few dissenting voices tempered, slightly, the chorus of praise: the researcher Olivier Roy and Mariam Abou Zahab, a research fellow at CERI who teaches politics at the Institut d'études politiques and the Institut national de langues et de civilisations orientales, were both guests of France Culture on 28 April; and the former Foreign Minister Hubert Védrine appeared the same day on France 2. In the print press, the only marginally dissonant notes were struck by Pierre Assouline in *Lire*,[47] by *Le Monde diplomatique*, which published in translation a highly critical piece by the British journalist William Dalrymple,[48] and by Philippe Lançon in *Libération*[49] The last of these, however, also published a very positive article by Didier François, a senior reporter and author of a major investigation of Al Qaeda whose conclusions were not dissimilar to those of Bernard-Henri Lévy's book[50].

All the reviewers, or nearly all, saw great pedagogic virtues in the 'faction' form, and tended to regard it as a severe indictment of the press for not doing its work properly. 'Once again, it's you who have really covered the story,' wrote Robert Ménard in congratulatory vein,[51] while for Alain Frachon of *Le Monde*, 'that investigation into the murder of Daniel Pearl in Pakistan, we could all wish we'd done it.'[52]

Does this book show up the press and print journalists, by underlining their poor work on the subject? The commentators were more right about this than they thought, but probably not for the reasons they had in mind. Because those who defended 'faction' as a valid and legitimate way of making the world understandable did so using perfectly acceptable argument. Bernard-Henri Lévy would surely always have taken good care to draw a clear distinction between fact and fiction. However, a more detailed scrutiny of the content of *Who Killed Daniel Pearl?* and what its author has subsequently said about it would suggest a somewhat more circumspect analysis of this narrative technique. In reality, Bernard-Henri Lévy's *Pearl* is an indictment of the journalistic profession, not because of the alleged scoops it contains, but because of the feeble criticisms it elicited from most journalists. Those panegyrists would have benefited from a more attentive reading of the book.

For starters, Bernard-Henri Lévy emphasizes the precautions he tried to take to avoid being noticed in Karachi: 'No stopping by the embassy. No grand hotel, where you're instantly spotted. Instead, just a little guest house on the road to the airport, right near the place where the cab was pulled over and I was forced to pay a bribe to the policeman during my first visit.'[53]

These details surprise Mariam Abou Zahab, who stands out in this affair as one of the very few specialists to have published an in-depth critique of Bernard-Henri Lévy's book. In it she explains that 'descending on a small guest house instead of the Marriott in the hope of passing unnoticed' is, on the contrary, 'the best way to attract attention.'[54] A city constantly patrolled by intelligence services of all nationalities and all sorts, Karachi despite its vast size is undoubtedly one of the hardest places in the world for a Western intellectual, investigating terrorism, to visit incognito. The British writer and journalist William Dalrymple, familiar with the region for twenty years, was equally amused by the hole-in-corner guest house. 'Pure James Bond ...'[55]

FAKE SCOOPS IN THE DEVIL'S HOUSE

Bernard-Henri Lévy does his utmost to dramatize himself, to fabricate fiction around his own character. It is a matter of style, a staging that often strays into fantasy. Through the 450-plus pages of his book he is the omnipresent narrator, constantly placed centre stage, usually against the terrifying backdrop of Karachi, in a Pakistan unblinkingly described as 'turning into the Devil's own home'.[56]

The diabolical reference, this image of the demon, runs all through the book, to the point of giving it an undeniable coherence of tone. A reporter is 'at the heart of darkness',[57] Bernard-Henri Lévy is 'in the mind of the devil'[58] (a slightly dubious play on the title of his first novel *Le Diable en tête*, or 'The Devil in Mind'), confronted with 'the newly possessed', exploring a 'silent hell' (p. xix), 'full of the living damned' who are strikingly depicted when the author finds himself inadvertently carried away by a passing Shi'ite street demonstration. 'The others, long-haired dervishes with wild, bloodshot eyes, are shouting murderous epithets against their Sunni neighbours, then suddenly, to a man, they stop and begin chanting incoherent litanies full of, I am told, blood, vengeance, and martyrdom' (p. 290). We are right in the middle of a cheap airport thriller.

Bernard-Henri Lévy describes himself surveying volatile zones amid apocalyptic urban landscapes. With one of his 'contacts', he ventures in mid-narrative into Aurangzeb Park, 'where the junkies hang out' in Karachi (p. 224), on the track of a scoop that emerges as something of a spectacular stage-effect. He learns through an alleged policeman that the brain behind Pearl's kidnap, Omar Sheikh, whom he believes to have been arrested by the police on 12 February 2002, had in fact given himself up to the authorities a week earlier through the good offices of the mayor of Lahore, a former ISI agent. Following this 'path to clarification' (p. 223), because he thinks it proves that the Pakistani secret services are implicated in Pearl's capture, the French investigator finds himself looking for a mysterious informer in 'one of the most squalid parts of the city' (p. 224) and rubbing shoulders with 'a reserve army of drugs and crime' which from a distance suggests 'members of some strange black-magic sect', trapped in a 'shady hellhole', a 'scorched esplanade turned into a dumping ground for syringes' (p. 226).

Things are hotting up. In his quest for the truth, the narrator-sleuth seems suddenly to have started taking the same sort of thoughtless risks as his American hero before him. As scoops go, however, this one leaves a lot to be desired. The episode of Omar Sheikh's premature surrender to the authorities was already old news to everyone in Pakistan. There is a reference to it in Mariam Abou Zahab and Olivier Roy's book, published in France in October 2002 – more than six months before Bernard-Henri Lévy's, and already in production during the writer's September 2002 escapade into the wasteland of hard drugs.[59] It seems unlikely that Bernard-Henri Lévy would not have known it.

A number of similar scenes in the book resemble simple misstatements of fact. On 24 November 2002 (p. 344) the writer enters the Binori Town *madrassa* (a prestigious Koranic school whose alumni include generations of mullahs and the future leaders of the Taliban regime in Afghanistan) by displaying, he writes, his expired diplomatic passport. In the course of this adventure he quotes his guide Abdul as saying, 'Don't even think about it! Very restricted place! As far as I know, no Western journalist has ever gone inside.' This seems rather dismissive of the French journalist Agnès Vahramian, who had taken her video camera into the school's classrooms and conducted two hours of interviews with young foreign students for France 2 in October 2002, hardly a month before Bernard-Henri Lévy's 'extraordinary' exploit. Mariam Abou Zahab remembered at least one other French TV crew (TF1 this time), and assured us that 'Binori Town has always welcomed Western journalists, and received hundreds from all countries after September 11.'[60]

More sensationally still, Bernard-Henri Lévy believes he has glimpsed a portrait of Osama Bin Laden in the *madrassa*, and leaves that 'house of the Devil' (p. 302) convinced that it shelters 'a logistics base for Al

Qaeda propaganda', since his suppositions lead him to think that it was inside this mosque that Bin Laden's cassette message claiming credit for terrorist operations (in Djerba, Yemen, Kuwait, Bali and Moscow) was recorded, and that, scoop of scoops, Osama Bin Laden stayed there several times in 2002 (both CBS and an Indian newspaper had reported this rumour at the time). 'Who said so?' Abou Zahab asked. 'And who can prove it? Where has Bin Laden *not* been seen since September 11?'[61] Randall Bennett added: 'It's speculation, pure and simple. There's no proof whatsoever. And in any case it's extremely improbable and illogical. There wouldn't have been any point.'[62]

'YOU DON'T PUT WORDS INTO THE MIND OF A DYING MAN'

In a more general way, the outlandish dramatization with which Bernard-Henri Lévy dresses up the data he throws to his readers is accompanied by innumerable factual errors. While many are too trivial to list here, it is worth noting some of the more striking and revealing ones.

For a start, the description of Pearl himself. In keeping with his vision of things determined by the struggle between good and evil, between light and darkness, Bernard-Henri Lévy portrays Daniel Pearl, a journalist he has never met, as a 'luminous character ... who had chosen to answer evil with good' (p. xvi), or, quoting Emmanuel Levinas, someone who felt 'an obligation to the world' [*l'obligé du monde*], or a 'just man', an 'old-fashioned man', 'the enigma of those "gentle men" of whom Dostoevsky speaks'. But Henry Samuel, who worked for the English language service of Radio France Internationale and was a friend of Pearl, disputed his view of the murdered man's character: 'I didn't feel that the Danny I knew had "an obligation to the world" or anything like that ... he didn't seem to me to be a man haunted by evil all the time'.[63] Marianne Pearl, whom he likened to a Vestal Virgin in the book and to Antigone on the radio,[64] has never replied publicly to Bernard-Henri Lévy and maintained an admirable dignity, refraining from all comment on the book. She met him in New York at her own request to convey privately, in the absence of any recording device, what she had thought of it. Although normally quick to put himself in the frame, he has never given an account of that meeting. (In 2005, she described him as a man 'whose intelligence is destroyed by his ego'.[65])

'Faction', Bernard-Henri Lévy might reply, permits literary appropriation of a character. But what are we to make of the long chapter he devotes to the journalist's execution? The sound of the steely blade slicing through the carotid artery, the victim's tears and gurgles. The reader is spared nothing, made into an unwilling accomplice, a voyeur despite himself, of the sordid spectacle forced on him by the narrator with manipulative insistence, at the same time scrolling through Pearl's imagined internal monologue: a narrative technique that raises ethical issues a good deal more fundamental than the mere questioning of the 'faction' form.

The use of video by these murderous terrorist groups is a trap, an unprecedented challenge in the history of contemporary media. Should the images be broadcast or not? The question is a serious one, touching on such essential principles as the right to information and respect for human dignity. In this context, the negligent attitude displayed in his book by Bernard-Henri Lévy – an author who claims to be a philosopher and one of whose earliest works was a reflection on violence and 'barbarism' – when he dwells upon this scene verges on cynicism. He must have known that Pearl's family, his wife and parents, had publicly declared that they did not want to see the videotape of his murder. 'I don't describe the video,' Bernard-Henri Lévy explained. 'It's anti-video. I wrote that scene precisely because the video existed and I wanted to give a different version of that moment from the one given by the video. If the video hadn't existed, I wouldn't have written that scene.'[66]

'How could he put words into the mind of a dead man?' Randall Bennett protests. 'That sort of "speculative philosophizing" is irresponsible. You don't put words into the mind of a dying man. He's sacrificed respect for truth to make a good show.'[67] In another different context, Jacques Derrida, a philosopher of an entirely different stature, alluded to the murder in 1993 of the South African communist and anti-apartheid activist Chris Hani (to whom he dedicated his *Specters of Marx*) in words that seem to apply equally well to Daniel Pearl: 'But we ought never to speak of the killing of a man as that of a symbol, not even an exemplary symbol in a logic of the emblem, a rhetoric of the flag or of martyrdom. A man's life, as unique as his death, will always be more than a paradigm and something other than a symbol. And that is precisely what a proper noun ought always to name.'[68]

Bernard-Henri Lévy does the very opposite in his book. 'Daniel Pearl is dead because he was a Jew. Daniel Pearl is dead, victim of the neo-anti-Judaism that is blossoming before our eyes. I've been talking about this neo-anti-Judaism for the past twenty-five years' (p. 393). In the video of the murder, before being decapitated, in the few seconds he is given to speak, Daniel Pearl intones: 'I am a Jewish American … on my father's side I come from a family of Zionists; my father is

Jewish; my mother is Jewish; I am Jewish … in the town of Bnei Brak, in Israel, there's a street called Haïm Pearl Street, named after my great-grandfather' (pp. 46–7). Then, still reciting from a script, Pearl delivers an anti-American tirade:

> Not knowing anything about my situation … not being able to communicate with anybody … only now do I think about some of the people in Guantanamo Bay who must be in a similar situation … and I've come to realize that … this is the sort of problem that Americans are going to have anywhere in the world now.
>
> We can't be secure, we can't walk around free as long as our government policies are continuing and we allow them to continue.
>
> We Americans cannot continue to bear the consequences of our government's actions, such as the unconditional support given to the state of Israel. Twenty-four uses of the veto power to justify massacres of children. And the support for the dictatorial regimes in the Arab and Muslim world. And also the continued American military presence in Afghanistan. (pp. 36–7)

The horror of Pearl's death is thus accompanied by the horror of the masquerade imposed on him by his murderers, the propaganda they forced him to recite and the anti-Semitic, anti-American hatred those words exuded. Did Pearl die 'because he was a Jew'? Did his execution herald a 'new anti-Judaism'? Once again, Randall Bennett thought not: 'Pearl didn't die primarily because he was Jewish. Those people don't like Americans, they don't like Jews and they probably don't like journalists either.'[69] In his book, however, Bernard-Henri Lévy asserts that Pearl 'is most surely a victim of modern anti-Semitism' (p. 392).

This religious, identity-based, exclusive reading is rejected by Marianne Pearl. 'We both came from all over the place. His mother was born in Baghdad, his father was born in Israel; my mother was born in Cuba, my father in Holland. There's some Buddhism (like her brother, of whom she often speaks, Marianne Pearl is a Buddhist), some Judaism. We came from America and France. We travelled everywhere, all over south Asia. We can't be categorized, except by fundamentalists.'[70] Describing the atmosphere in the house where she lived in Karachi with friends and helpers, when they were all searching for Danny, she added, 'People were in that house to find Danny; there were Jews, Buddhists, Muslims. Everyone felt violated in the same way. That's one of the main reasons why I wrote this book.'[71]

There is no doubt that to his captors Pearl's Jewishness would have represented an unbearable form of otherness, and through a sordid reasoning process constituted a motive for killing him. The problem is that on the pretext of giving his name back to a dead man, of paying 'homage' to his 'posthumous friend' (p. 454), Bernard-Henri Lévy turned him into grist for his literary mill and used him as a confessional standard-bearer, the object of a peculiar and worrying discursive performance.

INCOMPREHENSION: BERNARD-HENRI LÉVY AND OMAR SHEIKH

On the wider subject of Pakistan Bernard-Henri Lévy advances generalizations that seem plausible – the book's great snare – which even when illustrated with examples can turn out to be completely misleading. A case in point is his story of the kidnapping by the ISI of a prominent Pakistani journalist, Najam Sethi, in order to show how impossible it is for the press to work normally (p. 389). In fact, not only did Sethi himself tell us that he had been detained not by the ISI but by the Punjab police, but the respected British reporter Owen Bennett Jones, author of an authoritative study of Pakistan, says in so many words that it is an 'easy' country for the press.[72]

Bernard-Henri Lévy gets locations wrong,[73] misspells place-names,[74] and confuses democratic leaders with Islamist chiefs.[75] All these errors, which betray an offhand and over-hasty approach to the very complex and contradictory Pakistani landscape, fairly opaque to uninitiated outsiders, cumulatively force themselves on the reader's attention. But when the British journalist William Dalrymple pointed out his errors in the *New York Review of Books*, Bernard-Henri Lévy hit back denying all these blunders, jeering at a 'specialist' and giving an astonishing display of bad faith.[76]

He justified calling Pakistan 'the home of the Devil' by claiming that the expression 'came from a Pakistani, quoted as such' and anyway 'was not really about Pakistan'. In fact the expression appears in the book as of the introduction, and there can be no doubt that it's the narrator speaking: 'That same Pakistan that I saw turning into the Devil's own home' (p. xix). Bernard-Henri Lévy goes on to sneer at the British reporter for covering Karachi from the comfort of 'the glittering departure lounge' of its airport; Dalrymple had in fact been writing on Pakistan and India for seventeen years and had published several best-sellers (a Fellow of the Royal Society of Literature and the Royal Asiatic Society, he is best known for travel books on the Indian sub-continent, including *Xanadu*, *The Age of Kali* and *From the Holy Mountain*[77]).

Bernard-Henri Lévy also rejected the 'reproach' that he 'makes no distinction' between 'secular Pakistanis and their Islamist rivals', when 'the whole book (and more specifically its very last section, entitled "The Kindness of Islam", in which I make the apologia, rightly, for the popular, non-fundamentalist Islam of the "other Pakistan") pleads for this necessary, indispensable, vital distinction.'[78]

Indeed it does. To be precise, his eulogy of the 'kindness of Islam' runs from page 447 all the way to page 454. Barely six pages to compensate for the proliferation of demonizing descriptions, like the member of the 'wave of the faithful' (p. 290), 'foaming at the mouth, his face bathed in sweat', who 'brandishes a rock at the windshield'.

In another elision, Bernard-Henri Lévy mentions thinly and in passing, as it were between sentences (p. 70), the major *Vanity Fair* piece by the American investigative journalist Robert Sam Anson. Starting in August 2002, Anson had tracked down in impressive detail the mechanisms of the trap that caught Pearl. In the article, he recounted the scoop story written by Pearl and his *Wall Street Journal* colleague Steve LeVine on links between ISI and an ostensibly 'humanitarian' organization, Ummah Tameer-e-Nau, led by Bashiruddin Mahmood, former head of Pakistan's nuclear programme, accused of leaking nuclear secrets to Bin Laden. Anson also related another of the American journalist's scoops on Jaish-e-Mohammed, a group of Islamist radicals known for its violence and fully active despite being banned by Musharraf. Then came what triggered Pearl's fatal interest: a piece in the *Boston Globe*[79] revealing that, according to official US sources, the 'shoe bomber' Richard Reid[80] had belonged to a little-known Islamist group, Jamaat ul-Fuqra, led by a mysterious figure called Sheikh Mubarak Ali Shah Gilani who had not been interviewed by a journalist in ten years. Anson described the efforts to dissuade him by his contact Khalid Khawaja, an Islamist militant and ex-ISI agent, and Pearl's determination to get the interview despite all warnings. He instructs his assistant, Asif Furuqi, who makes contact, through a friend, with someone claiming to be in touch with Gilani – someone Furuqi does not realize is Omar Sheikh. The terrorist's trap is ready for the American.

A substantial part of what Bernard-Henri Lévy claims to have uncovered at such risk, putting himself tiresomely in the spotlight over more than 300 pages, was already set down in this article, in infinitely greater and more accurate detail and with far fewer risky allegations than in the Frenchman's book, which appeared nearly seven months later. Bernard-Henri Lévy claims to demonstrate his thesis with insignificant details, while persistently ignoring what the specialists say. The result doesn't hold water.

The most serious errors concern Omar Sheikh, the brain behind Pearl's capture (for which he has been condemned to death) and a central character in the book. First, though, he waffles a bit on the way his interlocutors say Omar Sheikh's name (p. 78).[81] More seriously, he presents the British terrorist as the lynchpin of a supposed objective alliance between the ISI and Al Qaeda (p. 398). One of the main conclusions of his book is that, in effect, Pearl was killed because he was investigating links between ISI and Al Qaeda and because he was 'busy gathering proof of Pakistan's collusion with the leading rogue states and terrorist networks of the world', by means of a double game successfully masking 'the most fearsome operations of nuclear proliferation' (p. 446) in passing to Al Qaeda the procedures and materials needed to make a nuclear weapon. So Pearl was supposedly the victim of a 'state crime' committed by the ISI or under its protection, aimed at safeguarding Pakistan's strategic interests (broadly speaking, relations between Pakistan and the US). 'This crime was not petty, a murder for nothing, an uncontrolled act of fundamentalist fanatics – it's a crime of state, intended and authorized, whether we like it or not, by the state of Pakistan' (p. 273).

'Danny Pearl was kidnapped and murdered in a joint operation by Kashmiri activist groups and Al Qaeda,' corrected Peter Bergen in 2004. Bergen, a member of the New America Foundation, professor at Johns Hopkins University and author of an essay on Al Qaeda,[82] added, 'It's probable that it was Khaled Sheikh Mohammed, military commander of Al Qaeda, who killed Pearl. Omar Sheikh was connected to Jaish-e-Mohammed, a group led by Maulana Azhar, who is close to ISI. When Sheikh turned himself in to the Pakistan authorities, it was to a former officer of ISI. So there are some links with ISI, but they're indirect. There's no evidence at all to implicate ISI as such in the kidnapping. Nor is there any evidence that ISI and Al Qaeda have as many links as all that.'[83]

In 2007 Khaled Sheikh Mohammed, detained at Guantanamo Bay for his alleged role in organizing the terrorist attacks of 11 September 2001, admitted to having killed Daniel Pearl. The confession, obtained (the US authorities specified) after the prisoner had been subjected to torture on numerous occasions, was corroborated by the FBI and the CIA. Using the latest police technology, their specialists thought they had identified the hand seen cutting the journalist's throat in the murder video.[84] It could well be the hand of the Al Qaeda boss, in the considered opinion of the *Pearl Project* report, the fruit of a three-year 'counter-inquiry' conducted by students at the University of Georgetown along with journalists.[85] According to their research, Omar Sheikh organized Daniel Pearl's capture but a completely different team, led by Khaled Sheikh Mohammed, took the decision to kill him.

Obsessed by the image of Omar Sheikh as a malign figure, a 'prince in the universe of Evil' (p. 375), Bernard-Henri Lévy exaggerates his importance and with reckless confidence assigns characteristics and roles to him that for the most part are matters of rumour. For example, he makes Omar Sheikh 'a perfect Englishman' (p. 87) swept for strange personal reasons into the dark madness of radical Islamism to become a secret financier of 11 September (p. 378) and 'bin Laden's favoured son' (p. 345), doubling as a spy in the pay of the most obscure forces in the entrails of the Pakistani intelligence services, a spectacular 'monster' (p. 83) whose biographical tittle-tattle he pursues right into the street where Sheikh's parents live in London. Peering in through the kitchen window, he notes for posterity the presence of 'a pretty tablecloth, egg cups, boxes of cereal, a pitcher of milk, flowered plates' (p. 88)... 'Tintin in the Land of the English Breakfast', mocked Tim King, Paris correspondent of the British magazine *Prospect*.[86]

Bernard-Henri Lévy visits the places Omar Sheikh would have frequented in England and reports at length on even the smallest incidents (the arm-wrestling tournaments, the lectures he skipped, the books he took out of the library, etc.). He focuses on arresting but trivial details, fabricates a sort of tabloid news story and completely misses one of the real keys to the character: his banality, his conformity to the new profile of the global jihadi which specialists in radical Islam have managed to establish more or less clearly.

A British subject, born in England to Pakistani parents, sent on a brief visit to Pakistan in mid-adolescence before attending the prestigious London School of Economics, Omar Sheikh is a perfect example of the 'products and agents of deculturation in a globalized world', the 'champions of a mythical and imaginary *umma* cutting across languages and nations' studied by Olivier Roy, director of research at the French National Centre for Scientific Research (CNRS).[87] 'When we are trying to understand the young radicals active today, it is pointless to blame the *madrassas* or theological schools ... In fact, the leaders of these radical internationalist movements are today pure products of Westernization,' Olivier Roy said more recently.[88] 'Islamic radicalism today, as I see it, in its terrorist form, is not a consequence – an exportation – of the conflicts in the Middle East, but a global Western phenomenon, with a slightly paradoxical side in the case of Omar Sheikh: here is someone who in a way, if I may put it like this, has exported Islamic radicalism from Britain to Pakistan.'[89]

Much like Bin Laden himself, the Afghani Gulbuddin Hekmatyar, Bin Laden's lieutenant Khaled Sheikh Mohammed, and of course Mohammed Atta, the presumed leader of the 11 September team, Omar Sheikh is an 'intellectual activist'. This is the view of Jason Burke, the *Observer* correspondent covering the Middle East and South-West Asia. Sheikh comes from the same social group as the first Islamist militants in colonial times, people who were educated, intelligent, with a good knowledge of the outside world, for whom radical Islamic militancy was an answer to the 'feeling of injustice' born out of the 'frustration of their social aspirations'.[90] Omar Sheikh was 'a Paki in England and a Gora [white] in Lahore', added Mariam Abou Zahab;[91] he 'found an identity and sense of belonging in Islamism'. But the insights offered by contemporary sociology are ignored by Bernard-Henri Lévy, who chooses instead to sketch the outlines of a character of his own invention. In the process he implicates very real actors in contemporary Pakistani life, starting with the ISI. Is Omar Sheikh merely an agent of the ISI, as he baldly asserts: 'an agent named Omar' (p. 239); 'I say "Omar Sheikh", and when I utter the words, I am naming the synthesis, in him, of the ISI and Al Qaida – that is the truth' (p. 375)?

To Mariam Abou Zahab and Olivier Roy, this matter is better stated in the conditional: 'He could be linked to the Pakistani intelligence services, most likely through General Mahmud Ahmed, the ISI director removed by Musharraf.'[92] The British reporter William Dalrymple would go as far as saying that he undoubtedly has 'strong links with Pakistani intelligence.'[93] What all observers of Pakistan seem sure of are links between the Pakistani military and certain terrorist groups. When the Pakistani military wanted a new army of surrogates to relaunch the guerrilla war in Kashmir and replace the leadership which the Indian army had decimated, they 'naturally' looked towards two new groups, Harkat-ul-Mujahideen and Lashkar-e-Taiba (the Army of the Pure), Jason Burke wrote.[94] Omar Sheikh trained at a camp run by Harkat-ul-Mujahideen in 1993. Then, arrested in India in 1994 for kidnapping tourists, he was freed after demands were made by a Harkat-ul-Mujahideen team.

'So radical Islamist movements are more or less autonomous instruments of the Pakistani government's regional policy,' specify Abou Zahab and Roy,[95] adding that 'the development of these movements is supervised by the Pakistani secret services in pursuit of two objectives: controlling the jihadis in Kashmir and Afghanistan by marginalizing their nationalist elements to the profit of "Islamic internationalists" based in Pakistan and plugged directly into the ISI; and intervening in Pakistan's domestic politics.'[96] These organized and structured Islamist networks constituted a sort of pond from which the leading officers of Al Qaeda could fish recruits in their turn. Pakistan thus became the 'central junction for the mobilization of radical Islamic networks'.[97] The Al Qaeda militants found refuge in Kashmir, in the Punjab and in Karachi, which would not have been possible without 'connivances' inside the ISI, Abou Zahab and Roy point out.[98]

'Omar Sheikh did visit Bin Laden in Afghanistan,' Randall Bennett told us.

> Interrogation of Taliban and Al Qaeda members confirmed to us that he was Bin Laden's 'favourite son' … but so were a lot of others. Al Qaeda, as its name indicates, is a 'base'. Those who become semi-leaders in the organization were, are and will be authorized to carry out actions in total independence. They don't have to ask permission. Omar Sheikh is part of Al Qaeda. He has his own cell. The people he worked with had made jihad in Kashmir with Al Qaeda. It was probably Khaled Sheikh Mohammed, one of Bin Laden's closest lieutenants and presumed 'brain' behind 11 September [arrested in Pakistan in 2003], who ordered the putting to death of Daniel Pearl.[99]

In 2011 Omar Sheikh was still incarcerated in Pakistan, but there were persistent rumours, picked up by the international press, that he might be released.

But Bernard-Henri Lévy cares not a fig for all this information and analysis. In his 2003 book, throwing caution to the wind, he even finds Omar Sheikh's spoor in the logistics of 9/11. If he is to be believed, the terrorist could have been a 'financier of 11 September' by arranging a decisive transfer of funds – $100,000 – to the Egyptian Mohammed Atta, the pilot of the first aircraft that crashed into the World Trade Center. But that is not all. The writer goes on to assert that 'the hypothesis, in other words, is no longer that Omar is the financier of 11 September, but that Omar is operating on orders from the ISI' (p. 322). In other words, 'the question we can no longer dodge, [is that] of the responsibility of the Pakistani secret service, or one of the ISI's factions, in the attack on America and the destruction of the World Trade Center' (p. 323). And on the basis that a big lie is more convincing than a small one, a few lines further on Bernard-Henri Lévy abandons the hypothetical mode more or less completely. 'Finally, concerning the ultimate responsibility of Pakistan involvement in the September 11 attack, it remains part of the great unspoken in the America of George W. Bush and Donald Rumsfeld' (p. 324). Unspoken, though, for the best of reasons. The possibility is not raised even once in the reports on September 11 from the intelligence commissions of the US Senate and Chamber of Deputies, since the identity of the main financier has been established. He is Mustafa Ahmed al-Hawsawi, a Saudi who has no connection with the ISI.

Pakistan as co-sponsor of 9/11 … could Bernard-Henri Lévy have been (so to speak) *on* something? He seems almost to admit it. 'Unless, of course, this is the investigator's own vertigo, investigating vertigo. Unless he too is sucked into the hole, swallowed in this matrix, carried off on this nightmare ride – the intoxication of a mystery that ends by thinning out to nothing.' (p. 325). Indeed.

THE 'CAUSE OF TRUTH', OR THE BOOK'S CENTRAL THESIS THROWN INTO DOUBT

With links both to Al Qaeda and the ISI, does Omar Sheikh constitute evidence in himself that the kidnap and murder of the American journalist could have been ordered by the Pakistan's intelligence services because he was investigating claims that they had been passing nuclear secrets to Al Qaeda? It seems very unlikely. Squeezed into two rushed chapters at the end of the book, it is nevertheless one of the more astonishing ideas to emerge from the 'investigation'. A massive scoop, if it were true. But eight years after the appearance of Bernard-Henri Lévy's book, the subsequent revelations concerning the transfer of so-called 'sensitive' technologies by Abdul Qadeer Khan ('father' of the Pakistani atomic bomb) have implicated Iran, Libya and North Korea. But not Al Qaeda.

'There's nothing to show that Pakistani scientists have "sold the recipe" of the atom bomb to Al Qaeda,' the American specialist Peter Bergen explained to us in 2004. 'However, Bin Laden when he was living in Kandahar did meet senior Pakistani nuclear scientists on two occasions, and they did talk about nuclear weapons. David Albright, the former UN inspector, wrote a report on the subject. But there's nothing to prove that Abdul Qadeer Khan had the slightest connection with Al Qaeda. Nor to my knowledge has he ever had any links with terrorist groups.'[100] Seven years on, the possibility that groups linked to Al Qaeda might acquire Pakistani nuclear technology remains a real source of anxiety to the Obama administration (as shown by the diplomatic cables between the US embassy in Pakistan and Washington published by Wikileaks at the end of 2010). But to this day, there is no evidence that this transfer of knowledge has taken place.

Unhappily for the narrator, all the clues indicate that he is wrong in his hypothesis regarding the investigation Pearl had in mind at the time of his abduction. That is at any rate what people close to the journalist affirm, including the editors of the *Wall Street Journal* and his father, Judea Pearl.[101] Randall Bennett is equally positive. 'Pearl was investigating Richard Reid, the shoe bomber. He wasn't looking into any subject that would have annoyed the ISI. Pearl wasn't working on the idea of Pakistanis selling the bomb to Al Qaeda. That's ridiculous.'[102]

So what are the established facts that might support the theory of criminal collusion between the Pakistani authorities and Al Qaeda, or of state involvement in the journalist's murder, or of the transfer of nuclear technologies to terrorist networks? According to Gilles Leclair, formerly head of the Anti-Terrorist Coordination Unit in France (he had conducted the enquiry into the attack that killed eleven French nationals in Karachi on 9 May 2002), 'one should properly speaking separate mere supposition from what has been proved legally.'[103]

'It's extremely difficult, because you're in a world of disinformation,' warned Mariam Abou Zahab in April 2003.

> You can never be sure of anything. Everything you say has to be put in the conditional. You're at risk of being manipulated by one side or another … The state of Pakistan shouldn't be confused with certain elements within the ISI. I think it's very risky to make an equation between the Pakistani government as a whole and Al Qaeda. There may be personal links between some Pakistanis and members of the Al Qaeda network, but that still doesn't mean that the Pakistani authorities are linked to Al Qaeda or that they had foreknowledge of the 11 September attacks, let alone that they were involved, as some in the US have been suggesting lately.[104]

None of these factual points was allowed to inflect Bernard-Henri Lévy's exegesis. Unperturbed, he intoned in the book:

> Following Danny, in his wake and in a way, in homage, I bring this modest contribution to the cause of truth that he loved more than anything else.

> I assert that Pakistan is the biggest rogue of all the rogue states of today.
>
> I assert that what is taking form there, between Islamabad and Karachi, is a black hole compared to which Saddam Hussein's Baghdad was an obsolete weapons dump.
>
> The scent of apocalypse hangs over those cities … (p. 446)

One who did read *Who Killed Daniel Pearl?* with care and attention was Hubert Védrine, the French foreign minister at the time of Pearl's murder. 'It's a great book, but it's a novel,' he said on television in April 2003, in Bernard-Henri Lévy's presence.[105] He went on to say he thought it 'very important for Bernard-Henri Lévy to specify in the succession of events which parts are investigation and which are his personal reconstruction, given the lack of data. It's very important in terms of the conclusions that should or should not be drawn from it. … Are there, in the final analysis, elements that show, not collusion between the Pakistani secret services and Al Qaeda – naturally that was known from the start – but involving the nuclear side? That's the most explosive aspect.' Eight years later, by 2011, Bernard-Henri Lévy had still not answered this question, or provided the slightest proof of the assertions advanced in his 2003 book.

Even during the broadcast Bernard-Henri Lévy made a mistake, or in any case exposed himself to damaging criticism, by parrying that objection with an attempt at a reprimand. 'It's not a novel. In a 550-page book, there are two scenes introduced as such: the moment of Pearl's decapitation and his assassin's internal monologue, the day before the kidnap. Those are the only novelized moments in the book. The rest is investigation.'

BANKRUPTCY OF THE FRENCH MEDIA

There is, then, a *Who Killed Daniel Pearl?* 'issue'. Most of the foreign sources – American and British for the most part – consulted for this counter-investigation were flabbergasted when they realized how seriously the book had been taken by the French media, over and above the splash of the event. How could such a book, whose pretensions to truth the author had explicitly defended, have remained unquestioned for so long? Why had the French media been such toadies? If they had no one competent on their own staffs, why had they not called in outside experts?

Then again, how could it be that even after being confronted (in the end) with his errors, Bernard-Henri Lévy at no point lost any credibility? In that sense at least, *Who Killed Daniel Pearl?* may well constitute a sensational event of French publishing during the first decade of the twenty-first century. It certainly was a turning point in Bernard-Henri Lévy's life. Taken unexpectedly seriously, he then found himself being consulted as a pundit, treated as the equal of seasoned researchers. The book enthroned him in a status for which he was substantially unqualified.

The abrupt change of treatment would hardly have mattered were it not for the fact that it seemed to legitimize a discourse that, far from displaying the seriousness and careful objectivity appropriate to any research work, spews out great chunks of morality. 'How does it work, in this day and age, the demonic?' Bernard-Henri Lévy wonders in the foreword to his book (p. xvii). And he carries on wondering to the end of his 'faction', which winds up with a 'call for the sharing of light' (p. 454). His vision of Islam is marked by relentless Manichaeism. 'I think, as I'm on my way again, of this other face of Islam, made of tolerance and moderation, disfigured by the madmen of God, or rather the Devil' (p. 453); 'Who will prevail, the sons of Massoud or Pearl's killers?' (p. 454); 'Who will prevail: the heirs of this ancient commerce of men and cultures that stretches from Avicenna to Mahfouz by way of the sages of Cordoba – or the madmen of the Peshawar camps who call for jihad and, belly strapped with explosives, aspire to die as martyrs?' (ibid.); 'How can the Islam of light triumph over this cadaver-hungry God, grinding bodies and souls in the melting-pot of a distorted law?' (p. xviii), and so on. Good guys and bad guys, as straightforward as a western. It's one reason why, perhaps, when reading his book one so often feels one is in Hollywood. Bernard-Henri Lévy was directing his own little movie as usual, as he has for thirty years now. The problem here is that he claims to have carried out an investigation.

Bernard-Henri Lévy's Manichaeism recalls another – that displayed by much of the French media in their coverage of radical Islam. Facts are distorted, the reality of the terrorist threat is wildly exaggerated in a tone of unbridled catastrophism, with xenophobia and Islamophobia lurking in the wings. Factual analysis, empirical data free from a moral charge, are rare or non-existent. On this level, a book like *Who Killed Daniel Pearl?* is revealing: perfectly pitched for the dominant media, reflecting the mean level of the discourse on the subject and at the same time endorsing it.

The way the book was promoted in the US – the English-language translation was published there by Melville House in September 2003 – laid strong emphasis on what its author called its 'anti-anti-Americanism', while its US publisher posed, not without symmetry, as a champion of 'anti-anti-French' sentiment.[106] Inoffensive in themselves, these terms nevertheless contribute to the fragmentation of public space into camps separated by ideological fault lines.

Written in the post-9/11 world, published on the eve of the US intervention in Iraq, can *Who Killed Daniel Pearl?* be considered a warlike book? One would assume not, since the author (in this book and in interviews) has made a point of dissociating himself publicly from any idea of a 'clash of civilizations'. And yet one has to bear in mind the total contrast between such virtuous declarations and what Bernard-Henri Lévy actually writes when discussing concrete situations involving political Islam. What we find in this book is looseness of language, a reading both homogenizing and polarizing that depicts a single Islamism, a single radicalism, referring to 'a world of radical Islamism', 'a jihadist syndicate' (p. 387), in wilful ignorance of the divergent objectives and means that separate the historic Islamist movements (Iran, the Muslim Brotherhood, Islamic Jihad, etc.) whose common purpose is to 're-Islamize' society, from Al Qaeda.

The simplistic opposition between two Islams (the dark and the bright) ignores both the differences and divergences between movements claiming to be Islamic, and the multiple non-religious dimensions (ethnic, geopolitical, political, economic and so on) that determine these movements' modes of action. By citing religion as the sole key to explaining the commitment of these radical militants, Bernard-Henri Lévy is helping to maintain the essentialist gaze that the West brings to bear on the conflicts ravaging Muslim societies. Olivier Roy, the Central Asia and political Islam specialist, defines Islamism more judiciously as a 'political and radical reading of fundamentalism'[107] (the latter term designating the wish to refocus exclusively on the founding texts of the religion). There is no homogeneous doctrine and no coherent overall ideology; there is no equivalence between terrorism and Islamism, nor is violence inherent in Islamism, which might just as easily favour a reformist project for society. Roy's viewpoint is shared by the sociologist François Burgat, the author of several books on political Islam in the Maghreb and the Middle East.[108]

But what good is all this erudite complexity in an intellectual landscape devastated by 9/11, radicalized by a toxic brew of fear of the other and centuries of ignorance? In a climate where a self-proclaimed tolerant humanist like Bernard-Henri Lévy can calmly wonder whether terrorism is 'the bastard child of a demonic couple: Islam and Europe' (p. 101)? Associating Europe and Islam, Western democracy and Muslim religion is, it would appear, so unnatural as to be morally reprehensible. Islam and Europe would seem to be incompatible, their meeting liable to produce nothing but a terrifying fusion of the worst tendencies on both sides. Bernard-Henri Lévy has often denounced the 'clash of civilizations' theory articulated by Samuel Huntington, but here he seems to offer a flagrant example of agreement with it. Once again the writer speaks with a forked tongue, a double discourse, a double language: on the one hand the public declaration (in interviews and articles) of impeccable intentions, amid appeals for tolerance and dialogue; and on the other a work that is the opposite, contemptuous and stigmatizing. It is hard to understand why this sentence was not picked up by more observers.

Unless, of course, Bernard-Henri Lévy in a moment of careless arrogance had only intended a literary flourish. For that sentence is really a self-quotation, a perfect echo of the opening sentence of *Barbarism with a Human Face*: 'I am the bastard child of an unholy union between fascism and Stalinism.' Perhaps, in this case, an irrepressible narcissism has upstaged a well-advertised set of ethical principles. But if that can happen, how solid can those principles be?

In France, *Qui a tué Daniel Pearl?* sold 129,200 copies in eight months.[109] For a book purporting to investigate the hidden side of the Pakistani secret services and the shady fringes of nuclear technology, this is quite a print run. The US publisher refused to disclose sales figures, but admitted, 'We distributed 50,000 copies, and sales have been excellent.'[110] Good enough in fact to encroach on sales of Marianne Pearl's book, published in the US under the title *A Mighty Heart*. Nan Graham, Marianne Pearl's editor at Scribner, told us later, 'We don't give out sales figures, but you can say that we have sold fewer than 50,000 copies. The reviews were exceptionally good, but I believe really that the appearance of Bernard-Henri Lévy's book a month before Marianne's, and his promotional campaign across the country, did deprive Marianne's book of sales and attention.'[111] Published in France on 23 April 2003, *Who Killed Daniel Pearl?* was rushed into print in the US in early September, some six weeks before Marianne Pearl's testimony appeared. Not exactly fair play.

When all is said and done, what do we learn from the warm welcome given to Bernard-Henri Lévy's book by media and public? Despite some serious refutations and equally serious (and obvious) reasons for doubting some of the 'information' in it, 'people' (hacks, critics, media intellectuals, their readers) are ready to 'believe'[112] that a nation state is deliberately organizing the transfer of nuclear weapons technology to the most murderous terrorist network on the planet, not because there is any evidence but because 'people' think that it is possible. It's possible, so it's probable, so it must have happened. Or if it hasn't happened yet, it soon will.

But 'people' have not been worried enough, even after all these years, to try to find out anything further. Where is this terrorist atom bomb? Is Al Qaeda going to become the next nuclear power? Have the newsdesks even tried to follow up on an issue they did so much to manufacture in the first place? Or perhaps 'people' think that you just suck 'information' in and pump it out, no big deal, just the noise of the world and its spectacle; that where Al Qaeda is concerned there's no point in 'trying to understand', in working and researching to build up a more accurate picture of the risks and threats posed by that terrorist nebula. As if it were a truism, as if everyone knew that when addressing Absolute Evil it doesn't matter what you say: truth, lies and error are all worth about the same.

With a few honourable exceptions, the French media failed in their duty over *Who Killed Daniel Pearl?* They did not register the book's factual errors and manipulative structure. But how could it have been otherwise, given the long history of reciprocal admiration and services rendered between its author and the journalists concerned? The media revel in heaping praise on Bernard-Henri Lévy's work, and he returns the compliment in his books and articles. So why should people knock themselves out criticizing Bernard-Henri Lévy? After all, one doesn't carp at what one admires. And as one journalist explained in 2004 on the TV programme 'Le Masque et la Plume' – a series renowned for the ferocity of its critical gaze – 'Bernard-Henri Lévy is intelligence in human form.'[113]

7 WAGING WAR FOR DEMOCRACY

Can one wage war for democracy? That is the weird paradox that Bernard-Henri Lévy defends. A damnably challenging exercise in intellectual acrobatics for an advocate of human rights. But it seems to link with the outlandish moralism that characterizes him and governs his Manichaean reading of the world. Thus, if he is to be believed, Islamism is a menace to the world as serious as fascism between the two World Wars. It was in the name of that Manichaean reading of history that he lobbied for an international military intervention in Bosnia. It was because he thought he had seen a war on civilians by Islamists in Darfur that he wanted the international community to use force there. It is because he accepts the comparison between the Iranian president Mahmoud Ahmadinejad and Adolf Hitler that he wanted to start a proxy revolution in Iran. And it is because we are living in a BHLian era that his discourse promoting muscular humanitarianism has had so much impact in Libya. Over and above this or that cause, the whole attests to a method.

FASCISM EVERYWHERE, ESPECIALLY IN ISLAMISM

Bernard-Henri Lévy loves colours. They are prettier than concepts and easier to understand. When the magazine *Elle* asked him in 2004 what his current struggles were, he replied, 'The same, in a way, as they were ten, twenty or thirty years ago. At one time we used to say, fascism. Or Stalinism. Well, this is the third stage, the third panel of the same will to purity, or in the literal sense, of the same integralism; and that is called fundamentalism. Brown, red or green, fundamentalism has only one face.'[1] Brown as the shirts worn by the Hitler Youth, red as the blood spilled over the communist flag, fascism can also be green, like Islam.

Bernard-Henri Lévy remains an anti-fascist; all that changes is the colour of the enemy. A rereading of geopolitics in the graphic palette he uses so freely: 'Algerian women tell us it is a form of green fascism';[2] 'In its fundamentalist form, Islam is in a certain way a third fascism, green fascism, after the brown and red fascisms.'[3] He even invented a 'Cambodian' variant in 1998, the 'green Khmers',[4] a geographically and chronologically insouciant neologism to designate the Algerian Islamists of the Groupes islamiques armés (GIA).

The problem is that 'green fascism' does not mean anything. The researcher Olivier Roy defines Islamism as a 'requirement to bring all aspects of social life under a single ideological model,'[5] based on a neo-fundamentalist and ahistorical relation to Islam. So it has little in common with fascism, a doctrine and political system rooted in the specific period between the World Wars, aiming to install a state dictatorship, always nationalist in practice, held together by a cult of the leader and, according to the definition given by the historian of fascism Pierre Milza, 'applying a totalitarian vision of relations between the individual and the State to the transformation of society'.[6] Bernard-Henri Lévy knows as much. The definition of fascism is a textbook classic of French secondary education.

In Pierre Milza's view, fascism is a

> totalitarianism that aims to replace the cultural hegemony of the old elites with that of the new ruling group, and at the same time integrate the masses into the resulting system. This implies, apart from various concessions and material advantages granted to the popular classes to obtain their support for the regime (but as cheaply as possible, without threatening the major interests of property owners), enrolling the masses in corporatist and paramilitary organizations supervised by the single party and aligning their individual members with a model adapted to the wishes of the government, via its monopoly of all the means of training, information and education. It is worth adding, to complete the list of all the criteria defining fascist totalitarianism, the control and management of the economy in what remains a capitalist framework, the use of physical and psychological terror developed in a systematic fashion (a characteristic shared with many other twentieth-century dictatorships) and – a much more specific and fundamental feature – the wish to substitute a 'new order', a new man, for the order and the individual shaped by decadent liberalism.[7]

By knowingly deforming the notion of fascism, Bernard-Henri Lévy reproduces one of the most recurrent leftist knee-jerk responses, the eagerness to discern a fascist hidden behind the most anodyne right-wing idea. He has even devised a 'civilizational' variant with his concept of 'barbarism' (see chapter 2). Just as Maoists and Trotskyists in the 1970s thought they were winkling 'fachos' out of every cranny, Bernard-Henri Lévy sees 'barbarians' and 'fascists' everywhere. The Front National is fascist,[8] Colombian paramilitaries are fascist,[9] Fidel Castro's regime is fascist[10]...

'It is not through indiscriminate use of the term "fascism" applied to absolutely anything and anyone ... that democracy will be defended most effectively against possible attacks by its enemies,' Milza noted, with some irritation already, back in the mid 1980s.[11] Such a careful use of language and striving for intellectual rigour are beyond the anti-fascist Bernard-Henri Lévy, his imagination trapped in the 1930s. Bernard-Henri Lévy's fascists can assume a more contemporary guise to become 'fundamentalists' when he assembles a random and diverse cohort to be denounced as a 'fundamentalist International':[12] the Serbian Milosevic, the Libyan Gaddafi, the Russian Zhirinovski, the Sudanese Hassan El-Turabi and others, with some of their distinguished forerunners for good measure – the Cathars, Hitler, the Khmer Rouge, and so on.

However, on this particular matter of fundamentalism, Bernard-Henri Lévy does make an attempt at definition. '[A] fundamentalist believes that there is a final solution to the questions raised by mankind. An anti-fundamentalist, by contrast, retorts: "No, no, humanity isn't sick, so it doesn't need to be cured"; or, "Humanity is incurable, man is a failed species".'[13] One cannot fail to be enlightened by this psychopathological definition in all its exemplary rigour. It allows fundamentalism, totalitarianism and Islamism to be confused with one another and to end by all designating the same enemy: 'The fundamentalism, mainly Muslim, embodied to a vertiginous degree by the Taliban.'[14] This reference to the Afghan movement of 'students of religion' is not fortuitous. The fundamentalism Bernard-Henri Lévy generally attacks is Islamic first and foremost, because 'it is our good luck that the Jews and Catholics are vaccinated against fundamentalism. They had their dose with the wars of religion and the Inquisition.'[15] This might seem a hasty assertion to anyone who had bothered to notice the discourse or antics of the born-again Christians who once enjoyed the support of George W. Bush, or of the Israeli Orthodox Jews of Gush Emunim (the Faith Bloc).

So Bernard-Henri Lévy makes Islamism the main enemy of democracy. 'Islamism' is a notion used in the same way as 'fascism' or 'populism': as turn-offs or anathemas to discredit utterly those he labels with them. However, by using these terms so loosely he is not only giving up on philosophic endeavour, he is undermining any chance of opposing the evils he denounces. He swamps his audience in the inevitability of the danger that threatens them. In the predominant key of an era that has thrown out, along with the bathwater of ideologies, the babies of theoretical systems and elaborated concepts, he is focused on the symptoms of the evils he denounces, but indifferent to possible modes of action.

French intellectuals have not set a shining example of relevance in their analyses of the Arab and Muslim world since the 1980s. With a few exceptions, French experts have overestimated the danger that Islamist movements might represent and endorsed, more or less openly, the established dictatorial regimes – in Algeria, Tunisia, Egypt and elsewhere – which claimed to be fighting them.

Bernard-Henri Lévy has followed that tendency in general. Even though he has taken very little interest in Arab societies, he joined the camp of the 'eradicators' on Algeria, those who claimed that the massacres of civilians carried out during the internal war of the 1990s had been committed exclusively by Islamists (see above, chapter 4). This reading of events served him well. Early in 2011, he went to Egypt after the fall of Hosni Mubarak, overthrown by the Egyptian revolution. He returned with a long reportage published over two pages by *Libération*.[16] Unsurprisingly, the text is favourable to the revolutionaries. There is nothing original in it, and appearing after the battle it passed unnoticed. However, the article focuses on the role of the Muslim Brotherhood in the uprising. And, without introducing any new material, it uses the presence of those religious militants in the demonstrations in Tahrir Square to cast doubt, not without caution, on their intentions. It is as if he had nothing to say about these Near Eastern societies that does not fit into a religion-centred reading.

'WE WILL ALL BE YUGOSLAVS!'[17]

'Over Bosnia a handful of us never stopped shouting that the carnage could be stopped and democratic Islam saved, and that this would not even cost very much. Instead of which there was a four-year delay before anything was done, at the price of 200,000 lives, millions of refugees and the radicalization of Islam. I remember my conversations with Mitterrand, his insufferable conceit, the irresponsibility and incompetence of Balladur and Juppé ...'[18] With his unequalled mediatic presence, Bernard-Henri Lévy can become a sounding-board, a megaphone of imposing volume for anyone seeking a hearing for their 'cause'. A role performed with exemplary emphasis when the first post–Berlin Wall war broke out in Europe with the conflict in former Yugoslavia.

In 1991 the Yugoslav Federation disintegrated. Between April 1991 and March 1992, the nationalist Serbia led by Slobodan Milosevic, which also controlled the former federal army, conquered a third of Croatia (almost as nationalist under the leadership of Franjo Tudjman), which had proclaimed its independence. But UN forces entered Croatia and halted the Serb conquest. The two provinces then set their heart on a third, Bosnia-Herzegovina. Populated by Serbs, Croats and Muslims (and led by a Muslim, Alija Izetbegovic), Bosnia was for three years subjected to an unequal, fratricidal, murderous war of aggression, in which Serbia supported the Bosnian Serbs led by Radovan Karadzic. At the centre of the conflict was the Bosnian capital Sarajevo, surrounded by mountains from which the Serbian army shelled the civilian population and sniped at will. The siege began in April 1992, and ended only with the signature of the Dayton accords in 1995.

The war was too complex to mobilize European opinion immediately. And the attention of governments was elsewhere. Worried, primarily, by the viability of the 'construction process' of a still-fragile Europe (the Maastricht referendum was due in September 1992), the Europeans were blundering about in the thicket of their old alliances.

Observing the impotence of the UN forces present at Sarajevo from April 1992 and the limpness of European governments, especially the French (Mitterrand was in favour of maintaining the frontiers of former Yugoslavia and hostile to armed intervention), Bernard-Henri Lévy embraced a just cause, that of the Bosnians, and for three years applied himself to making their voice heard by French public opinion. Throughout that period he tirelessly opposed the crazed nationalism of the Serbian president Milosevic and the Bosnian Serb leader Karadzic with support for a multi-ethnic, multi-denominational Bosnia.

He went to Sarajevo several times and made a film there, *Bosna!*. He organized a European tour for President Izetbegovic. He wrote innumerable articles and took part in TV broadcasts, conferences and seminars. He called for armed intervention. He repeatedly challenged the French government's refusal to lift its arms embargo (theoretically affecting both parties to the conflict, but in practice unfair to the Bosnians, who did not have access to the equipment and structures of the former Yugoslav federal army). He denounced the 'humanitarian alibi' – supplying food and medicine to escape the accusation of doing nothing – and the impotence of UN troops. And he brought the Bosnian question into the centre of the 1994 European elections by advancing the idea of a 'Sarajevo' list of candidates, but changed his mind on realizing that the Socialist leader for those elections, Michel Rocard, had already bagged the main demands put forward by the 'biodegradable' Sarajevo list.[19]

The great merit of Bernard-Henri Lévy 'is to have drummed up a debate – on human rights, humanitarianism, the image of Europe and the role of the European Union – at a time when political divergences and indecision were prevalent. … The interesting thing is that he triggered a moral mobilization in the face of international principles that did not allow for any solutions,' explains Sophia Clément-Noguier, researcher and senior lecturer at the Paris Institut d'études politiques.[20] But does mobilizing opinion ever influence political decision-making? Éric Chevallier, the French ambassador to Syria and Bernard Kouchner's deputy when the latter was the UN special representative in Kosovo, explains the mechanism in these terms:

> It's impossible for governments to act on all crises at the same time and with the same intensity. Of course they react most promptly to the ones in which major national interests are at stake. But not only to those, fortunately. The problem is that there are several dozen crises going on in the world at any one time. The only ones that escape the indifference we think so unbearable are those that manage to raise a political and mediatic fuss. In that framework mediatic intellectuals have a role to play although, obviously, they can't do the whole thing by themselves.[21]

Bernard-Henri Lévy was not alone in France in espousing the Bosnian cause. The review *Esprit*, his old enemy, and its inner circle (in particular the editor of *Esprit*, Olivier Mongin, the jurist Antoine Garapon, the international relations specialist Pierre Hassner and Véronique Nahoum-Grappe, researcher in contemporary social anthropology at the École des hautes études en sciences sociales) had become involved in 1991, before founding the Comité Vukovar-Sarajevo in May 1992, where they were joined by the film-maker Romain Goupil among others. NGOs, for example Médecins sans frontières which called for armed intervention, had been quick to get involved. But unlike them, Bernard-Henri Lévy chose his own mode of intervention: personalization.

During his first visit to Sarajevo (of which a long account appeared in Le Point, 27 June 1992), he recounts having been stopped with his companions (including Philippe Doust-Blazy and Jean-François Deniau, all having hooked up with a UN convoy) at a Serb roadblock outside the Bosnian capital. The wait lasted two days, the Serbs refusing to allow the convoy into the besieged town. Only the arrival of a CNN crew enabled the situation to be unblocked and the Frenchmen to reach Sarajevo. Two reporters who were there covering the Bosnian conflict recalled the arrival of the CNN crew at the Serb checkpoint: 'As soon as they arrived, the technicians rigged up a satellite telephone dish. BHL introduced himself: "I am BHL, French philosopher." The technician was visibly unimpressed but agreed to lend Lévy his satphone to make a single call. The call was to AFP and the message, although not strictly accurate, had the virtue of concision: "Say that I'm in Sarajevo".'[22] And a few hours later, he was.

Pro-Bosnian commitment mingled with self-promotion. Watching him strolling along the muddy trenches in his film *Bosna!*, it was impossible not to remember the images of his wedding to Arielle Dombasle a few months earlier, on the TV news[23] and in the pages of *Paris Match*. And it was also, surely, as the courageous 'intellectual' that Claire Chazal invited him onto her TV show to talk about about his play *Le Jugement dernier*, whose theatre performances were about to start.[24]

Publicizing commitment, making a display of it, does not always come off. What starts off as physical courage ends up as the staging of courage. In one famous and ridiculous example Bernard-Henri Lévy was interviewed crouching behind a low wall, head sunk between his shoulders and eyes darting nervously about, while in the background people can be seen starting to move normally. And there is a great deal of footage of Bernard-Henri Lévy in the Bosnian trenches, Bernard-Henri Lévy in Sniper Alley, Bernard-Henri Lévy under artillery fire ...

In 1996 on the TV programme 'Arrêt sur image' (Freeze frame), questioned by the journalist Philippe Meyer,[25] Bernard-Henri Lévy argued the need to appear on screen in *Bosna!* by saying, 'I wanted to illustrate the subjectivity of this film.' As ever, when Bernard-Henri Lévy mentions his 'subjectivity' he is about to simplify things to excess. In this case he is the first to admit it, saying that where Bosnia is concerned he refrains from going into the 'complexity' and the 'ins and outs of the situation.'[26] If analysis is lacking, however, there is no shortage of analogies. At one moment the Bosnians are the Spanish Republicans. At another, they are the British in 1942, refused supplies of weapons by the Americans. The inaction of European countries is an instance of 'Munichism' (a term that, along with 'the spirit of Munich', crops up in nearly all Bernard-Henri Lévy's public statements during the conflict), and François Mitterrand is accused of passive collaboration: 'I cannot help recalling, all things considered, the discourse of those who said in 1940: "The resistance are irresponsible people who are just adding one war to another and bringing down German thunderbolts on the heads of the poor French."'[27] From there it needed only a short step to make Serbia into a new Nazi Germany, a step that Bernard-Henri Lévy took explicitly in the account of his first visit to former Yugoslavia. 'Yes, Belgrade in that early summer was the strangest place. Blank looks. Lugubrious faces. Embarrassed demeanours. The lost look of the passers-by in the street. Diffuse anxiety. A feeling of guilt, too – as if here were an entire people emerging from a nightmare and trying to recover its senses. Germany in 1944 must have looked like this.'[28]

Bosna!, the film on the war in Bosnia, uses and abuses the same sort of montage: camps, exoduses, nationalist speeches. Images of the Second World War alternate with images from former Yugoslavia, linked by the commentary. 'After Auschwitz, people said: "We didn't know." Fifty years later, outside Sarajevo, they say: "We don't understand".'[29] Massacres of civilians, ethnic cleansing, genocide, all get jumbled up, with utter disdain for historical accuracy and to the detriment of any understanding of the specific stakes of the Bosnia conflict. Does Bernard-Henri Lévy know it, or is he carried away by his imagination? Eric Chevallier for his part points out that 'in order to mobilize people, to bring a neglected or forgotten crisis out of the shadows, you have to overstate the case. Everyone knows that the victim-culprit duality is seldom chemically pure. But the mobilization imperative sometimes forces one to exaggerate or play down certain nuances, and even so it's usually quite easy to tell which is which.'

But at what cost? 'Let Sarajevo fall, and that image of Europe will go down with it,'[30] Bernard-Henri Lévy prophesies. And what is 'that image of Europe'? 'It is that people could be Serb, Croat, Jewish or Muslim, they could belong to different "ethnic groups" or "nationalities" – while forming, for centuries, a pretty successful community.'[31] Unfortunately the Bosnian reality is a good deal more complex than that. 'You can't call it a real mixing, more a cohabitation of populations,' Sophia Clément-Noguier says cautiously.[32] 'There is, in the true sense of the term, a superficial multi-ethnicity, a sort of interleaving of peoples. But holding Sarajevo out as a multicultural town doesn't erase the historical enmities and imbalances between populations that have always agitated the city.' As Bernard-Henri Lévy knows, the Bosnia he defends is 'an idea. A certain idea of Europe or even, who knows, of human culture.'[33]

Most at ease when being indignant, Bernard-Henri Lévy neglects to formulate political proposals for the Bosnia to come, and thus loses all credibility. 'Sarajevo needed to be defended and it's very good to articulate what are anyway true and respectable political principles applied to a zone,' Sophia Clément-Noguier adds. 'But the problem is the failure to carry his own logic and reasoning through to their conclusion. Bernard-Henri Lévy stops being serious when he talks about solutions. He never worries about "aftermaths" or the implications of the things he says. But those are for politicians and soldiers to consider! It's too easy simply to brew up worthy ideas without ensuring the follow-up and resources to do anything about them. Reality is often much more complex than discourse.' A position that Bernard-Henri Lévy is happy to adopt, against those he calls 'Norpois' (from the name of Proust's ridiculous diplomat) or 'experts'. He flaunts his lack of interest in the consequences of what he preaches. 'Intervene, I said. … After that, I don't know … No, I don't know how or when the enormous fundamental problems created or magnified by this war will be resolved.'[34]

To mobilize the masses, heroes are needed, and Bernard-Henri Lévy found one in General Jovan Divjak. A Bosnian Serb and field officer in the Yugoslav federal army, he was one of the few Serb military men to remain loyal to his new-born country of Bosnia. Naturally, this confirmation of his ideal of a multi-ethnic Bosnia was pleasing to Bernard-Henri Lévy, and Divjak became a recurrent figure in his articles and one of the heroes of his film *Bosna!*. Ten years later, interviewed by Frédéric Dupuis for Canal Plus, Divjak recalled Bernard-Henri Lévy's courage when accompanying Bosnian soldiers in the front line. He also said that after the war he had founded an orphanage, which Bernard-Henri Lévy had promised to help, but nothing had ever materialized. When asked about this by the journalist, Bernard-Henri Lévy replied, 'I had the feeling I wasn't needed so much.' So, on to other campaigns. After the Canal Plus film was broadcast, however, Bernard-Henri Lévy (according to several sources[35]) sent Divjak a cheque. He would not have wanted the former Bosnian general to repeat too often what he had said to the Canal Plus journalist: 'Everything he did for Bosnia was for himself.'[36]

DARFUR: ALL UNITED AGAINST THE 'ISLAMIST MILITIA'

On 20 March 2007, a big meeting on Darfur was held at La Mutualité, the historic Paris venue for left-wing campaigns. The meeting was organized by Urgence Darfour, a collective chaired by Jacky Mamou, former president of the humanitarian NGO Médecins du monde, and by SOS Darfour. With the French elections only weeks away, the main presidential candidates were all either there, or represented (Nicolas Sarkozy was not present in person). Politically the evening was successful. The candidates signed a text that committed them to concrete action to stop the massacres, and held out the threat of boycotting the Beijing Olympic Games if the killing continued (Beijing was accused of supporting Khartoum). The conflict in that region of western Sudan, where since 2003 militias backed by the Sudanese army had clashed with local rebel movements, had already caused tens of thousands of deaths and nearly two million displaced persons.

The high point of the evening was Bernard-Henri Lévy's speech. After the publication – in the top national daily *Le Monde*, then in the mass-circulation weekly *Paris Match* – of his reportage on a trip with rebel combatants (entitled 'Choses vues au Darfour',[37] Victor Hugo again), he had become the most celebrated defender in France of the Darfur rebels' cause. It was François Zimmeray, former Socialist member of the European parliament and founder of SOS Darfour, who awakened him to this campaign to 'pierce the mediatic wall of silence'.[38] He organized a trip to Darfur for BHL, the former Socialist prime minister Laurent Fabius, and the president of the association SOS Racisme, Dominique Sopo. Air tickets and hotel expenses were paid for by the US association Save Darfur. This brisk guided tour of a few days paid Bernard-Henri Lévy off a hundredfold. In articles, in interviews with the broadcast media, in his public utterances, he spoke henceforth as a witness to the massacres (of which he had really only seen traces), rather than as the mere observer of a conflict he knew little about.

Bernard-Henri Lévy is an excellent publicist and did the job perfectly. He popped up all over on television, endlessly repeating the demands of Urgence Darfour – intervention by UN troops to protect 'humanitarian aid corridors' – and missed no opportunity to compare the Sudanese troops to Nazis and the inhabitants of Darfur to Jews facing extermination during the Second World War. To Bernard-Henri Lévy, Darfur was the 'first genocide of the twenty-first century'. The historical parallel, so customary in his rhetoric, struck a chord in many minds and seemed to win the majority of the political and media class over to the idea of an international intervention in Darfur. Urgence Darfour had pulled a master-stroke of public relations by getting Bernard-Henri Lévy on board.

But offstage, in the wings, things went a lot further. Bernard-Henri Lévy began supporting the chief of a Darfur rebel group. Abdelwahid Mohammed Ahmed al-Nur headed the Sudan Liberation Movement/ Army (SLM-A), originally the main Darfur rebel group (the first armed incidents, in February 2003, were claimed by the Darfur Liberation Front, which then became the Sudan Liberation Movement/Sudan Liberation Army). After starting – with others – the Darfur rebellion, Abdelwahid gradually lost touch with the terrain and by 2007, when Bernard-Henri Lévy first met him, he only led a minority faction of the SLA. However, he remained one of the rebel leaders seen as legitimate interlocutors by the international community.

Exiled in France between 2006 and 2010, Abdelwahid al-Nur naturally got in touch with the delegate-general of Urgence Darfour, Richard Rossin. Former general secretary of Médecins sans frontières, Dr Rossin was an old comrade of Bernard-Henri Lévy. They had met in 1979 on the 'Un bateau pour le Viêt-nam' committee, a group of humanitarian intellectuals and doctors formed to help the 'boat people', the seaborne refugees then fleeing from communist Vietnam in their tens of thousands. That was a founding episode in the epic of the 'French doctors', and a media thunderclap that resounded internationally. Modern humanitarian action won its spurs there.

Thirty years later Rossin, convinced by his secular and pro-democratic discourse, became Abdelwahid's adviser. But the Quai d'Orsay (French foreign ministry) was ill at ease with a troublesome exile refusing to take part in the current peace negotiations on Darfur. It did grant him a short-term residence visa but then, in 2007, appeared reluctant to renew it. He found himself threatened with expulsion. When he learned of the threat to his friend, Rossin called an old acquaintance, Bernard Kouchner. Kouchner, Nicolas Sarkozy's recently appointed minister of foreign affairs, was another veteran of the Vietnam committee, and probably the best known of the former 'French doctors'. Rossin threatened the Quai d'Orsay with a media campaign, published an angry opinion piece in *Libération*,[39] and lobbied his old friend BHL, who also started to fire broadsides in the media. 'I cannot imagine that my friend Kouchner could have a hand in infamous dealings of that sort,' he wrote in his weekly diary for *Le Point*.[40] The response was not long in coming. Rossin received a call from Kouchner's office: 'You must stop this. BHL

… it's really too much.' Abdelwahid got his visa. He stayed in France for two more years, and even wrote a blog for the website of Bernard-Henri Lévy's review *La Règle du jeu*.

Indeed, the Sudanese exile seems to have been much influenced by BHL's take on matters of religion. Thus he wrote in his blog, after visiting an exhibition at the Louvre, that some Darfur place names derive from the word 'Torah'. He gave the example of the village of Torong Tonga – a name that in Fur simply means 'the ancestors' houses', after the ruined old dwellings there. 'There isn't the slightest indication or the slightest belief to connect them with some hypothetical Jewish presence,' we were assured by Jérôme Tubiana, a researcher specializing in the region who since February 2011 has been a member of the UN panel of experts on Sudan.[41] Similarly he cites the nickname given to the rebels, 'Tora Bora' (which he spells 'Torah Bora'). The rebels themselves see it as a reference to the battle of Tora Bora in Afghanistan, since the first Darfur insurgents sought shelter from airstrikes in mountain caves and gorges, like Osama Bin Laden in Tora Bora. To Bernard-Henri Lévy, Abdelwahid was 'the soul of the Darfur resistance.'[42] Not everyone shared this pious view, however. Already criticized for refusing to take part in the Darfur peace process, the warlord's faction SLA/AW is accused of executing opponents. 'It is well established,' the researcher Jérôme Tubiana told us, 'that Abdelwahid's loyalists on the ground (many of whom are members of his family) killed, or had killed, a number of commanders who were a little critical or dissident.'[43] Were these killings ordered by Abdelwahid in person? No one has managed to prove it. But there are other accusations. In its 2010 report, the UN panel of experts on Sudan said that 'individuals claiming to act in the name of the SLA/AW committed acts of violence against displaced persons favourably disposed to the Doha peace process'.[44] These exactions were thought to have been carried out in particular in the Kalma and Hamidiya refugee camps in July 2010. Moreover, 'commanders acting on the authority of Abdelwahid Mohammed al-Nur have repeatedly denied aid workers and peacekeepers access to civilians in the areas of the Jebel Marra [the SLA fiefdom] under SLA/AW control'.

In this context, the UN experts wrote, 'actions by Abdelwahid Mohammed al-Nur have hampered the peace process and are further threatening stability in Darfur and the wider region'. So much so that some experts on this panel recommended that Abdelwahid be placed on the list of sanctioned individuals. On the website of *La Règle du jeu*, BHL feebly dismissed these serious charges. 'In the first place, I do not believe these stories of remote-control executions ... I do not believe in this oversimplified image of the obstinate warlord.[45] But he produced no evidence to back up his position. Rony Brauman, former president of Médecins sans frontières, was scathing about BHL's 'Brezhnev-style interview' of his Darfuri protégé, given that that individual was 'a warlord, a violence entrepreneur'.[46] Abdelwahid now lives in Africa, between Nairobi and Kampala. He has finally agreed to re-enter the political game in Darfur.

The Darfur campaign then faded quietly away. Once in power, Sarkozy and Kouchner did not send UN troops to intervene in Darfur, and did not set up humanitarian aid corridors.

But the arguments developed in the process had further effects, legitimizing an outside, essentially Western, intervention in Africa, and constituting a demonized enemy that one would be morally obliged to fight: the Islamist militiaman. According to the Urgence Darfour campaign, it was in the name of radical Islamism that 'Arab' militias controlled by Khartoum were terrorizing and massacring 'black' civilians in Darfur. Bernard-Henri Lévy went straight to the point in 2007 when he thought he could see, in the Darfur civil war, an 'ethnic cleansing enterprise' in which 'Arab' horsemen were 'opposing' local 'black' tribes. What he saw was 'radical Islam against moderate Islam'; 'in the heart of Africa, in the darkness of what may become, if we do nothing, the first genocide of the twenty-first century, another theatre for the only clash of civilizations that means anything, which is – as we know – that between the two Islams.'[47] Three years later this opinion had not shifted at all: 'In that battle, which is the only battle that counts, between democratic Islam and fundamentalist Islam, between enlightened Islam and the Islam of burqas, there is one essential front line, and it is Darfur.'[48]

This reading of the conflict is highly arguable, however. According to Roland Marchal, a leading Africa specialist, the civil war ravaging Darfur 'does not arise simply from the destabilization of a former modus vivendi between neighbouring groups; on the contrary, it is the crystallization of three different dynamics of unequal importance: destabilization of the political economy of a whole region, the misdirection of the role of the state, and the effects of the civil war in Chad.'[49] In Tubiana's view,

> there is no war of religion in Darfur, and Bernard-Henri Lévy is misled when he sees the conflict as a confrontation between 'radical Islam and moderate Islam'. That is to misunderstand both Darfur and the complex-

> ity of the Khartoum regime. A good proportion of the non-Arab élites in Darfur adhered to the Sudanese Islamist project some time ago, seeing it as a chance for them, as Muslims, to gain access to the levers of power in Khartoum. They were disappointed, but many did not support the rebellion until after the Khartoum regime had abandoned its Islamist ideology and become what it is now, a simple junta with power appropriated by a minority. What is being played out in Darfur is the revolt of a Sultanate proud of its three centuries of history, but kept on the sidelines of immense Sudan since the end of colonization, fifty years ago.[50]

So, despite widespread expert opinion that numerous causes – political, social, geopolitical (the roles of Libya and Chad, both neighbours), and even ecological, given the protracted drought in the region – are fuelling the bloody Darfur war, the campaign of Urgence Darfour and its mouthpiece Bernard-Henri Lévy chooses deliberately to favour a religious explanation as the basis for their commitment and demands. Presenting Darfur civilians as victims of fundamentalist Islamism serves a binary, Manichaean view of the world, with good Muslims on one side and bad ones, who have to be fought, on the other. It is a discourse that casts extremist Muslims as representatives of that ultimate evil, the crime of genocide, even though that interpretation too is arguable. The virtuous against the wicked, victims versus terrorists ... In its binary simplicity, the discourse around the Darfur conflict is an extension of the War on Terrorism initiated by George W. Bush and the neoconservatives. The mobilization around Darfur is thus an essential milestone between two historic events: the war in Iraq and the Western intervention in Libya in March 2011. A number of the same individuals who had mobilized for Darfur, using a number of the same arguments, spoke up four years later urging the West to cough up aircraft and ordnance to make war on Muammar Gaddafi.

IRAN: REVOLUTION BY PROXY

In March 2011, *Le Journal du dimanche* (*JDD*), the Lagardère group's mass-circulation Sunday paper, used a whole page to promote its new format. One of the bullet points read, 'When BHL defends human rights in Iran ... he does it first in the *JDD*.' In the background a portrait of the writer overlays a black lawyer's gown.

The advertisement is a fib on two counts. For one thing, Bernard-Henri Lévy has not written any more on the subject in that paper than in any other. For another, he has not been noted for defending human rights in general in Iran. The cause he had embraced a few months earlier was a much narrower one: saving Sakineh Mohammadi-Ashtiani from death by stoning. From August to December 2010 he placed his review, *La Règle du jeu*, and his connections, at the service of the international campaign to save the life of an Iranian housewife who had been condemned to death. The French writer's involvement in the campaign was as intense as it was brief. Above all, it was terribly full of holes.

The mobilization for Sakineh started in Germany, at the urging of the international committee against stoning animated by Mina Ahadi, an Iranian exile. In 2006 Sakineh had been condemned to death for the murder of her husband and to stoning for adultery. The first sentence had been commuted on appeal to ten years in prison in 2007, but a different court of appeal had confirmed the second sentence. At the end of June 2010, Mina Ahadi's association published an open letter from Sakineh Mohammadi-Ashtiari's children, Farideh and Sajjad: 'Please, save our mother'.[51] The tragedy of the Iranian mother threatened with an atrocious death moved the whole world, and initiatives to save her were legion, with demonstrations in Washington, Cologne, and Malmö. In early July the London *Times* published a petition demanding 'urgent international action' to prevent the sentence of stoning from being carried out. Among its notable signatories were the former US Secretary of State Condoleezza Rice, East Timor President and Nobel Peace Prize Laureate José Ramos-Horta, the actors Robert Redford, Robert de Niro and Juliette Binoche, and Bernard-Henri Lévy. A week later, Tehran announced that it was considering reviewing Sakineh's sentence.

Bernard-Henri Lévy led the mobilization in France. First by publishing a campaigning piece in the daily *Libération*, of which he was then a shareholder: 'Sakineh Mohammadi-Ashtiani must be saved'.[52] Then by publishing jointly, in his review and in *Libération*, a new appeal signed by French personalities (the philosopher Élisabeth Badinter, Juliette Binoche, Sarkozy's former justice minister Rachida Dati, former Socialist presidential candidate Ségolène Royal, but also the Nigerian writer and Nobel Laureate Wole Soyinka and the Somali-born feminist, Dutch parliamentarian and anti-circumcision campaigner Ayaan Hirsi Ali). The petition was lodged in the *La Règle du jeu* website, where signatures were still being solicited nine months later. Sakineh's face, pale and tragic in its Islamic veil, was permanently posted on the home page of the review's website, part of its logo as it were: a mascot despite herself. As if the Iranian woman's cause and BHL's were now inextricably connected.

The Frenchman bustled about, giving the campaign the benefit of his phenomenal networking dexterity. He published opinion pieces one after the other, fired off salvoes of interviews on all the media, organized a solidarity meeting in Paris, published daily letters of support from French starlets including Carla Bruni Sarkozy, and even retrieved his journalist's hat to conduct an interview with Sakineh's former lawyer.[53] He called on Sarkozy to do something, and when the head of state responded with a rather tepid statement making Sakineh Mohammadi-Ashtiani a symbolic French 'responsibility', rewarded him with pompous flattery: 'That is an inestimable relief, an encouragement to persist and, suddenly, the rebirth of hope.' It is no exaggeration to say that he churned it out by the ton. 'He was extremely rapid, very quick to react,' a journalist on *Libération*'s foreign desk recalled. 'Everyone on *La Règle du jeu* was involved and they rang us all the time. The *Libération* management always ran their stuff.'

Typically, Bernard-Henri Lévy dived in head first. In December, when the Islamic republic of Iran mounted a mock liberation of the woman who had now become the most celebrated Iranian prisoner, he wrote (once again in *Libération*), 'The Nazis used to hold mock executions. The Iranians have refined that and are mounting mock liberations. It's the same thing.'[54]

The problem was that all this frantic outrage and agitation ended by being counterproductive. Sakineh's defenders did not limit themselves to rousing the media, they wanted a showdown with Tehran. In early November, on the strength of a claim made by the international committee against stoning, Bernard-Henri Lévy and *La Règle du jeu* announced a scoop: Sakineh could be put to death on 3 November.[55] Demonstrations thronged the streets and messages of support for the doomed woman flooded in. Protests came from all directions. The appointed day arrived, and the prisoner was not executed. Might that have been the result of international pressures? Not according to the Quai d'Orsay. In a press release, the French foreign minister Bernard Kouchner explained that 'the Iranian minister of foreign affairs, Manouchehr Mottaki, assured me that the final verdict in the case concerning Sakineh Ashtiani had not been pronounced by the Iranian courts and that reports concerning her possible execution did not correspond with reality.'

Losing no opportunity to flatter the French president, Bernard-Henri Lévy immediately attributed the prisoner's non-execution to prompt action by Sarkozy.[56] The groups and individuals who had defended her publicly all rejoiced in the reprieve. But a week later, the housewife was shown live on Iranian TV confessing to the murder of her husband, a charge of which a court had found her not guilty in 2006. The production was spine-chilling, and its purpose was clear: to counter the international campaign around Sakineh by showing that the prisoner was alive and that, contrary to her defenders' assertions, she was not innocent.

This state propaganda operation incensed Karim Lahidji, president of the Iranian human rights league and vice-president of the International Federation of Human Rights Leagues. He held the campaign for Sakineh partly responsible, through its lack of prudence. 'They gave the Iranian regime the means to advertise itself. Not only is Sakineh still alive, and a very good thing too, but on top of that she's been presented to the world as guilty. At a stroke, the Iranian regime has been made to look merciful for leaving her alive. It's the world upside down!'[57] In the opinion of this jurist, a very early opponent of the Islamist regime and exiled in France for the past thirty years, 'this excessively mediatic campaign spread some dubious information that rebounded against it and damaged its own credibility.'

During the same period, Iranian human rights campaigners were trying vainly to alert the world to an unprecedented wave of executions inside their jails. Iran, like China, is one of the countries that make most use of the death penalty. But in 2010 and 2011 the frequency of state killings reached alarming levels. 'This is the worst wave of executions since the end of the 1980s,' states the annual report of the Iranian human rights league (IHR), which says that at least 546 individuals were put to death in 2010. In January 2011, just as the international campaign for Sakineh was relaxing its pressure on Iran, whose judicial authorities had announced that Sakineh's death sentence might be commuted, eighty-five people were executed, according to official Iranian sources reported by IHR. At least three of them had been arrested for links with the dissident movements of 2009. 'They're up to three executions a day!' Karim Lahidji exclaimed. 'And we haven't heard a word from Bernard-Henri Lévy on the subject. Why doesn't he denounce this butchery?'

While intellectuals, showbiz stars and politicians in Paris all had their eyes fixed on Sakineh, seventeen political prisoners held at Evine jail in Tehran, mainly students and journalists arrested in 2009 after the revolt against President Ahmadinejad, started a hunger strike in protest against the conditions of their detention. They had been held in complete isolation for a year and subjected to brutal interrogations. 'Those prisoners were waiting for the world to hear their voices and come to their rescue,' explained the London-based Shirin Ebadi (Nobel Peace Prize Laureate 2003). 'They were ready to go as far as dying, to sacrifice their lives to improve the living conditions in Iranian jails. But media attention was all focused on one person and they were ignored. They were finally hospitalized by force. Their struggle failed, and the conditions of detention today are becoming worse and worse.'[58] By April 2011, some of these prisoners had started a new hunger strike.

Shirin Ebadi, a lawyer, feminist and human rights activist, said in August 2010 on Radio Farda (a station that broadcasts in Farsi from Prague) that 'the Sakineh affair was brought into prominence by the Iranian intelligence service so that everyone would focus on that, and the hunger strike by political prisoners would be forgotten.'[59] So would it have been better if international intellectuals, artists and activists had not campaigned for Sakineh? 'My comments don't mean that I am against the campaign for Sakineh,' Ebadi explained, 'but I would prefer a campaign against stoning to a campaign for Sakineh. And I would favour a campaign for human rights, not just one against stoning. It's important to struggle against stoning, but everyone ought to be saved. All the media attention was concentrated on a single individual, Sakineh. To concentrate on just one case is to stifle other voices.'

Is Bernard-Henri Lévy ill-informed on Iran? The country is not his speciality, far from it. When the Iranian regime pronounced a fatwa on Salman Rushdie in 1989, he had expressed support for the writer. But it was the arrival in power of Mahmoud Ahmadinejad in 2005 and his violently hostile declarations on the State of Israel that really marked the beginning of Bernard-Henri Lévy's regular comments and interventions on the Islamic Republic. Nothing surprising there.

On 23 June 2009, as mass demonstrations contesting the re-election of Mahmoud Ahmadinejad were being brutally repressed in Iran, internet surfers could find on Dailymotion a video of BHL's 'address to Iranian youth' in French and English. Seated in front of his bookshelves, white shirt unbuttoned, the director of *La Règle du jeu* solemnly lectured the youth of Tehran: 'Whatever happens now, nothing in Tehran will ever be the same again …' He read his text frowning and shaking his forefinger, as if urging the French Resistance to stand firm on Radio Londres.

More surprising is his association with the Iranian businessman Amir Jahanchahi, a son of the shah's last finance minister, who conducts his business between London and Paris. In June 2009 he was to be seen at Bernard-Henri Lévy's side during a demonstration on the esplanade of the Trocadéro in Paris, in protest at the electoral fraud favouring Ahmadinejad. Three months later, in his weekly editorial for *Le Point*, Bernard-Henri Lévy plugged his book *L'Hitler iranien: En finir avec la dictature d'Ahmadinedjad*. Comparing the President of the Islamic Republic to the Führer was going to take some cheek, but Bernard-Henri Lévy seemed at ease with this far-fetched historical parallel. 'The similarities between the 1930s and our time (the policy of appeasement in dealing with Nazism and in dealing, today, with state-sponsored jihadism and its armed wing Hizbollah) are, alas, and in all due proportion, terribly disturbing.'[60] For the Frenchman would have found much in that prose that was familiar. 'By making radical Islamism a particular case, a variant, a comet's tail, of the worldwide phenomenon that was fascism, nearly a century ago,' Jahanchahi was taking up an idea that had long been precious to Bernard-Henri Lévy.

In June 2010 BHL organized, with much fanfare, an event supposed to be a summit meeting between representatives of the exiled Iranian opposition. Among those present were the film-maker Mohsen Makhmalbaf, the Kurdish exile Abdullah Mohtadi, the journalist and academic Alireza Nourizadeh, Musa Sharifi (a founding member of the democratic solidarity party in Ahwaz), Mehrdad Khonsari (adviser to the Shah's former prime minister Shapour Bakhtiar) ... and Amir Jahanchahi, largely unknown to the Iranian community either in Paris or London. When asked, Shirin Ebadi claimed never to have heard of him.[61]

Introduced by Bernard-Henri Lévy as 'founder-president of the green wave', the businessman was lined up with far more seasoned political personalities. The 'Green Wave' was in fact the name he had chosen for his newly-created organization. It had not been chosen by accident. Green had been the colour chosen by the former prime minister Mir Hussein Moussavi for his 2009 presidential campaign, and taken up by the thousands of demonstrators who had marched against Mahmoud Ahmadinejad. Everyone would see the Green Wave as designating the movements of opposition to Ahmadinejad in Iran. So when Jahanchahi, who had played no part in the revolts of 2009, appropriated the name of the Iranian revolution, it was in the hope of stamping his brand on that historic moment. 'The Green Wave is an umbrella movement, a financing structure for opponents of the present Iranian regime, whatever their political line, provided they undertake to respect democracy,' Jahanchahi's staff explained.[62] Its objective was to infiltrate Iranian institutions and work to disorganize the country. A sort of charitable foundation to promote activism and sabotage.

In Paris, on the stage of the Gabriel studio, normally used for recording light entertainment TV but made available to the Iranian oppositionists on 11 June 2010 through the unexpected help of the TV presenter Michel Drucker, Amir Jahanchahi delivered a radical speech calling for the overthrow of the Teheran regime: 'Until today fear reigned in our camp, the camp of the Iranian people; but after today, it should change sides and take over the other camp, the enemy camp, the camp of the dictator.'[63] What on earth was Bernard-Henri Lévy doing here? 'The birth of Jahanchahi's "green wave" needed to be made official,' Amir Jahanchahi's staff explained, 'a message had to be sent to Iran that he had succeeded in gathering all those people around him. BHL performed that service, he called the speakers to invite them to come and show the face of a united opposition.' And that is how, for the space of an afternoon, Bernard-Henri Lévy imagined himself an *éminence grise* of revolution in Iran ...

LIBYA: MUSCULAR HUMANITARIANISM

Early in March 2011, two French journalists were having morning coffee in the café of the Tibesti hotel in Benghazi, Libya. Since the start of the uprising against Muammar Gaddafi, the coastal city in the east of the country had served as the capital of the embattled insurrection. Reporters from all over the world had been pouring in to cover the civil war.

Bernard-Henri Lévy, a guest in the same hotel as the two special correspondents, spotted them across the room and sat down at their table. Without being asked, he informed them that the Libyan head of state's official visit to Paris in 2007, when he had been entertained for five days with great pomp and ceremony, had shocked him deeply, and that he had since broken off all contact with Nicolas Sarkozy (not strictly true: see above, chapter 2). The journalists listened without much interest. They had been bumping into the French writer for some days. As usual, he was travelling flanked by his friend Gilles Hertzog, a photographer and a bodyguard. The group seldom left the hotel. 'He spent his time in the cafeteria waiting for people to come and interview him,' a witness recalled. 'His ambition seemed to be to get interviewed by everyone. It was a media chase.' One evening, Hertzog, 'in the role of beater' as an observer put it, approached the special correspondent of a French daily paper and showed him a list of journalists. 'Which of these works for Agence France Presse?' he asked. The reporter pointed them out. A few hours later, the AFP wire carried a report that Bernard-Henri Lévy was in Benghazi, where he had met the insurgents' executive council.[64]

Within hours the news had been taken up by websites and radio stations, followed by national dailies.

However, there was nothing unusual in having met members of the Libyan Independent National Council. 'Everyone used to see them, it was very easy,' said Jean-Pierre Perrin, a reporter for *Libération*. 'All you had to do to meet them was go to the Benghazi courthouse, since most of them are lawyers, judges and jurists. At that time, they wanted nothing better than to talk to the media.'[65] As so often, Bernard-Henri Lévy had known where to find a receptive ear to put some positive spin on his self-publicity.

But the story was not over. Just a few days after the breakfast in Benghazi, journalists following the visit to France of Mahmoud Jibril and Ali Essaoui, representatives of the Libyan National Transitional Council received by Nicolas Sarkozy on 10 March, were astounded to hear Bernard-Henri Lévy himself announce that the French president had come out in favour of 'targeted defensive actions' in Libya.[66] He even listed the priority targets: the airports of Syrte and Sebha, as well as the Libyan 'guide's' command centre in Tripoli.[67] The writer made this announcement just after emerging from the Élysée palace, where he had been present at the meeting between the head of state and the Benghazi emissaries. Most surprised of all was the French foreign minister, Alain Juppé, who had not been informed and who on hearing the news practically fell out of his chair in Brussels, where he was holding talks with his German opposite number Guido Westerwelle. Nine days afterward, an international coalition led by the US, the UK and France opened fire in Libya.

What was Bernard-Henri Lévy doing at the Élysée? Why was he present at that very restricted summit meeting? If the writer is to be believed, all it took was a telephone call, made in March from a Benghazi threatened by troops loyal to Gaddafi, just after he had met members of the insurgents' council: 'Powerless to help alleviate so much distress, I telephoned entirely on the off-chance the President of my own Republic.'[68] Bernard-Henri Lévy's advantage over the general run of mortals is that he has Sarkozy's phone number. He explained to the President that the opponents of Gaddafi needed help and should be received. Then, 'President Sarkozy came up with the right reflex and replied, on the telephone, that he would receive Mr Abdul Jalil's envoys, on the date of their choice, and that his seeing them would amount to recognition.' As we know, the meeting later took place, causing Bernard-Henri Lévy to remark, 'I just know that at this moment I am proud of my country.'

At that moment, too, there began a concerted PR effort on the famous phone call, recounted many times over in article after article, often spiced with new details. For example in *Le Figaro*, the daily closest to the presidential majority, the narrative, apparently supplied by the party concerned, was given some extra historical spin. According to that version, the writer had not been content merely to record the Libyans' grievances, but had proposed directly to put them in touch with the French president: 'BHL invited his interlocutors to come to France, promising to do everything possible to get them into the Élysée. When evening came he managed, through his satphone, to reach Nicolas Sarkozy: "Would you be willing to meet the Libyan Massouds?"'[69] In *Le Point*, the weekly owned by his industrialist friend François Pinault, in which he had a weekly column, the version differed again. This time Bernard-Henri Lévy is supposed to have called the president before leaving for Libya.[70] But never mind the variations. Obviously we are being told a story. What does it say?

It says, of course, that Bernard-Henri Lévy is hot stuff. The most swooning eulogies were to be found on the website of his own review *La Règle du jeu*: 'It is written, once and for all, whatever else is said and done, that in the whole worldwide engagement for Libya, BHL was and will remain the "prime mover" in the sense of Aristotle's physics.'[71] In fact, the French ministry of foreign affairs had been in touch with the Benghazi insurgents before the writer's stage entrance. At the exact moment of his arrival in Benghazi, an official mission was on its way to the town headed by a dozen officials, shepherded by Jean-Marie Safa, an Arabic-speaking diplomat, and including two truckloads of equipment and medical supplies, *Le Monde* reported.[72] Among the French emissaries was a doctor formerly working at the '1,200' hospital, the biggest medical institution in the city. When they arrived, the paper explained, they met leaders 'who had already encountered the philosopher and asked what the French hierarchy was. They thought in effect that in the person of Bernard-Henri Lévy they had received a higher-ranking official, since he had introduced himself as an envoy of the Élysée.' Paris had not needed Bernard-Henri Lévy to meet the Libyan insurrection. So why give the impression it had?

Because it was useful to Sarkozy. 'The Élysée encouraged BHL to get in touch', ventured one source at the Quai d'Orsay. It was a sound investment. For after the Libyan episode that put him on stage, the writer lavished superlatives on the French head of state: 'This morning I saw a Sarkozy who on this point was terrific. ... We have a president who has taken the right decision. We should wish him luck.'[73] In another comment the president is described as experiencing 'real indignation in response to the image of these massacres, a genuine surge of heart and mind, utterly sincere.'[74]

In fact, by anointing Bernard-Henri Lévy as its leading spokesman the Élysée had pulled off a coup. He is the country's highest-profile left-wing intellectual; he had publicly supported the Socialist Party candidate in the 2007 presidential election, he had criticized the debate on 'national identity' started by Nicolas Sarkozy to win over far-right voters as well as his repressive policy on the Roma. He embodies to the point of caricature the French-style social democratic conscience, a bit old-hat, moralistic and self-consciously humanist. Who better to defend French participation in the first Western war in an Arab country since the Gulf War? The commandeering was two-way. Bernard-Henri Lévy, who had missed the boat completely during the wave of Arab revolutions of early 2011, speaking little, cautiously and too late, found in Libya the opportunity to make a thunderous comeback onto the political stage; while Nicolas Sarkozy, the most unpopular president since 1968, gained the favour of the brightest left-wing star of the Paris chattering classes. All of which helped to dispel memories of the huge diplomatic blunder made by the previous foreign affairs minister, Michèle Alliot-Marie, who in January 2011 had offered French security expertise to the Tunisian dictator Zine al-Abidine Ben Ali just days before he was deposed by his people.

But the affair also reflects an institutional anomaly: the concentration of all power in the hands of Nicolas Sarkozy and his advisers at the expense of the rest of the government, even figures as important as Alain Juppé, the new foreign affairs minister. Once again the writer would become an instrument in a dispute, this time at the very top of the French state, that was nothing to do with him.

On 22 March (a date marked in France as the anniversary of the first 'events' of May '68), Bernard-Henri Lévy organized a travesty of a summit meeting at the Hôtel Rafael, a first-class Paris establishment that is like his second home. An audience of hand-picked journalists, officials and politicians – including the former foreign minister Bernard Kouchner, recently sacked by Sarkozy – had beeen invited to meet representatives of the Libyan insurgents. The writer became a semi-official spokesman for the Benghazi combatants, and their host during their stays in Paris.

He had himself photographed – white shirt unbuttoned to the waist – in the control room of the Libyan insurgents' headquarters, poring over military maps with General Abdul Fatah Younis.[75] The press nicknamed him 'foreign minister Mk. II [bis]'. Soon he knew so much about French intentions that he may even have divulged a 'defence secret' without realizing it: he announced the arrival of French liaison officers among the anti-Gaddafi forces.[76] The news was only confirmed officially two days later.

The narrative worked like a dream. Whether on left or right, almost no one criticized France's going to war against Libya, with the exception of the Communist deputies. A few scattered individuals questioned Bernard-Henri Lévy's motives and methods, but their isolation rendered them virtually inaudible. It should also be said that he and his associates employed methods amounting to symbolic intimidation to silence any critics. The writer lambasted their 'supremacist neo-pacifism'[77] and once again, in classic fashion, raised the spectre of the Munich accords. As for Laurent Dispot, he wrote in *La Règle du jeu* that 'being anti-Nazi today, in 2011, unavoidably means destroying the Gaddafi clique's missiles and radar.' There is a drive to make out that opposing French missile strikes in Libya is tantamount to choosing (to call a spade a spade) the Nazi camp.

Looked at objectively, however, the composition of the Libyan insurgents' council could raise legitimate questions. It included ex-Gaddafi associates such as General Younis, former interior minister and founder of the Libyan special forces (Younis was killed in Benghazi on 28 July 2011 in unclear circumstances, hours after his arrest for alleged contacts with the Gaddafi regime), or Mahmoud Jibril, planning minister until a year before the insurrection and close to Saif al-Islam, one of Gaddafi's sons. Also a member was Mustafa Abdul Jalil, once a leading figure in the regime. As justice minister he had run a judicial system manipulated by the government; most notably he had been responsible for the detention for eight years of the Bulgarian nurses and Palestinian doctor falsely accused of deliberately infecting children with the AIDS virus (they were released in July 2007 following mediation efforts sponsored partly from Paris). Bernard-Henri Lévy has several times rejoiced in the 'non-Islamist' character of the Libyan rebellion. But Mustafa Abdul Jalil is a devout conservative Muslim. And, according to the special correspondent of the *New York Times* in Benghazi, Kareem Fahim, the volunteers fighting with the TNC include some 'Islamists who learned to fight in Afghanistan' against Western armies.

Under a regime as repressive and as long-lasting – nearly forty years – as Gaddafi's, it is hardly surprising that no structured opposition has managed to take shape. But the past, in some cases the very recent past, of these men who played key roles in the dictatorship indicates clearly enough that they are not angels of liberty, fighting for Good against the forces of Evil. Their political project for a post-Gaddafi Libya remains very hazy, and their taste for democracy is far from certain. But these questions are systematically ignored and even dismissed by Bernard-Henri Lévy. It is striking to see how far, once at war, he is willing to lower his standards in judging the democratic credentials of his new friends. From the first French air strikes on Libya on 19 March 2011, launching the international military offensive against the Gaddafi regime, Bernard-Henri Lévy has never stopped defending the justice and rightness of the war. He had not enjoyed such wide exposure in the French media for years.

This warrior approach to the defence of human rights is not a new development. The New Philosophers had initiated that rhetoric on human rights, ostensibly progressive but bolstering a socially conservative discourse, at the end of the 1970s (see above, chapter 4). Defending some of the oppressed out there – boat people, Afghan women, the Darfur populations persecuted by the Janjaweed, Georgian peasants under the Russian yoke, Iranian youth – instead of attacking the established order over here ... It could be called 'muscular humanitarianism', a soft bellicosity cloaked in righteous, well-meaning messianism.

The novelty in 2011 is that this current of thought seems to have become predominant. We are living in a BHLian era. The play could be entitled *Three States in Quest of Power*. Or how the political leaderships of France, the United Kingdom and the United States, fully aware of their impotence in the face of economic and social crises, the growing indifference of their fellow countrymen toward political institutions, and the rise of populism, are carving out a new space for political survival: the war for human rights and democracy. You flex your muscles, get out your fighter aircraft, bombers, missiles ... so many simulacra of strength and energy. Contrary to appearances, muscular humanitarianism thrives on the withering away of political authority. Contrary to the way it would like to be seen, it is an admission of weakness. And in that context its great success has been to recruit the majority to its cause; with the spectacular effect that no one dares to call themselves a pacifist these days.

In April 2011 the website www.bernard-henri-levy.com, exclusively dedicated to extolling the writer's life and works, posted a slogan in the form of an advertising banner: 'The art of philosophy is of value only if it is an art of war'. To have a war to his credit – though of course he was not the only detonator – is a pretty odd fate for a defender of human rights ... Nevertheless, Bernard-Henri Lévy is not strictly speaking a neoconservative. He was in two minds on Iraq as we have seen, was critical of George W. Bush, and has always proclaimed himself opposed to Samuel Huntington's theory of a 'clash of civilizations' between Islam and the West. Over the thirty-plus years of his public political life he has usually aligned himself with the oppressed (the notable exception being his commitment to Israel – see below, chapter 8).

But in the name of the right to humanitarian interference, he embodies a left-wing interventionist tendency that does not quail at war. This gunboat conception of human rights enables a tyrannical discourse to be clothed in manifest good intentions: in the name of democracy, the use of weapons can be legitimate. Whatever the consequences may be in terms of civilian deaths, ugly 'mistakes', 'friendly fire', aggravation of conflicts ...

By adopting positions on moral grounds, Bernard-Henri Lévy can emancipate himself from the constraints of pragmatism. He can get away with a very general level of discourse (action in the name of Reason, Democracy, Liberty, the French Revolution ...). That absolves him from having to decipher the political and social complexities of the conflicts he claims to (help) settle.

However, by 19 March 2011, when the 'coalition' started its attacks, what was going on was no longer a popular insurrection but a civil war, explains Patrick Haimzadeh, formerly a French diplomat in Tripoli. 'The binary scenario of good against evil and a people up in arms against an isolated dictator is therefore a Parisian philosopher's beautiful image, which unfortunately doesn't correspond to the realities on the ground.'[78] As for the main argument of those supporting armed intervention – the need to save the town of Benghazi from a threatened bloodbath – that too is moot, according to the French diplomatic adviser, for 'Gaddafi's forces (fewer than 1,000 men backed by twenty tanks at most, and without logistical support) lacked the means to unleash a "bloodbath" in Benghazi, a town more than 30 km long and with 800,000 inhabitants, let alone to "recapture" the whole of Cyrenaica, whose liberated inhabitants had access to weapons seized in the first days of the uprising.' No one can say for sure that such a massacre would not have taken place; but what is sure is that once the threat had been brandished, no one was able to cast doubt on its plausibility. It was an extraordinary feat of propaganda, comparable to pretending that the Iraqi army in 1991 was the 'fourth biggest army in the world', or that in 2003 Saddam Hussein had weapons of mass destruction, concludes Patrick Haimzadeh.

Muscular humanitarianism encourages an old vice of Western liberal democracy: the belief that there is no salvation outside it. And that is how Bernard-Henri Lévy, under cover of humanism, has come to reactivate the tetanizing slogan of the conservative revolutions of the early 1980s, coined by Margaret Thatcher: 'There is no alternative.'

But there are limits to this mixing of styles and causes. In May 2011, some Syrian intellectuals called for a boycott of SOS Syrie,[79] a petition in solidarity with victims of Bashar al-Assad's repression, because it had been signed by Bernard-Henri Lévy among other prestigious names. The reason for their anger was his 'hostility to the legitimate demands of the Palestinian people' and his 'culpable endorsement of the colonization of the Occupied Territories, including the Golan Heights.'[80] In early July, representatives of the Syrian opposition publicly refused to take part in a meeting organized by the review *La Règle du jeu* because of its active support for Israel.[81] Others did agree to sign the writer's 'Paris pledge', along with a handful of French politicians and artists. But measured against the violence deployed by Damascus's troops and the thousands of deaths it caused among the demonstrators of the 'Syrian spring', the undertaking, in a cinema in Saint-Germain-des-Prés, of a few personalities to 'accompany' them towards democracy seemed so literary, ethereal and out of touch as to be totally meaningless.

A METHOD

From the foregoing account – inevitably episodic and full of gaps, for there are plenty of other terrains which Bernard-Henri Lévy has visited and commented on – it is not impossible to deduce a method specific to him. It has several characteristics, functioning on different levels.

Firstly, and basically, a strong taste for parts of the world that are making the news; but not only those. Anywhere experiencing war, conflict or massacre stands a chance of seeing Bernard-Henri Lévy sooner or later. The list of countries he has visited is very long. There are a number of reasons for this ubiquity: curiosity, no doubt, and an undeniable energy. But also life conditions specific to Bernard-Henri Lévy. He is not on the staff of any journal. He does not have to ask anyone's permission to go here or there. He has professional obligations, but they are 'adjustable' when the need arises. Bernard-Henri Lévy has no job and is not attached to any university. He can travel when he wants and has the means to charter an aircraft quickly, or the connections to borrow one. This is what he calls 'being free'. And, in a sense, he is.

There is also a rhetoric, which consists essentially of historical analogy. Nazism, fascism, Munich are wheeled out in all sorts of contexts. And analogy engenders analogy. If Massoud recalls the Resistance (Bernard-Henri Lévy recounts having taken him a copy of General de Gaulle's memoirs), the Libyan rebels become Massouds when he wants Nicolas Sarkozy to meet them. Never mind the historical coherence of such references. The value of analogy is obvious: refer to the familiar; simplify; intimidate. Just as Bernard-Henri Lévy piles on the philosophical references in support of his most trivial reflections, so he accumulates historical references when thinking about a political situation. It makes an impression, and is often effective, but it runs the risk of diluting the situation's specificity.

The English word 'storytelling' has become fashionable in France, and in this context it makes particular sense. As well as using History, Bernard-Henri Lévy tells a story. To spin a good yarn means finding a hero: Massoud in Afghanistan, Izetbegovic in Bosnia, Abdelwahid Mohammed Ahmed al-Nur in Darfur, all these become heroes who recall many others. And Bernard-Henri Lévy takes the trouble to describe each as the leading character in an epic. The value of this procedure is obvious – to embody the underlying issue, and generate emotion – and its effectiveness considerable. But it can trample complexities and nuances underfoot.

Spinning yarns also means, all too often, distorting the facts. Algeria, Afghanistan, Georgia … the reasons for the distortion are various: misunderstanding, mythomania, approximation, the wish to simplify, to alert rather than to inform them, to defend a theory against the awkward truth.

Even Bernard-Henri Lévy's objective allies often mention his practice of placing himself centre-stage. It is undeniable that under some circumstances he has courageously exposed himself to danger. But he is mainly a patroller of corridors in the big hotels where the press tends to gather when a conflict looms. He has to be there, finding journalists who can report his presence, organizing meetings, getting himself photographed. The same modus operandi, time after time. It is, in fact, a more or less full-time job in itself. A job that would be pointless without journalists willing to include Bernard-Henri Lévy's presence in their despatches to Paris, as if this were news in itself and as if there were no newspapers to publish his own 'reportages', often quite poor compared to the work of reporters less into hotels and more knowledgeable about the issues.

The relentless self-promotion does inspire a question or two: basically, who is Bernard-Henri Lévy addressing? Who does he want to reach, and who does he reach? To put it another way, does Bernard-Henri Lévy really generate public debate? The answer seems to be on two levels. In his own estimation he is a sort of lookout, a harbinger of necessary causes. And it can happen that this function is fulfilled, as in the case of Bosnia, where the debate really did become a public matter. But most of the time, if there is any effectiveness, it only operates upward, only reaching his own circle of editorialists, politicians and a handful of 'fashionable' Paris intellectuals. Elsewhere, the tendency seems to be to talk less about the article on his meeting with the Benghazi insurgents, and more about the silly photo that illustrates it; less about what he says and more about the gesticulations with which he says it. One might regret the blindness of the public, those imbeciles who stare at the pointing finger instead of the moon; one might admire the selfless behaviour of the writer who (as Bernard-Henri Lévy never tires of repeating) does not hesitate to sacrifice his own image to ensure a hearing for the victims' voices. But either way, the main effect of his mediatic posture is remarkably consistent: it is Bernard-Henri Lévy himself who becomes the object of discussion, ultimately overshadowing the causes he claims to champion.

8 IS BERNARD-HENRI LÉVY LEFT-WING?

What is Bernard-Henri Lévy's place on the political checkerboard? Doubtless the answer to this question has changed since the 11 September 2001 attack, and the rightward drift of the intellectual field that followed. Taken up for their own purposes by the American neoconservatives to justify their war in Iraq, the defence of human rights and of the right to humanitarian intervention does not of itself place those who espouse it on the political left.

This ideological confusion is especially striking in the case of the ex-New Philosopher, who has made a habit of abusing his progressive comrades. A review of the major causes he has embraced over the last thirty years reveals that behind an apparently dissident discourse, he has consistently taken the side of established authorities. With regard to sexual questions, he displays the same archaic attitudes as the rest of the European left of the '68 generation. And when he involves himself in the Israeli–Palestinian conflict, it is as a propagandist for the Jewish State.

THE ART OF TESTIFYING AGAINST YOUR OWN SIDE

One of the mysterious things about Bernard-Henri Lévy is that he passes for a man of the left. He may even be seen as a 'leftist' intellectual by some associates of his close friend, the billionaire François Pinault (see above, chapter 2). In his own circle, however, he surely much prefers to seem a debunker of May '68. 'It's above all one of the blackest dates in the history of the French left,' he explained in 1977. 'The moment when it opted for Marxism as never before.'[1] Thirty years later, when the eradication of May '68 became a campaign mainstay of candidate Nicolas Sarkozy, Lévy belatedly saw virtues in a historic moment which had marked both the 'final struggle with senile Moscow' and the 'break with all those old European Communist parties tossed into the dustbin of what we were starting to call red fascism.'[2] The exact opposite of what he said about it in his youth.

In reality, if Bernard-Henri Lévy was ever a 'leftist', it was in the formal area of intellectual comportment, involving a Manichaean division of ideas between principles considered morally right and those considered morally wrong, disqualification of the analytical approach, and excommunication of naysayers by undermining their credibility with theatrical and unfounded abuse ('fascists', 'barbarians' and so on). In 1989, Paul Thibaud, editor in chief of the centre-left journal *Esprit* (whose relations with Bernard-Henri Lévy have been execrable since at least 1981, when *L'Idéologie française* was published) complained: 'Moral demagogy (which our historians have inherited from the "New Philosophy") perpetuates the Maoist habit of separating "right ideas", seen as beyond criticism, from condemned ideas, from which there is nothing to learn and which are unworthy of all discussion.'[3]

With regard to the opposition between the struggle for democratic principles, or high-minded politics more generally, and the problem of inequality, Bernard-Henri Lévy took up this simplistic dichotomy inherited from leftism for his own purposes, inverting the leftist order of priorities. He has never been strong on 'social' issues: the economy, unemployment, schools, poverty, jobs, wages, the family, none of that interests him. When challenged on it, he replied:

> The difference between me and many others, if you will, is that I am honest with myself. An intellectual is always, almost by definition, 'somewhat deaf on the social question'. Nothing irritates me more than the position of someone like Bourdieu who, from the heights of his mandarin status, played the 'great oracle of the social movement' for the rest of us. But hey, I make an effort. I try to go beyond this positional deafness. I am a deaf person, I repeat, who makes an effort to hear. In *Pièces d'identité*, once again, there is a long text that I wrote on the occasion of the commemoration of the birth of the Red Cross, in which I try to reflect on the new forms of poverty, of insecurity, twenty years after Coluche …[4]

There are indeed some pages of reflection on humanitarianism and charity, completely out of touch and displaying total ignorance of current thinking on social questions: the poor are boiled down to the image of a tramp glimpsed in passing on the boulevard Saint-Germain.

He hardly mentions social issues, either in his books, his interviews or his 'bloc-notes' in *Le Point*, ostensibly devoted to the issues of the day. He displays an equally lordly ignorance of matters requiring a modicum of technical knowledge: new technologies, ecology, intellectual property rights, international trade … all areas with one big drawback, namely that they resist his standard mode of analysis in terms of catch-all ethical principles.

In France and the rest of Europe, as the revolutionary optimism of '68 faded away in the late 1970s and 1980s, social movements gradually identified terrains of struggle that were more modest in terms of expectation – people no longer believed in a revolutionary break leading to a new society – and more concrete: ecology, alternative education, gay and feminist demands. During the 1990s the political landscape changed, with new activists appearing to press new causes such as rejection of job insecurity, access to healthcare, social protection, jobs and housing in a general return to the 'social question'. In France, the demonstrations and long railway workers' strike against the Juppé Social Security reform plan in 1995 opened a cycle of contestation that, through a sort of demand dynamic, continued until late 2010 and the campaign against the raising of the retirement age.[5]

Bernard-Henri Lévy completely misses this major political sea change. He approaches the twenty-first century with the mentality he had in 1977: braced against a revolutionary project that no longer exists. The resulting empty anti-messianism would have to find causes outside France to supply his vindictive factory with raw material. The ones he found included Bosnia in 1992, Pakistan in 2002, Darfur in 2006 and Libya in 2011 (see above, chapters 5, 6 and 7).

Anti-racist and anti-authoritarian – neither in itself necessarily associated with the political left – Bernard-Henri Lévy occupies a very particular place in the French political landscape. Despite a limited taste for sport, he embodies a character well known on the football field: the player who scores own goals. For it cannot be denied that the ex-New Philosopher never gets bigger audiences than when he lays into the ideological side he claims for his own, the left. To put it another way, since 2007 he has taken against the head of state's comments on the failure of Africans to make an entry to history, his discourse on national identity and his anti-Roma policy – each time to a lukewarm public response.

On the other hand, his criticisms of the Socialist Party (PS) as a 'great recumbent corpse', his attacks on Jean-Luc Mélenchon, leader of the Front de Gauche (a coalition of parties to the left of the PS), accused of 'taking people for morons' and propounding a 'socialism for ignoramuses',[6] and most of all his defences of Nicolas Sarkozy (see above, chapter 2) guaranteed media attention and lodged in people's minds. And basically, that is a constant of his thirty-five years of public life, since the New Philosophers whose most celebrated representative he was in the late 1970s came to public notice for their critique of the Marxist left (see above, chapter 4). So, what personal strategic record does he think that leaves him with, after all these years? That is one of the questions we would have liked to ask him, had he been willing to answer.

THE WORLD AS ONE GIANT BORDELLO

BHL TO THE RESCUE OF DSK: 'A NATIONAL DISGRACE'?

One is not always the best person to defend one's friends, as Bernard-Henri Lévy has now discovered to his cost. Rushing to the rescue of Dominique Strauss-Kahn, his 'friend for twenty-five years',[7] after his arrest on 14 May 2011 for alleged sexual offences against a New York hotel chambermaid, led him to score one of his finest own goals. Hardly had his text appeared on the *Daily Beast* website[8] when howls of protest rose from US journals and blogs, ranging in tone from the ironic to the openly indignant. His defence of the IMF director general must count among the least effective defence pleas in recent media history. Whatever really happened in the French politician's suite in the Sofitel and whatever his political fate following his return to Paris in early September 2011, the Strauss-Kahn affair generated mountains of chatter. The public comments by various parties, and in particular by Bernard-Henri Lévy himself, project meanings which deserve to be analysed in themselves, independently of the outcome of proceedings in the Manhattan criminal court.

'Another reminder that BHL is ten times the national embarrassment to France that Jerry Lewis or even Johnny Halliday ever was,' crowed Matt Welch, editor of *Reason* magazine.[9] In the opinion of *New Yorker* journalist Amy Davidson, the piece was 'so gnawing in its irrationality that I may have to spend some hard time leafing through French fashion magazines for a dose of relative sanity.'[10] Blogger Tom Scocca wrote waspishly on the *Slate* site: 'If your goal is to push back against the tide of public opinion condemning your friend as an arrogant, hopelessly entitled sexual predator, it's maybe not wise to write your defense from the point of view of an arrogant, hopelessly entitled sexist.'[11] Even the very conservative *National Review* expressed sharp disapproval, through the pen of Jonah Goldberg: 'Read this so you can understand that no one can take Bernard-Henri Lévy as seriously as he takes himself.'[12] And Scocca banged the spike home by remarking that 'if Lévy had made the case against Qaddafi in the way he makes the case for Strauss-Kahn, the Marines would be defending Tripoli.'[13]

The French writer had taken a severe kicking. But what was it about his article that had aroused such ire among American commentators? Two ideas, essentially. One, that his friend Strauss-Kahn is 'a seducer, for sure; a charmer, fond of women', but never the man we read of as 'this brutal and violent character, this wild animal, this ape'.[14] As if Bernard-Henri Lévy's friendship constituted a proof of moral probity, and as if charm and seductiveness could not coexist with a capacity for violent acts. Two, that the IMF boss had some sort of right to special treatment from the courts: 'I am furious, this morning, with the American judge who … seemed to think he was a subject of justice like any other.' As the author of a book on America, supposedly 'in the footsteps' of Alexis de Tocqueville (see chapter 10), he really ought to known about the US passion for equality …

Less serious, but just as damning, were the factual errors in his article. The claim, for example, that the accused Strauss-Kahn would have to prove his innocence, when the opposite is true: the prosecution had to prove him guilty, something that led to the collapse of the case against him on 1 July 2011. Another claim was that in big hotels the chambermaids work in 'housekeeping brigades' comprising two individuals and not alone, as Nafissatou Diallo was on 14 May in suite 2806 of the Sofitel in Times Square where Dominique Strauss-Kahn was staying. This assertion puzzled many commentators, among them Jon Stewart, presenter of 'The Daily Show': 'Only the French would call two chambermaids a "brigade" … A little-known historical fact: during the Second World War the German army that marched into Paris was really just a cleaning crew! They crossed the Rhine and went into Paris just to sweep up!'[15] Guaranteed to have the audience rolling in the aisles.

The US public has been spared the extension of this defence in the French media, where the same arguments were deployed in even more forthright terms. 'Do you believe … that I would have been his friend if I thought for one second that Strauss-Kahn was a compulsive rapist, a Neanderthal, a guy who behaves like a sexual predator with any woman he meets?' he demanded on France Inter.[16] As for equality before the law, the writer – still on live public radio – seemed to dismiss it as a pretence for the plebs. 'Of course, democracy says that everyone ought to be treated in the same way, but not everyone is "everyone". The president of the IMF, a man who was on the brink of becoming a candidate for the presidency of the French Republic, in handcuffs … it's obvious that he isn't just anyone.' And again: 'People know perfectly well that not everyone is the same.' This reasoning is pushed further still in another editorial. Not only is DSK not 'everyone', but to pretend to treat him in the same way as others creates an 'illusion of equality, which masks an injustice'.[17] How so? Because of the 'court of public opinion' which is 'reinventing class justice in reverse' by thinking: 'Rich bastards, it's the word of the poor that's sacred' … a 'prejudice' that he finds 'revolting'. In short, the victim of the affair, he explained a week after the arrest, and well before the prosecution collapsed on 1 July, is 'Strauss-Kahn, as from now. He is henceforth the victim of this sort of infernal circus.'[18]

Uttered by someone else – the president of the employers' federation for example, or an IMF spokesman – these remarks would hardly be noticed; they would fall into the natural order of things. But trumpeted by Bernard-Henri Lévy, defender of boat people and advocate of human rights, they catch the ear. So is it as his personal friend that DSK could not be guilty of the charges brought by the New York prosecutor? Is it because he is a big international political boss that he ought to be presumed more innocent than others? And is it because he wields great power that he ought not to be treated as a common nobody by the legal system? In half a dozen sentences and phrases, the justification of class privilege is laid bare. The spokesman of the oppressed suddenly pipes up as a member of the exclusive club of rich powerful white males over sixty. One might have been listening to the dissection of an exemplary case in a queer studies seminar, scripted by Judith Butler.

But readers of the first two chapters of this book will not be surprised. It is the oligarchy that speaks through the caricature of himself that BHL offers here, doing battle for the honour of one of his peers. Moreover, in an unconscious self-exposure, he resorts to a counter-revolutionary parallel straight from 1789 when he compares Dominique Strauss-Kahn's accusers to '*tricoteuses* [knitting away] at the foot of the media scaffold, there to applaud the media guillotine'.[19]

VIRILITY AS A WAY OF RELATING TO THE WORLD

These attitudes express more than a class discourse on Bernard-Henry Lévy's part. They also display the vision of a sexual order in which not only is the alleged female victim deemed not to exist, but in which, in a more general sense, virility constitutes the model relation to the world.

This is not all that surprising, for sexual metaphors have been surfacing in Lévy's discourse for a while. In March 2011, interviewed by Al-Jazeera on the consequences of the revolutionary 'Arab spring', he explained that henceforth 'it will be difficult to get a blowjob from Arab dictators when you're a European government'.[20] In 2006, he opened the account of a promotional tour of the US published in *Le Monde*'s magazine with the words: 'America was already a very old mistress. I wanted to know whether she could become a wife.'[21] A more forthright version had been circulating earlier, spread by a journalist on *New York Magazine* who claimed to have heard him say: 'I had a great fuck with America' – but BHL denied it.[22] In 2004, when the first version of this book appeared, he referred to us in conversation with a journalist from *Libération* as 'puceaux' (a scornful and vulgar slang term for male virgins).

A retrospective trawl through Bernard-Henri Lévy's innumerable interviews over several decades is quite instructive on his view of women. In 1977, asked by *Nice-Matin* why there seem to be 'so few woman philosophers', he answered: 'I think women have a more immediate sense of delight [*jouissance*], taking the word in its general sense ... It seems to me, in consequence, that the awful mediation of philosophical discourse is foreign to them.'[23] Since that is an old quote, we should accept that he could have evolved and might today, thirty-five years later, believe women capable of philosophizing after all. In 1984 he explained to the women's magazine *Elle*:

> To claim that women are sexually liberated [is] a gross illusion, [because] they aren't, [and you could even say] they never will be. ... Contrary to what they imagine, nothing has changed for them. On that level, even if they think they are functioning in a totally new way, we've all seen those women who strive, quite pitifully by the way, to bend to the image, to standard patterns imposed by fashion, the various currents of society, and who don't manage to do it, since that image is absolutely unreal. Don't make me out to be saying women haven't evolved, that they haven't conquered freedoms held hitherto by men. But as for sexuality ...[24]

So as well as not really being equipped for philosophy, women remain in sexual subjection. But there remains a way to worm their way back into the writer's esteem: stay subordinate all over. For (as he confided to *L'Express* in 1993), 'I find powerful women somewhat less desirable than others. Men know about power, they've explored it all over. What's fascinating about a woman is her strangeness. If she's obsessed with power she becomes familiar, too alike. She no longer attracts.'[25] In the same year he told *Le Parisien* that he found woman executives 'not very sexy' and that 'women are bad at money'. When the journalist asked whether he would like to be a woman, he ended the interview with the words: 'I like being a man too much'.[26] As his wife Arielle Dombasle puts it: 'He is a wild animal, he's a big predator.'[27]

History does not relate whether he shared his thoughts on the low sex appeal of powerful women with Hillary Clinton, but he did have a theory on the reasons for her failure in the 2008 Democratic primary. For a start, she hadn't worn enough skirts: 'A style that's too stiff, almost masculine, in the image of those tailored slacks she has worn throughout the campaign.' Later, on a more serious note, he blamed feminists: 'American feminism, in its reactionary version, has chosen to punish Hillary and her criminal liberalism.' For the former First Lady had aroused 'the hatred of a whole swathe of female voters for this fellow-being, this sister in whom they have never been able to recognize themselves'.[28]

In short, women are sex objects lacking the capacity for abstract thought, who ought not to be burdened with too much money or too much power, and who are also extremely jealous. A miserable enough existence, but it is possible for them to sink even lower by failing the terrifying 'cheap tart test', described at length by the writer in an interview for *GQ* in 2009, published uncut on BHL's personal site. 'At one time, incidentally, I had a test that I called the "cheap tart test": if I was dining with a girl who dithered for hours before deciding what to eat, it was going pretty badly. And if I said "So have the cod with spinach" and she then sank into an even more sidereal contemplation of the menu while muttering "Where's 'at then, can't see it", it became frankly out of the question.'[29]

A HIGHLY SELECTIVE FEMINISM

Scraps of everyday, macho, bloke-in-the-pub discourse, really. A scattering of thin, fanciful references that in aggregate outline a highly stereotyped discourse on women behind a mask of gallantry and cultivated eroticism. Deciphering the internal jigsaw would hardly be worth the trouble if BHL's sexual worldview ended there. But the picture has hidden depths. After his first media-borne flowering in the late 1970s, the ex-New Philosopher has occupied the stage as a tanned playboy in shades, the famous white shirt nearly always unbuttoned ('the finest cleavage in Paris' is one BHL nickname). In public utterances he regularly stands up for hedonism, pleasure and playful badinage, and disparages puritanism, primness, 'political correctness'. In his fashion, he is a critic of the moral order. Except that this liberal display from the moral point of view accompanies, not to say underscores, a discourse protective of the existing social order and gender hierarchy by means of a feminism that is highly selective in its causes and heroines.

It would be wrong to claim that Bernard-Henri Lévy never takes up the cause of women. He was one of the first supporters of Taslima Nasreen, the Bangladeshi writer threatened with death by Islamist organizations for her critical declarations on Islam. He also bestirred himself to draw public attention to the fate of Ayaan Hirsi Ali, a former Dutch parliamentarian of Somali origin, when she was condemned to death by extremist Muslim groups in Amsterdam for involvement in a film by Theo Van Gogh (who had already been murdered). And of course he was among the first Europeans to join the campaign to save the Iranian housewife and mother Sakineh Mohammadi-Ashtiani from being stoned to death (see above, chapter 7). The fact that all three were being persecuted in the name of Islam escaped no one. Their cause contributed to the emergence of new political alliances in France between certain feminists and the advocates of secularism, who came together for example in defending the publication of caricatures of the Prophet first printed by the Danish newspaper *Jyllands-Posten* in 2005.

Bernard-Henri Lévy participated in that movement, as always in the name of freedom of expression and the defence of individual liberty. He supported the 2010 law forbidding the wearing of the niqab (a veil that hides the entire face) in public, the latest avatar of a French legislative offensive aimed at unveiling Muslim women launched more than twenty years ago. But he was not the first intellectual to do so, nor the most extreme ideologue of the movement in which he is a follower rather than a leader (the journalist Caroline Fourest and the former director of *Charlie Hebdo*, Philippe Val, are both much more committed zealots).

The problem with this militancy is that it is filled with enormous, silent gaps. Bernard-Henri Lévy has nothing to say about the prevalence of domestic violence and incest, the withdrawal of funding from family planning and abortion clinics, gender discrimination, wage imbalances, sexual harassment or the low proportion of women on parliamentary benches and in company boardrooms. Nothing either, or very little, on the structural difficulties experienced by Western women in the social field. And nothing on Muslim feminism, a religious and political movement that tries to reconcile religion with the desire for emancipation.

DEFENCE OF THE ELITE OF NOT-QUITE-DEAD-WHITE-MALES

When a major international scandal erupted over a proven sex offence – the one committed thirty-five years earlier by Roman Polanski against a thirteen-year-old girl, Samantha Gailey, not the one alleged against Dominique Strauss-Kahn – BHL chose to defend the offender. And without noticeable restraint. In his view the Polish film director was being 'hunted down like a terrorist', threatened with extradition 'like a former Nazi',[30] pursued 'by hatred', 'as in the dark days of McCarthyism at its fiercest'.[31] Interviewed by *Haaretz* in May 2010, the French writer compared the Polanski affair to the Dreyfus affair and the treatment of Soviet dissidents, 'those moments when everything focuses on a single face'.[32] The vindictiveness against him, 'that wish to see the artist's head aloft on a pike' – note the recurrence of counter-revolutionary imagery – is 'immorality itself'.[33]

The website of *La Règle du jeu* published a petition of support for the film-maker and presented him as the victim of 'infamy'. Bernard-Henri Lévy started an intense international campaign on both sides of the Atlantic, with frequent editorials and interviews, a world scoop with the first interview with the Polish cineast under house arrest in his Swiss chalet, and a petition signed by celeb artists (Jean-Luc Godard, Paul Auster, Milan Kundera, Isabelle Huppert[34]). He euphemized the statutory rape of Samantha Gailey, usually referring to it as the 'abduction of a minor'.[35] He insisted that Roman Polanski was the victim of his own notoriety, which was the sole reason for the ferocity 'of this prosecutor, greedy for recognition and glory, who wakes up one fine morning to deliver him, like a trophy, to the vengeance of enraged electors'.[36]

There may be some truth in this. Had he been less famous, the director might not have had to suffer the thunderbolts of US justice more than thirty years after the event. But, of course, it was also because he was a renowned artist that Samantha Gailey joined him in 1977 for a photo session in a Californian villa. The sexual offence committed was thus sanctioned from the start by his status as a star of the cinema. So there is a certain poetic justice in that same renown being the cause of his legal torments. It may not be so absurd to take such a view. 'Does the brotherhood of fame endow you with a lifetime exemption from accountability?' wondered Eve Ensler, the author of *The Vagina Monologues*. 'Being an artist does not make any of us exempt from the laws of humanity – in fact, it actually makes us more responsible to them.'[37]

What is most striking in this sequence of adopted causes is their contradictory nature. Why fight for Taslima Nasreen, Ayaan Hirsi Ali and

Sakineh Mohammadi-Ashtiani, and not for today's Samantha Gaileys? It's true that Polanski's victim stated clearly that she had no wish to see the director prosecuted thirty years later. But the refusal to prosecute does not nullify the offence. Surely that, too, deserves to be considered? For in what way is a proven sexual crime, even an old one, less serious than a death threat to a well-known writer or to a former parliamentarian employed by a powerful conservative US think tank? It is a question of scale of values. BHL's misadventures in the land of the sexual question illustrate it wonderfully: people create the objects of scandal that suit them. Obsessed with 'fascislamism', one of the concepts he boasts of having invented, the erstwhile New Philosopher outlines an arbitrary geography of indignation, one that is socially and racially marked, in the symbolic sense. According to this hierarchy of values, the threats Muslims pose to women are manifestly far more serious than those posed by powerful old white guys. That is how the moral libertarianism paraded by Bernard-Henri Lévy serves a conservative social discourse, for it boils down to defending the interests of the dominant elite: white, male and over sixty. Instead of using his gift of the gab and networking skills to gain recognition for the political and social rights of minorities, he sets them against one another.

Once again the writer poses a problem more interesting than he is himself: that of the fissures and archaism of the *soixante-huitard* European left. Unable to adapt to the new, shifting axes of dominance, it remains stuck in a political emancipation agenda forty years out of date.

A FRIEND TO ISRAEL

FULL SUPPORT, TO THE POINT OF EMBARRASSMENT

On 5 June 2011, nearly three months into the war against the Gaddafi regime, the Libyan rebel forces issued a corrective communiqué referring to Bernard-Henri Lévy. It said that the National Transitional Council (NTC), the political body representing the insurgents fighting the Tripoli regime, 'vehemently rejects what has been reported in some media as Mr Bernard Lévy's comments on the future relationship between Libya and the Israelis'. The communiqué continued: 'The NTC is surprised by Mr Lévy's comments', and – intriguing detail – 'Mr Lévy was received as a special envoy from the president of France, and relations with Israel were never discussed.'[38]

What was going on? The event had passed unnoticed at first, but three days earlier Agence France Presse (AFP) had come up with a considerable scoop – if it turned out to be authentic. A real breakthrough in the history of relations between Israel and the Arab countries: the NTC was apparently prepared to recognize the State of Israel and maintain 'normal relations' with it. That was the 'verbal message' that Bernard-Henri Lévy had come to deliver to the Israeli prime minister, Benjamin Netanyahu, on behalf of the Libyan Council. The future regime 'will be a moderate and anti-terrorist regime, concerned with both justice for the Palestinians and security for Israel'. At least, that is what the French writer told the press agency. The Israeli head of government's services limited themselves to confirming the meeting, without saying anything on its content.

But the diplomatic thunderclap fell flat. In reality it had been an enormous faux-pas by the French writer. The NTC did not beat about the bush. 'Libya is a member of the Arab League and the Organization of the Islamic Conference,' the communiqué continued. 'These two organizations have a very solid and clear position on the Palestinian question. With this in mind, Libya firmly commits to the already firm position taken by the Arab world on the Palestinian question, and will support the aspirations of the Palestinian people to achieve their inalienable rights and their desire to establish an independent state with Jerusalem as its capital.' Radically opposed to Muammar Gaddafi the insurgents might be, but they were not ready to mark their differences with him by entering into official relations with Tel Aviv.

'As I'm Jewish, and a friend of Israel ...' Even on Al-Jazeera, where he introduced himself with those words in March 2011,[39] Bernard-Henri Lévy has never hidden his support for the Israeli state. It is a constant in his public utterances, whether made in France, the US or Israel. 'He's one of the great defenders of Israel, and he does it in fine, resonant language and with great physical courage, and I believe that that is how he is perceived here,' we were told from Jerusalem by Claude Sitbon, a sociologist and historian who knows the Israeli francophone community well. The writer often goes there to give talks. He has an honorary doctorate from Tel Aviv University and another from the Hebrew University of Jerusalem, in addition to the Scopus Prize awarded by the French community of the latter establishment.

In 2000, with Alain Finkielkraut and Benny Lévy (former leader of a late-1960s Maoist group, Gauche Prolétarienne, and former secretary to Jean-Paul Sartre), Bernard-Henri Lévy founded the Institut d'études lévinassiennes in Jerusalem. It is a study and conference centre with no particular academic authority, and occupies a marginal place in local intellectual life. Having become a scholar devoted to the study of the Scriptures, Benny Lévy (who died in 2003) was 'a sort of guru for those returning to their Judaism or those lacking the courage to plunge straight into an understanding of Judaism,' in the opinion of Esther Benbassa, a historian of modern Judaism and study director at the École pratique des hautes études. 'He was a choice contact for French Jewish former leftists, because he was a man of their generation who had come back to the Torah, and by the same token represented a sort of unattainable ideal who offered a French reading of Judaism. I don't think Benny Lévy was known in Israel as an authority on Judaism. He wrote in French and gave in his lectures a vision of the Torah accessible to French-speakers. He was the symbol of a certain Jewish accomplishment for a group in quest of its own Judaism. So Benny Lévy became a tutelary figure for some people.'[40]

Although he still gives lectures there, it is not through the Institut d'études lévinassiennes that BHL has become known in Israel, but thanks to the reprinting of some of his opinion pieces by the centre-left daily *Haaretz* in recent years, making him a household name for many English-speaking readers. He is sufficiently well-known to be received in the highest Israeli government circles, from the Likud to the Labour left, since he is also close to the former prime minister Shimon Peres.

A ZEALOUS SPOKESMAN FOR THE ISRAELI DEFENSE FORCES

That rare social dexterity – unique for a French intellectual – gave him access to the top ranks of the Israeli Defense Forces (IDF, also known by the Hebrew acronym, Tzahal), which found in Bernard-Henri Lévy one of their most zealous spokesmen. Indeed it is not unreasonable to suggest that over the years a close collaboration has been established between the writer and the IDF staff. In January 2009, aiming to report on the Tzahal offensive in the Gaza Strip, he travelled 'embedded … with an elite unit', as he put it in an article published on three continents.[41] So he describes entering after dark, accompanied by a major and four reservists, the Abasan al-Jadida district 'in the suburbs of Gaza City', and rejoicing not to find the sort of wholesale destruction visited on the city of Grozny, in Chechnya, or some parts of Sarajevo. The implicit message was that Israeli shelling had not been as destructive as claimed.

In fact, however – according to *Le Monde*'s Israel correspondent Benjamin Barthe[42] – he was not in the outskirts of the Gaza capital at all, but in 'a big village, more than twenty kilometres south of Gaza'. Contrary to what BHL seems to believe, Abasan al-Jadida is not a suburb of Gaza

City. At that juncture in the poetically-named 'Operation Cast Lead' military operation – 13 January, four days before the ceasefire – foreign journalists were having great difficulty in reaching the operations zone or entering the Strip at all. Most of them would have to wait for hostilities to end before setting foot in Gaza. BHL did not only have the privilege of going there accompanied by an armed convoy. He also had ready access to the highest dignitaries of the Israeli army and the state: Prime Minister Ehud Olmert, Defence Minister Ehud Barak, and Youval Diskin (erroneously named 'Yovan Diskin' in the article and again in its reprinted version in the anthology *Pièces d'identité*), boss of Shin Bet, the Israeli internal security service. All three were extensively quoted by the French writer who, by contrast, did not quote a single Gaza inhabitant. Two Palestinian militants, Mustapha Barghouti and Mamdouh Aker, were briskly quoted and dispatched in a few lines. On the other hand, the author had time to wax lyrical about the two pianos in Ehud Barak's 'long' drawing room and on the 'pianist minister' playing his instruments 'like a virtuoso', contributing to the mythical image of an army filled with artistic generals and commanders inhabited by a 'deep distaste for war'.

Even before the appearance of a news feature so favourable to the Israeli Staff, the provisional casualty figures from this lightning campaign (just over three weeks in all) were surely dismaying: at least 1,000 Palestinians killed and nearly 5,000 wounded, according to the chief of Gaza's emergency services, Mouawiya Hassanein, quoted by AFP. In mid-January the UN agency responsible for Palestinian refugees, UNRWA, denounced the shelling of a school where families had taken shelter. The Israeli offensive in Gaza caused 1,450 deaths on the Palestinian side, the majority civilian, according to local medical sources, and thirteen on the Israeli side. There was no shortage of awkward questions to put to those music-loving Tzahal officers, but none are raised in the article.

BHL did not seem entirely at ease with his position as an embedded reporter. 'I know, having avoided it all my life, that the "embedded" viewpoint is never the best one,' he wrote, as if it was an exceptional practice for him, tried for the first time. In reality it was nothing of the sort. BHL is an old travelling companion of Tzahal. When the Israeli army attacked Lebanon in 2006 after the capture of two of its soldiers by Shia militiamen from Lebanese Hezbollah, Bernard-Henri Lévy turned up for another of his 'war reportages', published all over Europe.[43] He did not set foot inside Lebanon but visited Sderot, Haifa and Acre, towns in

Israel that had taken Hezbollah or Gazan rocket fire. He passed through the Labour Party's headquarters where he met the defence minister, Amir Peretz, and spoke to foreign minister Tzipi Livni; he visited the parents of Gilad Shalit, the soldier kidnapped by Hamas (who reminded him of the parents of Daniel Pearl, the US journalist murdered by Al Qaeda). He also met the former prime minister, Shimon Peres; but he did not talk to a single Israeli opponent of the war, not one Palestinian refugee and no one from Lebanon.

During the well-orchestrated tour, he came across a group of Israeli artillerymen. With their 'extreme youth', their 'stunned look at each discharge', their 'childlike teasing', their 'relaxed, unrestrained and even carefree' demeanour, they seem 'the exact opposite of those battalions of brutes or unprincipled pitiless terminators that are so often described in the European media'. But the most extraordinary occurrence, still according to the article, was a transcendental and historical one: the sudden disappearance from before his unbelieving eyes of those frolicksome IDF soldiers and their replacement by reincarnations of the International Brigades, the battalions of volunteers who had joined the Spanish Republicans in 1936 to fight General Franco's troops. They were no longer soldiers who had just shelled and wrecked part of neighbouring Lebanon at the cost of several hundred civilian lives; no, they were 'that joyous scramble of battalions of young republicans' described by Malraux; 'an army that is more friendly than it is martial, more democratic than self-assured and dominating'.

Anniversary magic: it was on 17 July, the 'anniversary of the day the Spanish Civil War began', that Bernard-Henri Lévy landed at Tel Aviv. And the significant connection is fascism, 'this fascism with an Islamist face, this third fascism, which is to our generation what the other fascism ... [was] to our elders'. To put it plainly, today's extremist Islamist militias and the states supporting them, Iran and Syria, play a role equivalent to that of the Axis powers led by Hitler's Germany in the 1930s. So today's Israeli military are not just artists who make war reluctantly: they have taken up the torch of the founding epic of European civil disobedience. This is more than scoop journalism. It is prophecy.

It should be noted that in 2006, Bernard-Henri Lévy managed to find an excellent guide for a quick sortie to the Lebanese front, in the person of Lt-Col. Olivier Rafovitch (as he spelt his surname), with whom he passed 'like a whirlwind through a deserted Druze village'. Olivier Rafowicz also happens to be an Israeli army spokesman to the foreign media; French-born and a perfect French speaker, he is more specifically in charge of French journalists. But Bernard-Henri Lévy makes no mention of his PR duties, as if he were with an ordinary soldier. But BHL is not an ordinary reporter. A French journalist familiar with Israel and the Palestinian territories remembered seeing him, at the end of that expedition, 'arrive at Tel Aviv airport accompanied by Olivier Rafowicz, the Israeli army's French press officer, in uniform. BHL hoped Rafowicz's uniform would get him into the VIP lounge, but it didn't work. Then he got on the plane and the soldier left.' He added: 'I've been going to Israel for thirty-five years, and no army officer has ever seen me off.'[44]

Olivier Rafowicz remembers those few hours spent with the French writer in 2006 very well.[45] In a message posted on the writer's promotional website, bernard-henri-levy.com, he writes: 'It seems to me that a man like him, who enjoys international renown for his lectures, books and radio and TV appearances, can play an extremely important role in support of States [...] And, therefore, I think this is very important for Israel and for Tzahal.' Not a bad bit of puffery, for a press relations professional. And a recipe that works, tested over time; indeed, he adds that 'for more than ten years now, in practically every crisis of international scope between Israel and its neighbours, Bernard-Henri Lévy has joined me and been present on the ground'.

This camaraderie began in 2002, during the second Intifada. 'The Israeli authorities had given him permission to join us in the field. He was with us in the operations room,' recalled the soldier, who at that time was already acting as a minder for journalists. It was still going strong in 2009, during Operation Cast Lead in the Gaza Strip. 'By the Israeli government's decision, for security reasons, the press was not permitted to enter the Gaza strip to cover the conflict from inside,' Rafowicz recalled. 'It was then that Bernard-Henri Lévy made contact with the highest Israeli authorities, and once again requested to see what was happening from inside.' Nor did the soldier doubt the success of this new PR stunt: 'After a few intense hours spent with soldiers and officers on the ground, BHL returned satisfied to have fulfilled his mission.'

PRAISE FOR TZAHAL'S 'PURITY OF ARMS'

All the attention lavished on the French writer by the Israeli military authorities was not wasted. Bernard-Henri Lévy no longer misses an opportunity to praise the IDF. When he received his honorary doctorate from the Hebrew University of Jerusalem in June 2008, he rejoiced in being the repository of the value of 'Purity of Arms'. He had no need to explain what it meant, for all Israelis are familiar with this Tzahal doctrine, a principle written into its code of ethics: 'The IDF servicemen and women will use their weapons and force only for the purpose of their mission, only to the necessary extent and will maintain their humanity even during combat.' In his acceptance speech for the Scopus Prize, also awarded by the Hebrew University of Jerusalem, he said he believed that 'the Israeli miracle endures', thanks to the 'purity of arms' and the dream of remaining 'an exceptional country submitting to rules of conduct that are themselves exceptional'.

However, the doctrine of purity of arms has come under growing criticism in Israel, being judged increasingly theoretical, misleading and remote from the actual behaviour of the soldiers. The *Haaretz* journalist Gideon Levy makes fun of its 'archaism.'[46] And after the Jewish State's army had fired on demonstrators marching on the Israel–Syria frontier, even the former Mossad chief Zvi Zamir declared in June 2011 that 'by firing on unarmed people, Tzahal is eroding its purity of arms.'[47] But BHL still wants to believe in it.

In May 2010 he opened a very classy forum organized by the French embassy's cultural service, on 'Democracy and Its Challenges', by declaring: 'I have been in other countries, other wars. But never have I seen, as here in Israel, a democratic army that asks itself as many moral questions as the army of Israel does.'[48] He cites no source, but the remark echoes the words of the former prime minister (and fierce opponent of the Palestinians) Ariel Sharon, interviewed in 2004: 'Tzahal is the most moral army in the world.'[49] Ehud Barak had used the quote himself in 2009, to refute alleged exactions by his troops during the Gaza military campaign.

In any case it is an extravagant judgement, both for its vagueness and its implicit claim to discern in Tzahal some generic principle of moral behaviour. By an unfortunate coincidence, the day after that sentence was uttered the Israeli armed forces attacked on the high seas a humanitarian flotilla chartered by the pro-Palestinian association Free Gaza, in an attempt to break the blockade of the Palestinian territory. Nine militants died in the attack. The episode aroused a chorus of international protests, led by the UN Secretary General Ban Ki Moon. An emergency meeting of the UN Security Council was called. Washington demanded explanations. Demonstrations took place all over the world. Politically the operation was a fiasco for Israel, whose image was lastingly tarnished by it.

In France, a voice rose to denounce the 'mechanism of demonization' brought to bear on the Jewish state. On 7 June, Bernard-Henri Lévy published in *Libération* – a paper of which he is a shareholder – an opinion piece in which he rails against 'the confusion of an era in which people fight democracies as if they were dictatorships or fascist states'.[50] Entitled 'Why I defend Israel', this text is not specifically a defence of Tzahal. But, published in the post-Gaza flotilla context, that is certainly the meaning it acquires. The author uses it to roll out one of his favourite arguments: since Israel is a democracy, the only one in the region, it can only behave democratically, with no major contradiction between its respect for human rights and the freedom of its citizens. It is a purely theoretical defence, of principle alone, and underlies a sort of spiral argument tirelessly pumped out by the writer: Israel should be defended because it is a democracy, it can't be criticized because that would be playing the game of the dictatorships surrounding it, and because Israel's struggle with Hezbollah and Hamas is legitimate, then practically any means of waging it is acceptable.

This viewpoint, disconnected from the realities on the ground, enables him to repeat some untruths about the Gaza blockade. That, for example, it 'is only concerned with weapons and the materials for making them'. This is a way of delegitimizing the Gaza flotilla and is, besides, false, as the *Libération* journalist Christophe Ayad noted in his reply: 'For three years, the ban has covered preserves and pasta (no doubt used in the composition of weapons of mass destruction), school exercise books and ballpoint pens (well known to be convertible into rockets).'[51] In *Haaretz*, which translated and published BHL's editorial, the journalist Gideon Levy was even more severe: 'Shouldn't a great intellectual like you, of all people, be expected to know that people, including Gazans, need more than bread and water? … How can you ignore the context? There have been forty-three years of occupation and despair for millions of people, some of whom may wish to become Bernard-Henri Lévy, and not just pass their lives in a battle for survival.'[52]

Gideon Levy has got it right. Conspicuously absent from BHL's discourse on Israel are the Palestinian people. He hardly ever mentions them. Thirty years of going on about the Jewish state, Judaism, the diaspora, Jewish identities, not to mention the permanent state of war of Israeli society, its fears, terrorism, rocket fire and so on, all as if the Occupied Territories did not exist. You talk 'as though you were the IDF spokesman,' Gideon Levy observed in his reply to BHL. Perhaps he did not know how right he was.

A POSTMODERN AGITPROP ACE

Much of the above will surprise people who are not really familiar with Bernard-Henri Lévy's writings, as it reveals a militaristic point of view far removed from his image as a partisan of peace in the Middle East. The fact is that the French writer is by no means a hawk, of the kind who, like Ariel Sharon, lobby incessantly for more settlements on the West Bank of the Jordan. In 2003 he was personally involved in the Geneva Accord process, an unofficial peace plan launched on the initiative of a former Israeli justice minister, Yossi Beilin, and a former Palestinian information minister, Yasser Abed Rabbo. He took part in a support meeting in Paris organized by a group close to the Israeli Labour Party, Les Amis de 'La Paix Maintenant' (Friends of 'Peace Now'), and the weekly *Marianne*. He marched onto the stage at the Mutualité (the historic setting for meetings of the French left) between Beilin and Rabbo and, arms raised, received the plaudits of the audience before delivering a long speech which nearly caused a diplomatic glitch.

'Bernard-Henri Lévy tried everything to get himself mentioned in Beilin's speech on 1 December in Geneva,' a negotiator told us. 'I got a phone call from Yossi Beilin who said: "A gentleman who introduces himself as the greatest French philosopher telephoned me, he is of the Jewish faith, do you know him? Who is this man?" Bernard-Henri Lévy wanted to be publicly enthroned as the ambassador for the Geneva accord, but, to avoid upsetting anyone, there was an absolute veto on that.'[53] Others defended him, however, and insisted that he played a significant role in promoting the peace plan, especially in the US where he had just finished a tour to promote one of his books.

Once associated with the Geneva Accord, Bernard-Henri Lévy went on to give it a particular slant, in disagreement with some of the negotiators. Speaking from the platform at the Mutualité, he said: 'I think that for Israel it's a good plan, because for the first time Palestinian leaders, eminent personalities like Mr Rabbo who was a minister, and Yasser Arafat, are making this considerable sacrifice, breaking the colossal taboo that locks the Palestinian consciousness which is the old question of the right of return. For the first time, in this plan, Palestinians are giving up that mirage they used to flash before their people, that mirage of the right of return.'

A peremptory assertion qualified by Ari Arnon, an Israeli negotiator of the Geneva Accord charged specifically with the Palestinian refugee question:

> I wouldn't say the Palestinians have abandoned the right of return. It's more complicated than that. There are eight pages on the issue in the Geneva Accord. The expression 'right of return', a very abstract concept, certainly doesn't appear in the agreement, but we do go into detail on how to resolve the refugee problem. It's very important to bear that in mind, when a lot of commentators are giving an erroneous interpretation of these – actually very precise – data, through ignorance or for political reasons. The Geneva Accord doesn't recognize the right of return as it has been understood in the past, meaning the right of Palestinians to return to their ancestral villages now inside Israel. In that sense Bernard-Henri Lévy is right. But what's written down is a lot more cautious, purposely so.[54]

A similar interpretation comes from Marc Lefèvre, of Les Amis de La Paix Maintenant and organizer of the French collective supporting the 'Two peoples, two states' appeal. 'You can't say that the Palestinians have renounced the right of return in clear and unambiguous language. What you can say is that they have made a significant advance in the direction of a de facto renunciation of that right through the practical modalities of return that they have accepted: a limited number of refugees permitted to return to Israel after acceptance by the state of Israel … It's what you could call a "constructive ambiguity".'[55]

So Bernard-Henri Lévy had permitted himself to expose, like a bull in a china shop, the fragile product of years of negotiation. Pascal Lederer, academic and organizer of Une autre voix juive (A different Jewish voice), who could not speak at the meeting because of the boycott of Les Amis de La Paix Maintenant, thinks that 'the meeting at the Mutualité was also a political operation attempting to drag Geneva as far to the right as possible. For some of the official supporters of the accord, it was a way of avoiding self-criticism, of making people forget how very seldom they had mentioned the Israeli army's crimes against Palestinians.'[56]

In 2010, Bernard-Henri Lévy backed another non-governmental initiative in favour of peace in the Middle East, J Call, 'the European Jewish Call for Reason', in the wake of the US movement J Street. The J Call signatories demand a viable, sovereign Palestinian state and an end to the occupation of Palestinian territories. As members of the Jewish diaspora, they want to influence Israeli policy towards a resumption of the stalled negotiations with the Palestinian Authority. They are also seeking to create a new political space distinct from the existing representative bodies of the European Jewish communities, which often fall into line with whatever Tel Aviv decides. In this sense, J Call is on the side of Palestinian rights. But only up to a point, and not without ambiguity. Their call for the creation of a sovereign Palestine is motivated primarily by the wish to guarantee Israel's future existence. The issue, they explain, is one of ensuring 'the survival and security of the state of Israel' by ending the 'unprecedented isolation of the government of Israel in the international arena' and thus halt 'the unacceptable delegitimization process that Israel currently faces abroad'.

These anxieties are perfectly legitimate and wholly logical on the part of notables in the European diaspora. But they carry political implications. If the first priority is to protect the interests of the state of Israel, rather than to act in accordance with international law or to ensure the Palestinian people's right to self-determination, then that will inflect the answers to the questions that have troubled and obstructed the peace process for several years. Where will the frontiers be? How will Jerusalem be shared? What happens to the wall? What right of return for the refugees? 'J Call was a way of channelling the grumbling in the community after the military offensive in Gaza,' is the retrospectively critical judgement of one of its French signatories.[57] The initiative thus highlights an element of back-pedalling by the Israeli left on its critique of colonization, even as these Europeans of the diaspora seek to dissociate themselves from Israeli political life. It is now easier to understand why Bernard-Henri Lévy is involved, albeit not as a leading spokesman.

At the same time that he was supporting J Call, he was much more in the public eye storming against the 'Boycott, Divestment, Sanctions' campaign launched by the Palestinian militant Omar Barghouti. It was 'disgraceful', BHL protested, an 'appalling' campaign, because 'you boycott totalitarian regimes, not democracies.'[58] That old chestnut again.

At the end of January 2011, the Parti des Indigènes de la République, which campaigns against racial inequality and pockets of neocolonialism in French political and media circles, staged a symbolic trial of BHL. The accused was sentenced to 'suffer the reading of his entire literary output, press articles included' as well as to participate in the demolition of the 'wall of shame' in Palestine and the refurbishment of the 'tunnels of hope' between Egypt and Gaza. The main indictment was 'Frenzied promotion of imperialism and Zionism'. But the terms of this indictment are off target.

For Bernard-Henri Lévy has invented a far more subtle register of discourse, one that delivers both propaganda and the antidote to that propaganda. Postmodern agitprop: speaking up for an army of occupation, Tzahal, but in the name of a fantasy of emancipation (international brigades, the right of self-determination) for its Palestinian adversaries. A spherical, perfect rhetoric that eludes critical grasp and prevents the speaker from being nailed down politically. Imperialist? No, anti-fascist. Zionist? No, in favour of creating a Palestinian state. Pro-Tzahal? Only because of its moral values. It becomes impossible to criticize him, because the judgement is always off to one side. The parry seems infallible.

Like a communist intellectual travelling in the USSR after the Bolshevik revolution, he sees only what he wants to see of Israel, almost always overlooking the suffering of the Palestinians. But unlike the organic philosophers of the French Communist Party, he is no Stalinist. On the contrary, he takes a very different line to a lot of Israel's defenders, always avoiding the starkly security-focused discourse of realpolitik, which argues for repression. No, it is in the name of human rights that he defends what are basically militaristic and colonialist positions; by means of a staggering inversion of meaning that leaves criticism speechless.

9 THE NIGHTMARE OF ENDLESS NEW BEGINNINGS

Could it all be over for BHL? Something of the sort seems to be indicated by the decline in his bookshop sales and the short lives of his books, and the resounding failure of Public Enemies, *his correspondence with the writer Michel Houellebecq, launched with much marketing and advertising fanfare in 2008. Add to this the regrettable 'Botul affair', which tarnished his big comeback as a philosopher in 2010, and the appearance of serious competitors on his own terrain as a media intellectual.*

THE DECLINE IN SALES

For thirty years, since *Barbarism with a Human Face*,[1] Bernard-Henri Lévy has produced repeated best-sellers in all genres: *Le Diable en tête*, his first novel, stayed in the best-seller list for twenty-one weeks,[2] his *Éloge des intellectuels* for eight weeks.[3] *Adventures on the Freedom Road* sold between 80,000 and 100,000 copies, *Les Hommes et les femmes* between 100,000 and 150,000, *Les Derniers jours de Charles Baudelaire* about 180,000;[4] *War, Evil and the End of History* sold nearly 100,000 copies,[5] *Who Killed Daniel Pearl*, 129,200.[6] *Sartre: The Philosopher of the 20th Century*, with 'only' 27,500 copies sold, is an exception.[7] Still, over that period Bernard-Henri Lévy sold more than a million books, an enormous number.

For some years now, however, his books have sold less well in France, and the decline has become steeper. *American Vertigo*, his book on the US, sold 90,400 copies, still a genuine best-seller by the standards of the French market. But a year later *Left in Dark Times*, meditations on the French left published after Ségolène Royal's defeat in the presidential election, ran out of steam after 29,500 copies. That would be an excellent commercial result for any other author of essays, but it is a mediocre one for him, barely a third of the sales of his previous book. 2008 was similarly slight, with *Public Enemies*, his correspondence with Michel Houellebecq, selling just over 39,000 copies despite its highly publicized launch campaign. But 2010 brought a collapse, with *Pièces d'identité*, a thick anthology of recent writings, finding only 2,600 buyers. That would be poor for any author; for the ex-New Philosopher it is catastrophic. In its defence, the collection is enormous (1,300 pages), and the series *Questions de principe*, of which the book is the eleventh volume, has never sold well. *De la guerre en philosophie* (the book involved in the Botul affair), which was published at the same time, sold a mere 4,200 copies.[8]

There are other indicators. 'These are short-lived books,' one bookseller explained. They sell very poorly from a few weeks after their publication, something confirmed by the weak sales of pocket editions. The same bookseller, who runs a large provincial outlet, noticed in June 2011 that since its publication in 2007 he had only sold eleven copies of the pocket edition of *American Vertigo*, and had none in stock. After checking, he found that there were only another eleven copies of that pocket edition in the 200 independent bookshops served by his network – remarkably few, he thought. Asked whether he had sold any copies of *De la guerre en philosophie*, he answered in the affirmative. But after consulting his computer, he said that of the twenty-five copies he had ordered, he had sold a grand total of two.

This decline could be attributed to a more general crisis in French book publishing. But that would not be strictly true. For others, writing in a similar register, have been highly successful in the shops (we will return to this later). Who buys Bernard-Henri Lévy's books? 'Magazine readers who don't read philosophy,' explained the manager of the non-fiction and philosophy department of a big bookshop. Is this readership losing interest in the essayist and his works? The rest of this chapter attempts to unravel this new BHLian mystery.

LITTLE-LOVED PUBLIC ENEMIES

The campaign was launched from *Le Journal du dimanche*. On 15 June 2008, a 'little bird' told the paper that Teresa Cremisi, the CEO of Flammarion, was to announce in two days' time, to an audience of booksellers, a book to be published that autumn with an advance print run of 100,000 to 150,000 copies – a staggering amount. It was a two-hander by authors as yet unnamed. If the news did not throw the country into turmoil, mild interest was certainly taken in literary Paris, which wondered who the hands might belong to. In early September, Michel Houellebecq let slip that he was to be one of the mystery book's authors. Everyone was agog to know who the other might be. Carla Bruni? Lionel Jospin? The fiendish Maurice G. Dantec? Well, no. Not until 21 September, a few days before the book appeared, did it emerge – again in *Le Journal du dimanche* – that the lucky partner was Bernard-Henri Lévy. The book would be co-published by Grasset which – like *Le Journal du dimanche* – is owned by the Lagardère group.

In fact, *Le Journal du dimanche* more or less turned itself into a publicity leaflet for the occasion. The 21 September article went on: 'We already have some information on what promises to be an event … Huge polemics on the horizon. Because these are not just two great authors and two big sellers, they are also both redoubtable brawlers, men who enjoy a punch-up. They make a lot of noise separately; one almost shudders to think what they could produce together. If the correspondence between the "media-savvy" philosopher and the "depressive" novelist manages to unite the enemies of both men, we can be sure the success will be immense.'[9] No further details were given, since no one had yet read the book. The publishers had made an exclusive deal with *Le Nouvel Observateur* to divulge some of the choicer passages in its 2 October issue. But *Libération* – remember that Bernard-Henri Lévy is a shareholder – obtained a copy and unveiled the content in its issue dated Wednesday 1 October. A publicity campaign had started that recalled the great days of *Le Jour et la Nuit* (see above, chapter 2).

The strategy reeked of pure publishing hype and no one was taken in, journalists least of all. But the articles that sprang up everywhere, purporting to expose the people behind the strategy, helped in effect to reinforce it. Others joined in happily, for example Jérôme Béglé in *Paris Match* (another Lagardère possession), who seemed to see himself as Bob Woodward: 'The secrecy had to be perfectly maintained. After informing me of the tenor of the secret book about which the most improbable theories were circulating, the Flammarion group's CEO Teresa Cremisi invited me to read it as discreetly as possible in her office. I spent the afternoons of last Thursday and Friday doing so. … Each evening, the precious document was replaced in a locked cupboard in the director's office. As emails, requests and sometimes threats rained down, the publisher begged me to maintain absolute secrecy on what I had read. All I could do was put a few notes into a diary …'[10]

The reviews were unanimously positive overall, give or take a few preliminary reservations. Jérôme Garcin in *Le Nouvel Observateur* recognized that 'the most exasperating aspect of this lament for two voices is the way two men who already enjoy fame and fortune enthrone themselves as "public enemies", pose as victims of a system they have both successfully abused and cannot refrain, like misunderstood geniuses, from sometimes piling paranoia on top of megalomania'. He notes nevertheless that the book 'contains letters that are forceful, radical, even moving'. 'But it is when they argue about literature that they give the true measure of their encounter. ... The complacent dialogue between the two so-called public enemies then becomes a fiery conversation between two incontestable book-lovers.'[11] In *Libération*, Claire Devarrieux too notes that 'this correspondence reveals a vanity one had not thought to be so entrenched. But 'the tandem works well', 'BHL's philosophy lesson is bracing', and in the end it is a 'thrilling book'.[12]

Le Journal du dimanche's very eulogistic review was called, in allusion to Balzac, 'Splendeurs et misères des écrivains',[13] a title that appeared two days later in *Les Inrockuptibles* which (for once) found the book 'moving': 'We are indebted to both for some beautiful and forceful pages'.[14] But Jacques-Pierre Amette in *Le Point*[15] (where Bernard-Henri Lévy has had a weekly diary for twenty years) took a fairly original line: for him the book provided an answer to Donald Morrison, who wondered in *Time* magazine 'what remains of French culture?'[16] This is what remains, suggests Amette; a storm of excitement over a conversation between two writers, a conversation reported on in Europe and even in America. Full circle, so to speak: the book interests journalists because it interests journalists.

It should be noted that all these reviews (and there were others) covered more or less the whole spectrum of the French print media, and were published in the space of a few days. No one remotely interested in current events could have missed the plaudits. Nor was the campaign limited to the written press; during that week radio and TV joined the party, with slots on the eight o'clock news on France 2 on 5 October, the 'Grand journal' of Canal Plus on 6 October, etc. And yet, despite everything, the public was less than enthusiastic. In December, after two months in the bookshops, sales were hardly over 30,000 (out of a print run of 120,000). This was a blow for the publishers, who had to cover a big loss. In addition to the cost of production, there was talk of a €300,000 advance for each of the authors.[17]

The failure of this book can be analysed on different levels. Firstly, an obvious mistake in the marketing strategy: why make a big secret of the identity of such mainstream authors, regularly seen and heard already?

Booksellers saw through it at once – even before the book came out, as two of them told *Livres Hebdo*. 'A Flammarion executive called to persuade me,' recalled one. 'I took fifty. When the authors' names had been unveiled, he called again to get me to take more. I refused.'[18] The other was more explicit: 'If you're going to do this Mr X business, make it a real Mr X! Houellebecq, BHL, that won't make anyone's mouth water!' And the retailer added that if it had been his responsibility alone, he would not have ordered any copies at all: 'But my shop manager didn't dare. It's going to take a shedload of hype to shift them.'[19] There was plenty, but not enough to do the trick.

Apart from the way it was launched, the book 'felt' fabricated. Of course, not everything in *Public Enemies* is worthless, but at no time does the reader believe that there was any need for the correspondence. The book's title and its starting point – 'Why are we so detested?' – as well as their extravagant fooling around, show in themselves that the authors, rather than talking to each other, are courting the reader with reasons to love them. Houellebecq, like an attention-seeking younger brother, does it by painting himself as thoroughly odious. Bernard-Henri Lévy, like the swottish elder, boasts about the range of his talents. Anyone would have known that without opening the book. And give or take the odd detail (those extraordinary passages on the 'pack' of those who dare to criticize them), the reader is never surprised. Both egos are too powerful, in their different ways, for much to emerge from six months of sporadic exchanges. More than the content of the emails, it is the gimcrack side of the book's construction that makes reading it so tedious.

But perhaps, paradoxically, that is the key to the work's moderate success abroad, notably in the US where it came out in January 2011. With each author earnestly embodying a different stereotype of the French intellectual (cynical, libidinous introvert with fag-end stuck to lower lip versus brilliant seducer quoting at least one author per sentence), their signposted exchanges doubtless have the same sort of charm as the Paris reconstituted on Hollywood film sets. On that level, the book was quite favourably received. It took the *New York Times*, in a review accurately entitled 'Two guys from Paris', to display a little acerbity: 'One way to read this book, a dialogue between two famous French authors, is as a comic novel, a brilliant satire on the vanity of writers.'[20] And further down: 'BHL does a wonderful parody of philosophizing, that is, saying something quite banal in a very complicated way. Talking about "that dimension of intersubjectivity on which Epicureanism (and

Leibnizianism too, for that matter) founders," he deduces that "what is in one today will be in another tomorrow, that by the end of our exchanges that which forms part of my essence at the moment of my writing to you may perhaps have entered yours." In short, people influence one another.' But what really shocks the reviewer are Bernard-Henri Lévy's boasts that he was on the trail of Daniel Pearl when everyone else had forgotten him, that he had made Ayaan Hirsi Ali's case a national cause when no one knew who she was, or that he had been to Sarajevo 'before everyone else'. 'This is the false braggadocio of what Germans call a *Hochstapler*, something between a boaster and an impostor, a well-known comic figure in European literature.'

Be that as it may, what is perhaps most astonishing of all is that this is the book in which Bernard-Henri Lévy comes closest to coming clean. Of course he has always, from the start, talked endlessly about himself. But here and there in *Public Enemies* the tone changes: he talks about his father, an adored, remote figure, about his childhood when he spent hours imagining the orations at his own funeral; about his relation to Judaism. Moments of manifest sincerity, quite rare in the essayist's texts, but which struggle to emerge from this long string of poses and, more worryingly, are patently of scant interest to most people outside his circle of journalist friends. We must therefore move on.

THE BOTUL AFFAIR, OR, PHILOSOPHY DOWN THE TOILET

ON THE 'COURT JESTER'

Intellectual life can be cruel. Citing by name a fictitious philosopher ruined Bernard-Henri Lévy's bid for seriousness in *De la guerre en philosophie* (Grasset, 2010). But the joke ceased to be funny when the laughers were accused of anti-Semitism, and the journalist who exposed the howler got into trouble with her editor.

Just over a year after the flop of his correspondence with Michel Houellebecq, Bernard-Henri Lévy published simultaneously two books whose purpose was to summarize the direction of his work. *Pièces d'identité*, the eleventh volume in the 'Questions de principe' series, is a collection of articles, speeches, correspondence etc., nearly all published between 2004 and 2009. This fat tome predictably addresses almost all the writer's favourite subjects: himself, his relationships with literature, art, Jewishness, Sartre, the US, and his causes over the previous five years (Darfur, Georgia, Afghanistan …). The second book to appear in early 2010 was more original. Entitled *De la guerre en philosophie* (On war in philosophy), it was essentially a rewriting of a lecture given on 6 April 2009 at the École normale supérieure in the rue d'Ulm in Paris, under the title 'How I philosophize'. That is what this short 130-page volume, a 'programme-book' according to its dust jacket, is for: to explain the way Bernard-Henri Lévy conceives in his own case the art of philosophizing.

The stakes were higher than one might think. As we know, in a career of thirty-five years Bernard-Henri Lévy had never really worked as a philosopher, in the sense usually understood. With the exception of the Sartre biography, his work on texts consists mainly of sprinkled-on quotations, never sourced and often chucked in out of context. Not the slightest sign of an attempt at systematization. Although there are constants among his references (Lacan, Althusser, Levinas, Sartre) and themes, it is far from easy to discern any real coherence or vaguely rigorous positioning. However, Bernard-Henri Lévy knows philosophy well, he is manifestly soaked in it – his 'principal concern', he calls it in the first few pages of *De la guerre en philosophie*[21] – and owes a great deal to the label of 'philosopher' which he trails around even into the most improbable situations. The whole object of this book was to identify some main connecting threads, to expound a different way of doing philosophy and being a philosopher, to legitimize once and for all a standing that would justify a place among the great thinkers. As usual, the pre-launch press campaign was impressive (including a big interview in *L'Express* on 4 February, a week before publication, with the editor in chief Christophe Barbier, a long portrait in *Paris Match* and another in *Le Point* signed by Christine Angot, an interview in *Le Journal du dimanche* on Saturday 6 February). Everything was ready for the consecration.

But three days before it came out, on 8 February 2010, the book suddenly became a huge joke. On that day a *Nouvel Observateur* journalist, Aude Lancelin, published the fruits of her observant reading on the BibliObs website. On page 121 of *De la guerre en philosophie* Bernard-Henri Lévy attacks these 'allegedly fleshless philosophers … all those friends of the transcendental who would have us believe that their thought has given up, given up for good, their corporeality and their sources of confusion'. On page 122, after giving Althusser as an example of such dry sticks, he goes on: 'Or then again Kant, the so-called sage of Königsberg, the lifeless and disembodied philosopher par excellence, of whom Jean-Baptiste Botul demonstrated soon after the Second World War, in his series of lectures to the Paraguayan neo-Kantians, that their hero was an abstract fraud, and a pure mind purely in appearance.' This is one of the very rare exegeses to which Bernard-Henri Lévy refers in the book. It has all the trappings of scientific authority (an unknown thinker, the post-war era, Paraguay …) and enables the 'philosopher' to conclude his critique with a stinging: 'Kant, that furious madman of thought, that concept freak, all of whose *Critique of Pure Reason* could be read, in that case, as the narrative of a private drama, a secret and encrypted autobiography …'[22] Old Immanuel put firmly in his place, by the alliance of the warlike thinker and the perceptive commentator.

Except that Jean-Baptiste Botul didn't exist. Jean-Baptiste Botul was a made-up character. Not only had the fake philosopher been wholly invented by Frédéric Pagès, a journalist on the *Canard enchaîné*, and a group of jolly fellows in a 'Society of Friends of Jean-Baptiste Botul', but little effort had been made to maintain the illusion since 1999 when Botul had first appeared in the groves of academe. His name suggests a nasty illness; his life story is pretty unusual (he met Proust, Cocteau, Zweig, Zapata and Pancho Villa and had flings with Marie Bonaparte and Simone de Beauvoir, without leaving a trace anywhere), and his oeuvre hardly credible (*La Vie sexuelle d'Emmanuel Kant*, *Landru précurseur du féminisme*, *Nietzsche et le démon du midi*, *Métaphysique du mou*[23]). Botul has certainly been quoted a few times, but usually in books produced by individuals connected with the Botul Foundation for Botulism, which since 2004 has awarded a Botul Prize for which 'the necessary but not sufficient condition for becoming a laureate … is membership of the Botul prize jury'. Although Botul's alleged texts are extremely well-written, the overall hoax is as coarse as it is funny. In 2007 the journalist Roger-Pol Droit had a lot of fun with it in a very clever piece in *Le Monde des livres*[24]… a supplement BHL apparently does not read.

The moment it went online at BibliObs, *Le Nouvel Observateur*'s culture website, the news of Aude Lancelin's piece went viral, tweeted and retweeted and all over Facebook. So heavy was the hit-rate that the server crashed and the article was moved to NouvelObs.com, the weekly's main website. It was taken up next day by the French press, and the day after that by European and US print media. Everyone let rip with plays on words, 'Botul' supplying quite a few. The joke had gone international.

The reason for all the fuss, obviously, was that the joke was on Bernard-Henri Lévy: an oxymoronic collision between the schoolboy joke and the pompous intellectual, a sort of 'self-pieing' as the *Canard* rightly pointed out (see above, chapter 3). Because, as one journalist accurately put it: 'It's court jester stuff. A pratfall on the ballroom floor in front of the assembled company. It's trivial, but it sticks in the mind.'

The whole incident contains a cruel irony. Bernard-Henri Lévy has invented a great deal in the course of his life, and part of his work has consisted of self-invention (see most of the preceding chapters). That he should find himself citing a joke philosopher invented by someone else is a punishment of which only the unconscious is capable.

It is a further irony that in the very book in which Bernard-Henri Lévy works to prove that he is (in his fashion) a philosopher, here he is on page 122, six pages before the end, offering blatant proof of being a lightweight in his dealings with philosophy. In just three lines Bernard-Henri Lévy himself gives the evidence – surplus, of course, but so droll and so obvious – of a frivolous approach to work, which no one would criticize if he had not spent thirty-five years trying to make people believe the opposite.

Suddenly, whole new questions arose: had Bernard-Henri Lévy really read the stuff he quoted? Did anyone at Grasset check over his texts? If a gaffe like that had got through, how many others had there been, that no one had noticed?

HOW TO WRING THE NECK OF A 'HILARIOUS STORY'

So the mistake is less harmless than it might seem. On the same evening that the article appeared online, Bernard-Henri Lévy was on the set of the Canal Plus 'Grand Journal' where, with an embarrassed laugh, someone risked a mention of Botul. 'It's a hilarious story, really, most frightfully amusing,' the writer replied with a tight smile, before going on to recommend Botul's writings, especially *La Vie sexuelle d'Emmanuel Kant*.[25] An hour earlier the *La Règle du jeu* website had published, to establish a pre-emptive fire-break, the 'bloc-notes' scheduled to appear in *Le Point* three days later.

The first part was obviously devoted to Botul: 'So I let myself be taken in as were, before me, the critics who reviewed it when it came out; as in the past Pascal Pia and Maurice Nadeau were taken in by the fake Rimbaud invented by Nicolas Bataille and Akakia-Viala. … The highbrow hoax being, as you know, something of an École normale tradition, I even confess to feeling a certain pleasure at having let myself be caught out, in my turn, by such a well-crafted mystification.'[26] Bernard-Henri Lévy played it very well. He laughed, complimented his tormentors and claimed his place in the proud lineage of victims of literary hoaxes.

But he did not maintain that line for long. A few days later, at the microphone with Nicolas Demorand on the radio programme 'Matinale de France Inter', the tone had changed: 'Listen, it was amusing for five minutes, now I think we've had enough. It's stopped being so funny. I'm not in stitches anymore.'[27] A little later, he expanded on that: 'I find that what started as an agreeable hoax, as a schoolboy prank, is in the process of turning weird and it's starting to go a bit off. ... It was funny, and now it's getting nasty. That's my personal impression.' When the journalist asked what he meant by 'off', Bernard-Henri Lévy explained that he was referring to criticisms levelled at a man not for what he does, but 'for what he is'. The word anti-Semitism was not used, but everyone understood.

His friends, as so often, were less cautious. In *L'Express* Christophe Barbier, perhaps vexed after publishing a long interview with Bernard-Henri Lévy a week before the book's launch without mentioning the non-existent Botul, explained that he saw in the animosity against the writer what Bernard-Henri Lévy himself had identified: proof of the 'national gene predisposing us to fascism in this country'.[28] No mincing of words there. Philippe Boggio, always at hand when needed (some years earlier he had been asked to write an official biography of the Master when critical investigations were being prepared), denounced a 'délit de faciès' (expression for random police interrogation of individuals, most usually people of colour, whom officers 'don't like the look of').[29] Rhetorically mentioning 'investigating cops' and 'totally Stalinist ... vigilance committees', he ended the piece with an isolated and definitive phrase: 'Bernard-Henri Lévy, that Jew.'[30] A similar rhetoric flowed from the pen of Ségolène Royal: the candidate defeated in the presidential election, whose confidant Bernard-Henri Lévy had been during the campaign (see above, chapter 1). She flew to his rescue with a long op-ed piece in *Le Monde*.

In support of the idea that the roar of laughter could have had anti-Semitic undertones, Royal advanced an argument already used by Josyane Savigneau in a *Le Monde* article and by Boggio who, ever the conscientious journalist, had written in *Slate*: 'Florent Latrive, in charge of Libé Labo, confirmed on Thursday 11 February the closure of the forum following an article about BHL's mistake, owing to the "dozens of comments, often insulting (insulting, not 'critical') and anti-Semitic" that the *Libération* site received.'[31] Florent Latrive's eyes widened on reading that, for the comment thread had never been opened. Boggio had misunderstood: he had not opened the comment thread for preventive reasons, as *Libération* lacked the staff during that weekend to moderate it – as would doubtless be necessary, in view of the mass of vitriolic and anti-Semitic remarks that had accompanied two articles published earlier on Bernard-Henri Lévy.

This story within the story underlines two facts. Bernard-Henri Lévy is the target of a manifest anti-Semitism expressed largely on the internet: just googling his name will provide chilling confirmation of this. And there is also a use made of that anti-Semitism, by him, but especially by those who defend him, to invalidate any fairly tough criticism and to see any mockery as the expression of a 'fascism' which is hardly even latent. The accusation had a paralyzing effect: everyone stopped sniggering.

At *Le Nouvel Observateur*, people had stopped sniggering some time before. The appearance of Aude Lancelin's piece on the magazine's website, then in the weekly itself three days later, caused some agitation. On 10 February Jean Daniel, founder of the journal, friend of Bernard-Henri Lévy and an eminent figure in French journalism, got involved through a post on his blog, elegantly contriving to offend no one.[32] Denis Olivennes, publishing director of *Le Nouvel Observateur*, lacked his predecessor's lightness of touch when the Botul affair arose. Although he did not react on the day Aude Lancelin's piece appeared on BibliObs, the amplitude of the clamour next day goaded him into sending the journalist a furious email, so furious that the Authors' Society reacted in its turn. Although the body seldom interferes on editorial matters, it released a communiqué to praise 'the moral and professional stance of the journal.'[33] That did not stop Olivennes, who wanted to publish a text in defence of Bernard-Henri Lévy in the journal: having failed to control his troops, he needed to dissociate himself from them.

The text never came out, either because Olivennes yielded to the opinions of the journalists he consulted, or, as one would hope, because he became aware of the absurdity of the move. Having access to a copy of this aborted exercise in journalistic courage, we quote here a few extracts, which illustrate the embarrassment afflicting Denis Olivennes and the rhetorical circumlocutions to which it reduced him: 'He asks for trouble, does BHL. For a start, he has everything: he's handsome, wealthy and smart. So at least he might keep his head down. But no! It isn't a promo, it's a media spectacular by a rock star. … For all that, the pleasure of putting BHL down after having celebrated him … leaves a sour aftertaste.' The entire text works in this seesaw way, conceding a little to excuse much: 'One might not like his books, but they are not worthless'; 'One is free not to share his positions, on the Middle East for example, or to be exasperated by the narcissistic affectation with which he puts himself at the centre of his combats for just causes. But in the end, he is seldom mistaken and his commitments are disinterested'; 'In a word, there is something unfair about the animosity towards him. He has certainly asked for it. But that doesn't mean he deserves it.'

Accusations of anti-Semitism, pressure on a journalist: one can only be dumbfounded by the scale of what started as a great peal of laughter at the demonstration of a fraud by the author of that fraud himself. But among the arguments advanced in defence of Bernard-Henri Lévy, there is one that merits closer attention: suppose that regrettable mention of Botul was preventing *De la guerre en philosophie* from being read? Suppose focusing on that one gaffe was leading people to overlook a good book on philosophy? Many people suggested as much.

THE SELF-INVENTION OF A NON-PHILOSOPHER

So let us take them at their word. Let us see what is in this book. Let's read it seriously and try to follow the arguments step by step, to understand how he philosophizes. Firstly, following the teaching of his master Althusser, he explains what it is to believe in philosophy. Next, the master's second lesson, doing philosophy means making, 'in other words shaping, manufacturing'.[34] And Bernard-Henri Lévy wonders whether he has been faithful to that lesson. Here, just before the twentieth page, we start to worry. For the disciple describes three 'concepts' that he has 'made' over the course of his career: 'French ideology', 'will to purity' and 'fascislamism' (pp. 19–20). 'Concepts' which, with all the goodwill in the world, cannot be said to have permeated thought in general, and which would be very hard to find in any philosophical writings other than his own. He adds, 'I have just given three examples. There must be others. Many others. Let us move on ...' (p. 21). Why the rush? People would like to see other examples. Never mind. Another time, perhaps.

Thirdly, Bernard-Henri Lévy asserts, unlike almost everyone else (including Nietzscheans, Deleuzeans, Derridians, postmodernists, Levinas and Heidegger), the need for a 'system'. A brave move, these days. What is his own system, then? It is a 'special system'. 'It is an open-ended system. Lacunary. That is not closed. It is a system that accepts within it the demon, not of the absolute, but of the infinite' (p. 24). Right: so Bernard-Henri Lévy's system is a system that is not a system. Interestingly, it is a system that can say everything and its opposite since, at the same time, its characteristic is that it is not systematic. OK. But 'a system for doing what, finally?', wonders Bernard-Henri Lévy (p. 27). Well, certainly not for doing the same as all those dullards who, 'from Plato to Auguste Comte' (p. 27), wanted either to discern a system in the world, or to impose their systematic readings of the world. No, for Bernard-Henri Lévy, the world is not a system, it is a ruin, and the system is what makes it possible to avoid total collapse. And it is because the world is like that that the philosopher has to make a system. Brilliant. End of first chapter.

In the chapters that follow, Bernard-Henri Lévy justifies not having students by saying that 'the university is not the right place to philosophize' (p. 36). He explains that his thought does not measure itself against 'adverse hypotheses' (p. 41) because he does not believe in philosophical dialogue – in a great moment, he makes an exception for the couples Benny Lévy and Sartre, Deleuze and Guattari 'or, more modestly, Michel Houellebecq and myself' (p. 42). Because for him philosophy is assertion, philosophy 'is an art of war' (p. 50) and one philosophizes well when one philosophizes against. He quickly adds that his way of philosophizing is not to comment, not to read slowly and ruminate, but to practise a 'piratical reading', 'reading as fly-over' (p. 59). He defines himself as 'a philosopher who does not quote' (p. 68) but who looks for inspiration outside philosophy and who, above all, addresses dead philosophers as if they were alive. That gets us three quarters of the way through, and the rest is along similar lines.

Even without Botul, it is difficult to take *De la guerre en philosophie* seriously. It is not that it does not show a real love and a real knowledge of philosophy, but that there is something absurd about the laborious attempt to present as an art of philosophizing what is at best – and that's saying a lot – a relationship with philosophy. And there is something upsetting about the shabby arguments to which Bernard-Henri Lévy is reduced in the effort to persuade us – to persuade himself – that that relationship with philosophy is a philosophical relationship. Advancing three non-existent 'concepts' and promising a thousand others of which it is hard to find the slightest trace; claiming a system that is not a system and not giving even the beginnings of a notion of it; confusing the perfectly justifiable absence of students with the more disturbing absence of exegetists, and the wish not to teach, equally justifiable, with the wish not to be studied, and so on and so forth. Botul, far from doing Bernard-Henri Lévy a disservice, may have saved him from having this book read for what it is: an attempt at self-constitution as a philosopher which does the exact opposite.

BERNARD-HENRI LÉVY, BEATEN AT HIS OWN GAME

'AND ONFRAY DETHRONED BHL'

For a long time Bernard-Henri Lévy reigned alone over the small country of French media intellectuals. Others were of course allowed to play walk-on parts: Philippe Sollers as the erudite cynic and string-puller in the world of publishing, Alain Finkielkraut as the reactionary vexed by his epoch, Jacques Attali as the thinker of the economy and the future, Luc Ferry as the academic lost to the Republic's gold, Pascal Bruckner as the enemy of repentance, Régis Debray as the repenter … Without counting the shooting stars. But until very recently, no one had threatened the primacy of the author of *Barbarism with a Human Face*; no one had been able either to broaden his spectrum or to strengthen his position enough to assert himself as a durable figure of reference. If maintaining that position sometimes cost Bernard-Henri Lévy a scuffle with an adversary, the odd punch-up soon forgotten by the history of thought (like the one with Debray over the NATO bombing in Kosovo[35]), it was chiefly done by dint of an energy, a squatting of the territory and a nose for networking which nobody could compete with. So that when, in October 2010, *Marianne* published a silly survey that found Bernard-Henri Lévy to be the intellectual best known to the French, no one was remotely surprised. But, to anyone up to speed, things were already changing.

On 21 May 2010, a few months after the Botul business, *Le Nouvel Observateur* published a piece no one had ever expected to see. Headlined 'And Onfray dethroned BHL', it explained why Bernard-Henri Lévy was France's top media intellectual no longer. That place, the journal said, would now be occupied by Michel Onfray. The reasons for the reshuffle were on several levels. First, book sales, with Bernard-Henri Lévy's collapsing while Michel Onfray's were colossal: 172,800 for the *Traité d'athéologie* (Grasset, 2005), then 93,500 for *Le Crépuscule d'une idole, affabulation freudienne* (Grasset, 2010), an ambitious attempt to deconstruct Freud.[36] Next, Onfray had managed to start newsworthy controversies in media-intellectual circles. His Freud book, 'Twilight of an idol', had the triple advantage of selling very well, getting coverage in the mainstream press (at its launch it got the front pages of three big French weeklies, *Le Point*, *Le Nouvel Observateur* and *Marianne*) and generating debate (being publicly attacked by such eminent characters as Élisabeth Roudinesco, Jacques-Alain Miller, Alain Finkielkraut, Étienne Balibar, Jean-Luc Nancy and Alain Badiou).

No matter that he was a Grasset author, who had published his first book in Bernard-Henri Lévy's series.[37] His success cast a shadow. Making his usual use of the 'bloc-notes' in *Le Point* for the dirty work of dismissal, Bernard-Henri Lévy wrote on 29 April 2010, 'Michel Onfray complains that he is criticized without being read? Well then, I have read him. … And honesty compels me to say that I emerged from that perusal even more dismayed than might have been predicted from the few reviews which I, like everyone else, had already seen.' The book, he went on, was 'banal, reductionist, puerile, pedantic and occasionally downright ludicrous', apparently reflecting 'the famous "valet's viewpoint", which, as Hegel has taught us is seldom the best angle from which to judge a great man, let alone a great oeuvre'. After developing the flattering adjectives listed above, the piece ends on a note of sour malice: 'Psychoanalysis has been through it before, and will recover. I am not so sure about Michel Onfray.'[38]

The following week, also in *Le Point*, Michel Onfray replied, starting off in ironic mode: 'A writer known for his rectitude, his morality, his independence; a philosopher admired for his virtue, his probity and honesty; an individual respected for the seriousness of his work, the profundity of his analyses, the breadth of his vision; the exegetist of Botul now known worldwide can at last express all his dark thoughts about me in France and abroad, by activating an international network that will cost him dear in every sense[39] … An article in my favour from the Great Helmsman of Saint-Germain-des-Prés would have caused me the greatest distress.'[40] It is clear that for both parties, Freud is merely the pretext for a struggle on a different terrain.

Ostensibly, the two men are opposed in every way. On one side, the wealthy heir and École normale graduate who lives in Saint-Germain-des-Prés, travels the world to defend victims abroad but serves the powers that be in his own country. On the other, the son of an agricultural labourer and a cleaner – underlining the elegance of the 'valet's viewpoint' jibe – who created the Popular University of Caen, claims to have little interest in Parisian life and positions himself on the far left. Indeed, Michel Onfray's first public criticisms of Bernard-Henri Lévy were based on this opposition. Invited by *Le Nouvel Observateur* to comment on *Left in Dark Times*, Michel Onfray attacked the book on the level both of form – 'Stiffened by the assaults of the distantly syllogistic war machine of his book, who could still risk not thinking like Bernard-Henri Lévy?'[41] – and of content, broadly reproaching Bernard-Henri Lévy for defending a 'right-wing left' and demanding: 'When will people talk openly about the role of the caviar left in the exceptionally good health of the Front National since Mitterrand's renunciation of the left in 1983?'[42] Two years later, he returned to the fray with a hostile piece on Bernard-Henri Lévy's arguments in defence of Polanski (see above, chapter 7). Writing in *Libération*,[43] he accused the writer of bad faith and class solidarity. 'Sodomizing a thirteen-year-old girl after getting her drunk: is that a crime, yes or no?' Michel Onfray may have attacked Bernard-Henri Lévy repeatedly, but it is noticeable that until 2010 the latter seemed, publicly at least, to attach small importance to the youngster's tantrums. It took the success of *Crépuscule d'une idole* to goad Bernard-Henri Lévy into retaliating, which suggests that what peeves him about Onfray is not so much his political ideas and aggressiveness as the place he is taking in the media-intellectual field.

For, where the life of ideas is concerned, they are under the same constraints. Both believe that philosophy and thought can exist outside the traditional university setting and should reach the widest possible audience, and thus their legitimacy is subject to their book sales and the publishing/media loop. This in turn imposes postures that are similar in certain respects: writing polemical books, giving proofs of seriousness without being too rebarbative or too theoretical, inventing a media persona that is both singular and flexible enough to comment at any time on the most varied issues. For some years Michel Onfray has excelled at this art. He has a feel for the way the wind is blowing and is good at choosing trendy subjects (against God, against psychoanalysis ...). His books are cleverly launched (*Crépuscule d'une idole* was embargoed before publication), carry a heavy punch and appeal to people who want intellectual stimulation without having to read philosophy. He skilfully parades, from France Culture to the lowest-rent talk shows, his persona as an anti-elite ranter. The shirt is sometimes white, but always under a black pullover. As a media philosopher Michel Onfray imposes a less glittery style, more radical and skirmishing, that visibly reduces Bernard-Henri Lévy to the defence of a faded, consensual oligarchy. Could this be the end of an era?

WITH SARKOZY: COMPETITION FROM THE 'ANTI-TEACHER' ALAIN BADIOU

The author of *Left in Dark Times* has suffered another setback in recent years. At the end of October 2007, a few months after Nicolas Sarkozy's election to the presidency of the Republic, the philosopher Alain Badiou published the fourth volume of his *Circonstances*, subtitled *De quoi*

Sarkozy est-il le nom?[44] Launched discreetly by the small and exacting Nouvelles Éditions Lignes, the book was an unexpected hit: the 3,000 copies printed sold out in four days. From reprint to reprint, the book sold 26,900 copies,[45] unheard-of for Alain Badiou who is little known to the public at large and little read outside universities. The book was a violent critique of Sarkozyism, on both substance and form, and offered a conceptual armoury which the honorary professor at the École normale supérieure had drawn from his analyses of Marxism and Maoism.

Just as people were starting to talk about Badiou's book, Bernard-Henri Lévy was spreading himself all over the papers and TV channels to promote *Left in Dark Times*, and consequently explaining that the left was on the brink of death. For someone who wanted to be among the first opponents of the new government's policies, the coincidence was very awkward. Bernard-Henri Lévy was not only being overtaken on his left – not difficult, admittedly, there is considerable elbow room there – but also, and worse, his place as top intellectual opponent was being snaffled by an old Maoist and École normale man. A bit much. Especially as in *Left in Dark Times* he had attacked Alain Badiou for his opposition, in 1999, to the NATO air strikes on Serbia, blinded though he may have been by his denunciation of the Empire involved in that war. He had presented Badiou as a paradigm of one of the French left's numerous failings: 'A failure of intelligence and of heart. The end of political considerations, precisely when we were claiming to sharpen them. These bad teachers, these anti-teachers, so strangely devoted to undoing what in politics is the hardest thing of all to construct: a way to get people to worry about other people's suffering.'[46] When this 'anti-teacher' became the person to whom a disabled left turned to try to understand Sarkozyism, there was good reason to take umbrage. Especially since the press and public were starting to take an interest in Alain Badiou, 'in the shade for forty years and then suddenly in the glare of the footlights.'[47] His portrait was sketched, he was hailed as a 'philosophy star',[48] a 'contested but central figure in French intellectual debate,'[49] the 'new herald of anti-Sarkozyism,'[50] the 'guru of anti-Sarkozia';[51] he was invited on television, interviewed in the papers and made one of the characters in Jean-Luc Godard's film *Socialisme*.

So Bernard-Henri Lévy attacked Alain Badiou on a rather sensitive point. On page 36 of *The Meaning of Sarkozy*, the English translation of the book, Badiou writes: 'I propose to call Nicolas Sarkozy the Rat Man. Yes, that suits him, it's well deserved.' Explaining what he means by 'rats', he says 'The rat is the person who needs to rush in to the duration on offer, not being in any state to construct a different one.' In fact, the use of the name in the book precedes this definition. It appears on page 4, designating those leaving the sinking ship of the left to join Sarkozy's UMP. And here is New Philosophy embarked in that movement: 'A certain number of personalities represent this posture, this possibility – the avant-garde rats for the construction of Sarkozy's UPU. Indeed, all they are doing is extending, completing and giving a definitive form to the broad movement of counter-revolutionary renegacy that began in 1976 with the clique of the "new philosophers".'[52]

The argument itself is on target (see above, chapter 3), but the use of the word 'rat', even though it refers to one of Freud's five classic analyses and, beyond that, to the Pied Piper of Hamelin, is unfortunate to say the least. Several readers objected, and Bernard-Henri Lévy seized upon it to disqualify Badiou's critique in a March 2008 'bloc-notes' in *Le Point*: 'I take up the book again, which appeared after the elections, in which the philosopher Alain Badiou, claiming to quote Freud (poor Freud!), no longer calls the president by his name but calls him "the rat man", just "the rat man", like in one of those propaganda films shown in cinemas under the Occupation.'[53] There follow a few lines which say a lot, in Bernard-Henri Lévy's view, about what comes to the surface under 'a certain sort of anti-Sarkozyism', before concluding unambiguously: 'And I end by thinking that here, whether we like it or not, is something symptomatic: the question is no longer the meaning of Sarkozy, but the meaning of anti-Sarkozyism.'

Some months later he reiterated the attack in the pages of *Le Monde*. 'In a recent book, *The Meaning of Sarkozy*, Alain Badiou permitted himself in his just struggle against "foulness" to reintroduce some zoological metaphors to the political lexicon ("rats", "the rat man") which Sartre in the preface to *The Wretched of the Earth* had nevertheless shown, unarguably, to be an invariable mark of fascism.'[54] Throwing the suspicion of anti-Semitism on Alain Badiou is not new. Since 2005 and the appearance of *Circonstances 3. Portées du mot 'juif'* (*Polemics*, Verso, 2006) he has been regularly attacked on this matter. Bernard-Henri Lévy – and he was not alone – therefore knew very well what he was doing by advancing these references full of unspoken implications.[55] Anyone hoping for an inch-by-inch discussion of the arguments advanced by Alain Badiou – and a critique too of his proposed solutions, in particular his 'communist hypothesis' – might as well give up. In the presence of the paralysing suspicion of anti-Semitism, the rest is just snippets of contradiction tossed back and forth.

Alain Badiou's reply was scathing. After noting the recourse to the insinuation of anti-Semitism by 'enemies of any politics other than the one they quite wrongly name "democracy"', he denied any possible connection between his use of the word 'rats' and the Jews and, addressing 'the leading light of the media intellectuals committed to the Restoration, Bernard-Henri Lévy', he wrote: 'I claim the right to use "zoological metaphors" – I don't have a hang-up about them. It is characteristic of politics that there are enemies, even if capitalo-parliamentarism presses its domination to the point of trying to make us forget this. And why the hell, if there are real enemies, shouldn't I be allowed to insult them?'[56] And the polemic continued, just as poor on Bernard-Henri Lévy's part. In his 'bloc-notes' of 8 January 2010, headlined 'Why the debate on national identity ought to be stopped', he wrote, 'I do not believe, like Alain Badiou, that Sarkozyism might be a "transcendental Pétainism".' Why? We are not told, although it would have been interesting to criticize that notion which occupies a lot of the last part of *The Meaning of Sarkozy*. But it is apparent that Bernard-Henri Lévy, so prompt to denounce the 'French ideology' he boasts of having identified – and that he accuses Badiou of lifting from him – sees it everywhere except in the politics of the Sarkozy government. Alain Badiou becomes the left adversary par excellence, the automatic whipping boy, for reasons that are easy to understand (his attitudes to communism and Maoism, his critique of parliamentary democracy) but that are never subjected to the least rational scrutiny.

That critical task, necessitating a proper reading of Badiou, was left by Bernard-Henri Lévy to a young writer-philosopher who had scores to settle with the professor of the rue d'Ulm: Mehdi Belhaj Kacem. He enjoyed precocious glory with some astonishing novels, enough indeed to earn the acronym MBK in the small world of literature, before becoming a philosopher and publishing books which do with concepts what his early novels did with words: bash them together in a not untalented but confused way. Belhaj Kacem began his career as a political and intellectual radical, and had been a pupil and admirer of Badiou before breaking with him. His resulting status as a 'trophy of war'[57] was attested by a fat book, *Après Badiou*, published in early 2011 in Bernard-Henri Lévy's collection at Grasset, with a dust-cover blurb signed 'BHL'. Any doubts as to BHL's implication in the book's existence are laid to rest in the first paragraph: the 'present text' was 'occasioned at the request of the review *La Règle du jeu*' and the first chapter is dedicated to 'the person who shoved you into this hole [Alain Badiou], as well as to the one who got you out, Bernard-Henri Lévy.'[58]

The procedure is admirably direct and labour-saving: get a disenchanted former disciple to do the demolition job. Badiou's interpretation was unflattering: 'Plainly, Mehdi Belhaj Kacem thought that being my friend did not pay him enough, or quickly enough, and that being my enemy would be highly profitable: all he had to do was sell out to those people, many and powerful, who have long been my enemies. I have no other comment to make on this banal story of mental corruption.'[59] Despite the violence in form and content of *Après Badiou*, however, the project misfired. Alain Badiou's aura had manifestly withstood the combined onslaught of the New Philosopher and the young turncoat.

Any weapon will do, to stay master of the field. Perhaps that is how the title of *De la guerre en philosophie* should be understood. It is hard to tell whether Bernard-Henri Lévy will win this fight against those encroaching on his territory. In France the competition is getting tougher. There are plenty of people who are more controversial, more hard-working, more radical and less risible. The space is shrinking. Time to conquer fresh lands.

10 BHL WORLDWIDE

The first decade of the twenty-first century started poorly for Bernard-Henri Lévy, whose star was fading in France, but 2006 saw a spectacular comeback based on the reception of his book American Vertigo *in the US. This success owed little to chance and much to a systematic effort to conquer the US media, which helped in its turn to find him a new space on the web in which to spread his word and flaunt himself.*

AMERICAN VERTIGO, 2006: A FRENCH TRIUMPH

Early this century a large part of the French press started retailing what sounded rather a good story: get this, Bernard-Henri Lévy has conquered America! It was all supposed to have begun with *Who Killed Daniel Pearl?*, whose American translation was published in 2003 by Melville House. 'On a subject extensively covered by the American media, the French intellectual has succeeded in attracting 70,000 purchasers' (other sources claimed 200,000). 'A figure rarely attained since Jean-Paul Sartre, which places the author in the front rank of French authors translated over there, alongside Jacques Derrida and Alain Robbe-Grillet', said *Paris Match* in 2004 in a piece soberly entitled 'BHL, American star.'[1]

Of course, parts of Bernard-Henri Lévy's output had been finding their way into US translation for years – *Barbarism with a Human Face* being a major example – and the US press had followed the trajectory of this curious phenomenon since the 1980s. But that work of 'faction' on the murder of a US journalist in the post-9/11 context (see above, chapter 6) gave a considerable boost to his notoriety. And the French press revelled in this new accolade. People marvelled that *Vanity Fair* in 2003 devoted a long article to the French intellectual[2] – without mentioning that its author, Joan Juliet Buck, is a fashionable denizen of Saint-Germain – and quoted the *Vanity Fair* editor Graydon Carter to explain what Americans liked about the essayist: 'What gets to me about Bernard-Henri Lévy is his UFO side. He isn't like any kind of writer we have over here' (or here either, Graydon, one is tempted to say). 'Everything he's resented for in France is a plus for us.'[3] The *Paris Match* journalist who quoted these remarks may not have known that Graydon Carter's book skewering the Bush administration, *What We've Lost*, was to be published a few months later in France by Éditions Grasset. No matter, though, the machine was up and running.

Following another translation from Melville House (*War, Evil and the End of History*, 2004), the French intellectual stepped another rung or two up the ladder of US celebrity when the respected *Atlantic Monthly* thought of him for a journey through the US in the footsteps of Alexis de Tocqueville. *Paris Match* once again kept the French up to date on the details: 'I hesitate to accept,' Bernard-Henri Lévy told the magazine in May 2004, 'because it's a titanic job, a year's travelling from Miami to Seattle through *l'Amérique profonde* ...'[4] The hesitation was brief, and the contract soon signed with the *Atlantic Monthly*. A year later, in early May 2005, the first of the seven sections appeared.

Instant triumph, *Le Monde* reported from New York: 'From the first instalment, according to early estimates, sales of the *Atlantic* are up by 20 per cent'; 'The coverage has been exceptional: cable networks, national radio, print media, lectures in the New York Public Library and at the New School. The TV journalist Charlie Rose, the Bernard Pivot of contemporary America, has had Lévy on his show four times since 2003, in spite of a French accent usually thought a disqualification for American television.'[5] But the real earthquake was yet to come, with the appearance in January 2006 of the book containing the collected *Atlantic Monthly* pieces, *American Vertigo* (Random House, 2006).

To start with, it was put about everywhere that this was the first time a French author's book had come out in the US before coming out in France (two months later). That is not true, but never mind. Then, we were treated stage by stage to Bernard-Henri Lévy's success in promoting his book. For example the debate with William Kristol at the Johns Hopkins University School of Advanced International Studies in Washington: he defied the neoconservative and summoned him to disavow creationism. 'Resignedly, Kristol complied,' wrote the Washington correspondent of *Le Monde*.[6] The end of her piece is truly baffling: 'The Frenchman prophesies that the most radical conflicts are only just beginning. "The end of dialectic could signal the end of History, but perhaps also the birth of tragedy," he told the petrified audience.'

The flower of the French press was clearly present, since *L'Express* carried another account of the Washington encounter in which, as if by magic, Francis Fukuyama – author of the celebrated *The End of History* and not mentioned once in the preceding article – also makes an appearance, only to be unhorsed in his turn by the extraordinary BHL. 'In English, BHL remains BHL, displaying an astounding eloquence, peppered with delicious Gallicisms, charming mistakes and five-syllable concepts. The miracle happens: he flattens his contradictors amid laughter and applause. ... His interlocutors, ill-served by their accountant look, smilingly give way.'[7] KERPOWed by our BHL ...

Leaving Washington in flames, he set New York alight two days later with his talk at the New York Public Library, in the somewhat over-excited view of *Le Figaro*: 'Six hundred people had swarmed in (with half that number again having to be refused entry) to see the show with its two stars: Bernard-Henri Lévy, interviewed by Tina Brown, former editor of *Vanity Fair* and the *New Yorker*. ... Laid-back, funny, passionate, he came up with a spectacular actor's turn in front of an audience of connoisseurs, with his wife Arielle Dombasle and the grande dame of American cinema, Lauren Bacall, in the front row.'[8] The entire nation seemed afflicted by this thirst for BHL: 'From Manhattan, where in less than a week he spoke to nearly 4,000 people who had paid from $15 to $25 depending on the talk, to San Francisco then Miami, by way of Philadelphia, people jostled to hear him and many had often to be turned away,' wrote *Le Figaro*'s New York correspondent.[9]

The careful orchestration was again apparent in a press release from the cultural services of the French embassy, rejoicing officially at the French intellectual's success in remarkably similar language: 'In less than a week, nearly 4,000 people travelled to meet BHL in New York, some of them paying a sum of $15 to $25 to attend lectures held at the New York Public Library or at the 92nd Street Y, in bookshops or at think tanks.'[10] The *L'Express* journalist, in lyrical mode, described the exit from the glorious Library building: 'In a Pavlovian reflex, BHL and Arielle both donned their film-star dark glasses. Their company, machine-gunned by photographers, headed towards Fifth Avenue at a slow, triumphal pace.'[11] A few days later, still in New York, he filled the 900 seats of the 92nd Street Y, where he was interviewed by his friend Adam Gopnik before a 'captivated crowd'.[12] 'He repeated the exploit the following day, his last evening in New York, standing up like a crooner on a platform in the biggest bookshop in town, Barnes and Noble in Union Square.'[13]

Le Figaro reported that a week after hitting the stores, *American Vertigo* had sold 86,000 copies and was already in the *New York Times* and *Los Angeles Times* best-seller lists. Other cities were added to the triumphal tour: Chicago, Portland, Seattle, Houston. 'In Boston, the demand was such that the venue of the event had to be changed at the last minute, not once but twice. Finally everyone ended up in a church. A publishing miracle.'[14] And for bountiful good measure, *Le Monde 2*, a weekly supplement of the evening daily, in March 2006 published a piece by the essayist himself, 'BHL, an American diary'[15] – going over the book tour in detail, and repeating from the inside everything that the French journalists present had already said. And changing very little. The piece contained the same old sentences, repeated almost word for word. Who copied whom?

By spring 2006, the popular weekly *VSD* was able to claim: 'Over a few weeks, BHL has become a sort of federal figure, the "guy on TV" who is starting to be recognized and stopped in the street, quite far out in the Houston suburbs'; for 'BHL has relaunched the American debate on democracy, on Iraq, on Bush, on "New World values". He has got Americans talking to each other. He has awakened them.'[16]

THE BHL OPERATION SETS UP SHOP IN AMERICA

AN EFFICIENT PROMOTIONAL MACHINE

Since then, the French press has regularly gratified its readers with little items on Bernard-Henri Lévy's American success. When the translation of his correspondence with Houellebecq was published, when he was interviewed on a major TV network, when Arielle Dombasle sang in New York ... What could explain such an obsession? The answer involves the strange genesis of that improbable book, *American Vertigo*. Why should the *Atlantic Monthly* have gone looking for Bernard-Henri Lévy to travel the country in the manner of a present-day Tocqueville? He admitted himself that he really began to read Tocqueville properly for the occasion; and despite frequent visits to the US, his writings hitherto had shown no great interest in the country.

The first reason has to do with image. That is what appeals to *Vanity Fair*, and was explained by William Murphy, publisher at Random House, six months after the book appeared: 'I believe all the reasons that make Bernard-Henri Lévy detested by some in his country will get him adulated here, because he belongs to that curious and rare species, the flamboyant intellectual.'[17] He put it another way, a few months later: 'American intellectuals are grey, dusty and voiceless.'[18] In fact, Bernard-Henri Lévy enjoys a highly serviceable image in the US. He embodies the stereotypical Paris intellectual (brilliant, pretentious, metaphysical, charming, chic), but in a version globalized enough not to upset American interlocutors too much. He is at home in New York, in a suite in the Carlyle, so much so that in 2007 he wrote the preface to a book on the hotel[19] and is said to be considering buying a suite there. His English is rough and ready, but good enough to express what he means under all circumstances.

And when the time came to launch *American Vertigo*, Random House came up with the resources to market that image. William Murphy explained that in budgetary terms, promotion of the book 'was in the same category as Salman Rushdie, Robert Kaplan or Norman Mailer'.[20] Bernard-Henri Lévy's book tour was a promotional juggernaut that hardly touched the university campuses but aimed, beyond the media, at the big, often prestigious venues for lectures with an admission charge, midway between seminar and show. The man aroused sufficient curiosity to fill those halls, unusually for a French author. He is manifestly at ease in that hybrid register. And he cares enough for success to lend himself to the game of editorial marketing.

> Exhausted this morning. Exhausted with having to reply, ten times a day, to the same questions. … And still half asleep when I have to start, on the telephone from my hotel room, the *n*th live interview, which can last an hour, with some Midwestern radio station. Then, to relieve the boredom, I watch CNN with the sound off. Then to my computer: Amazon.com, of which a friend had warned me that because you can follow the progress of the best-seller lists live, it has become an addiction cum nightmare for American authors. And I quickly become aware of a most distracting feature for a writer accustomed to our good old French lists, with their slow weekly rhythm: here, it changes all the time; I have the impression that it winks and blinks, at least for the top few titles, almost as fast as the stock market figures in the left corner of the TV screen; until at the idea – surely fanciful, but never mind – of a Wisconsin farmer clicking his online 'order and pay' button while listening to his radio, I wake up and apply myself to the game.[21]

The purpose was clear at least: the BHL business was setting up shop in the US.

Parallel to the campaign organized by Random House, Bernard-Henri Lévy put his personal friendships to work to broaden the promotional scope. One contact was Diane von Fürstenberg, the super-rich fashion designer and New York celebrity. Their acquaintanceship dates from the 1970s, but had been revived in 1994, when Bernard-Henri Lévy arrived to promote his film *Bosna!* and von Fürstenberg put him in touch with the people who mattered in New York. This connection became a constant of the writer's transatlantic efforts. And it worked: 'In New York, I owe her everything, or nearly; what little status I enjoy, the credit I have, the welcome given to my ideas or to my ideological battles, all that I owe to her.'[22]

It was at his old friend's home, for example, that in 1994 he met Charlie Rose, host of the eponymous chat show broadcast on the PBS public network since 1993. Charlie Rose has regularly invited his 'friend' Bernard-Henri Lévy to hold forth on his very high-profile platform, which regularly showcases all those who count in US intellectual and political life. Since Charlie Rose had been one of the people the Tocqueville imitator had featured in his *Atlantic Monthly* trip, this was a fair exchange. When *American Vertigo* came out, Diane von Fürstenberg again played the part of carriage-trade press attaché, and on 24 January 2006 held a dinner in her friend's honour in her house in Greenwich Village. One of the journalists present gave a run-down on the four hundred people at the dinner:[23] they included the *Vanity Fair* publisher Graydon Carter, the celebrated journalist Dominick Dunne, the US ambassador to Paris under Clinton, Felix Rohatyn, and the diplomat Richard Holbrooke. American friendships are useful in the same way as French ones, another example being Bernard-Henri Lévy's relationship with Christopher Hitchens, formerly a journalist with the left-wing *Nation*, more recently at *Vanity Fair* and *Slate*. They met in 1994 and since that time Hitchens has written supportively of all or nearly all of Bernard-Henri Lévy's books, and has been prompt to reply in print whenever his friend comes under attack in the US press.

HERALD OF ANTI-ANTI-AMERICANISM

It would be mistaken, however, to attribute several years of US interest in Bernard-Henri Lévy to the sole influence of his friendships and the resources mobilized by his publisher. There is also a political reason, summarized in the argument used by the *Atlantic Monthly* editor Cullen Murphy to justify his idea of sending Bernard-Henri Lévy off in the footsteps of his esteemed compatriot: 'I had known his work for a long time. And he was a Frenchman who had never been viscerally anti-American. He seemed to me the one we needed, in the aftermath of 9/11 with Americans under pressure to reassess their place in the world, to hold out to us the mirror of a foreign gaze.'[24] Random House publisher William Murphy put it in similar terms: 'Bernard brings style and boldness, and, because he is anti-anti-American despite being French, a rather positive and progressive gaze to bear on our country in which the ideological divide prevents any proper debate.'[25]

The phrase 'anti-anti-American despite being French' is pretty odd, if you think about it. It suggests an ontological contradiction between the two terms from which Bernard-Henri Lévy is somehow exempt. In fact something along those lines is what the writer thinks himself: 'I was very quick to take the measure, I believe, of what is unhealthy and murky in French anti-Americanism. That anti-Americanism "on principle" is of a piece with all that is worst about French thought.'[26] Lo and behold the spectre of 'French ideology', applied to anti-Americanism – which is in any case, as he explains elsewhere, a 'metaphor for anti-Semitism'.

This question of French anti-Americanism, of its origins and forms, is quite complex, certainly more so than the essayist makes out. Of course, there does exist in France an anti-Americanism that can be associated with anti-Semitism; but presenting anti-Americanism as a generalized and necessarily suspect sentiment proceeds from that simultaneous tendency to exaggeration and reduction that is so characteristic of Bernard-Henri Lévy's rhetoric. On the other hand, the usefulness of the procedure is undeniable: it makes him appear as the Frenchman who loves the US. Something the *Wall Street Journal* confirmed in its review of *American Vertigo* titled 'French Kiss', which noted the scarcity of 'persons of substance who profess a love for America.'[27]

William Grimes commented in the *New York Times*: 'Mr Lévy, France's leading critic of reflexive anti-Americanism, is the French intellectual most likely to give the United States a sympathetic read.'[28] While a detestation of America would indeed have been an unfortunate precondition for a year-long journey and a book, making an interpretive framework of anti-anti-Americanism is somewhat distorting, quite apart from its coarseness as a strategy. *American Vertigo* is not of course completely free from criticisms of the US, but, as the Harvard political science professor Glyn Morgan explained to *Le Monde diplomatique*: 'Bernard-Henri Lévy is far too polite a visitor to expose us to the more shocking pathologies of the United States … For, thank God, he has come primarily to compliment America. He finds its people open, welcoming and astonishingly free from the francophobia he expected.'[29] Well, yes: not all Americans are fearsome francophobes. And it could be that not all French people are carriers of the americanophobia gene ... But this role as the great intercontinental peacemaker plays a big part in Bernard-Henri Lévy's American existence.

As the decade from 2000 advanced, this existence became very important to the BHL enterprise, on several levels. Firstly, because success in the US guarantees incomparable kudos in France, for an intellectual just as much as for an actor or sportsman. Next, because the list of French intellectuals who have made a career in the US, in some cases gaining recognition there before doing so in France, is short and prestigious: Jacques Derrida, Jacques Baudrillard, Étienne Balibar, Jacques Rancière, Alain Badiou, Bruno Latour. Even though their audience is not the same as Bernard-Henri Lévy's, the mythology works twice.

But that existence also gives him a new qualification and new pretexts for giving his opinion: Bernard-Henri Lévy has become an expert on the United States. He spoke up to explain the reasons for Bush's re-election in 2004. Then, because he had met Barack Obama at the 2004 convention for the investiture of John Kerry and had seen him as a future president, he became the inter-epoch Obama pundit, writing portraits and think pieces and taking part in discussions on topics such as 'The record and future prospects of Barack Obama's policy'.[30] He explained that the US ought to inspire the French: 'America has lessons to teach us';[31] 'How ethnic difference enriches citizenship';[32] 'I prefer the American left.'[33] Whether comparing France with the US, supplying heavyweight analyses of neoconservatism and creationism or elaborating on 'Sarah Palin's pants',[34] Bernard-Henri Lévy airs his new expertise in media overjoyed to have a new reason to give him a platform. The fact is, he explained when discussing the US's attitude to its intellectuals, 'contrary to what one would think, the US media respect them and give them time to explain their thoughts and introduce their books. Head-to-head interviews lasting thirty minutes are not unusual, for example with Charlie Rose. Writers are not alibis but personages who are listened to, appreciated, dissected, and not only in New York. Here too, we have much to learn from the United States.'[35]

FEROCIOUS CRITIQUES

The situation was richly ironic. For although *American Vertigo* sold well in the US and Bernard-Henri Lévy had filled auditoriums and expressed himself widely in the media, it cannot be said that this success was based on his knowledge of America. Part of the US press, apart from finding the author delightfully sketchable, certainly found some of the issues raised by his book intriguing; but a large number of critics focused, sometimes very wittily, on the superficial character of the French intellectual's work.

Thus, an article in the *Los Angeles Times* drew an unkind comparison with Tocqueville:

> Other than the fact that both De Tocqueville and Lévy are French, they have almost nothing in common. ... Although he fondly admits to keeping Jack Kerouac's *On the Road* by his side during the journey, his second-most-referred-to text must be the complete back issues of *Vanity Fair*. Here is his list of 'typical' Americans to interview: Barry Diller, Norman Mailer, Woody Allen, Warren Beatty. De Tocqueville met and talked to John Quincy Adams, Sam Houston, Daniel Webster and Andrew Jackson, but he also interviewed farmers, craftsmen and local merchants, and he discoursed passionately about the state of American schools, American poetry, American language – even American marriage. ... The pattern of using high-profile individuals as oracles of local wisdom is Lévy's primary working method. Montana equals Jim Harrison, North Carolina equals Charlie Rose, Los Angeles equals Sharon Stone.
>
> Whereas peppering a magazine article with famous names makes for a quick and jazzy read, *American Vertigo* begins to sound less like *Democracy in America* or *On the Road* and more like 'Celebrity in America' or 'On the Make'.[36]

Adam Cohen in the *New York Times* goes straight to the point: 'Entertaining as Mr. Lévy's book is, "Democracy in America" – 170 years old, and notoriously difficult to distil – still provides far greater insight into contemporary American democracy.'[37] Also in the *New York Times*, William Grimes thought that 'Tocqueville's shoes, and his footsteps, still look very large.' Although he admitted that 'Mr. Lévy is, in some ways, a good travelling companion', he went on: 'but because he lives almost entirely inside his head, he does a remarkably poor job at communicating the sights, sounds and smells of American life. There are many moments, riding in the car with him, that you want to tell him to shut up for five minutes and take a good look at what's out the window.' Before adding: 'He is lazy.'[38] In the *Boston Globe*, Alex Beam observed courteously: 'I can't take Lévy seriously at all.' Reading his first instalment in the *Atlantic*, the phrase 'Detroit, sublime Detroit' caused Beam to 'burst out laughing.'[39] The US press overflowed with digs of the same sort, without counting the mentions of sentences rendered incomprehensible by the heaping up of references, or meaningless montages of words. These are writing habits for which he is never held to account in France, although they have been a mainstay since the 1970s of what in Paris is called 'the BHL style'.

But the piece which undeniably did most damage appeared on the front page of the *New York Times Book Review* on 29 January 2006, from the pen of the journalist and humourist Garrison Keillor. After listing the people met by Bernard-Henri Lévy, Keillor adds: '... but there's nobody here whom you recognize. In more than 300 pages, nobody tells a joke. Nobody does much work. Nobody sits and eats and enjoys their food. You've lived all your life in America, never attended a mega-church or a brothel, don't own guns, are non-Amish, and it dawns on you that this is a book about the French.'[40] Keillor angrily pinpointed the book's platitudes, its commonplaces, its 'childlike love of paradox', its lists of rhetorical questions, before ending: 'Thanks, pal. I don't imagine France collapsing any day soon either. Thanks for coming. Don't let the door hit you on the way out. For your next book, tell us about those riots in France, the cars burning in the suburbs of Paris. What was all that about? Were fat people involved?' The same basic critique had been made elsewhere, but this very funny piece in a prestigious slot in the paper packed a resounding punch.

Typically, the attack elicited a two-phase response. Initially, American friends took up their pens in his defence. On 13 February 2006 Martin Peretz, then editor in chief of *New Republic* and an old friend, wrote an enthusiastic review of *American Vertigo*. Christopher Hitchens, another old friend, published a piece in *Slate* on the same day, headlined 'Garrison Keillor vulgarian. In defense of Bernard-Henri Lévy'.[41] This defence essentially consisted of spotting instances of francophobia in Garrison Keillor's article, which, horror of horrors, even went so far as to say: 'As always with French writers, Lévy is short on the facts, long on conclusions.'[42] This argument was developed by Bernard-Henri Lévy to invalidate Keillor's criticism (which had crossed the Atlantic, although in a low-key way): 'Just imagine Jean-Pierre Pernaut reviewing an American intellectual's book for *Le Monde des livres*,' he sneered.[43] It is true that Garrison Keillor is a radio presenter and a very popular journalist who has devoted books, and part of his career, to describing his home state Minnesota; but to compare him with the blandly avuncular, 'regionalist' TV newsreader Jean-Pierre Pernaut is merely insulting. Who in France, though, would dare to contradict Bernard-Henri Lévy? He went on: 'Is this the Midwest's reaction to an intellectual, foreign to boot, arriving to explain what an American is, where he comes from and what he can reasonably hope for? Is this the big symptom of francophobia I spent a year looking for without finding it, now being served up on a plate, but too late, the book being finished?'[44] Of course, it's francophobia ... what else could it possibly be?

But once again, never mind. The whole business raised some slight discussion in the US, sold in France as a nationwide controversy to make Bernard-Henri Lévy into the French intellectual that shook up the US. He has acquired a new dimension, enabling him to step outside a parochial French field that's too constricting for him. A syndication contract now ensures that his articles appear at the same time in the international press. BHL Inc. has become a multinational, and is going digital.

BHL 2.0

A 'DOUBLE WAR MACHINE'

'I am often credited in my country with having understood early on, thirty years ago, how to make "good use" of the media,' explained Bernard-Henri Lévy modestly to the *Herald Tribune*.

> That may be. But what seems to me far more certain, and something I am far more proud of, is having grasped, before many others, the marvellous uses of the Internet for an intellectual of my species; its effectiveness in the battle of ideas, its aptness for conserving and perpetuating the traces of individual thought against the grain. The Internet as the world's trash-can? The realm of the instantaneous and ephemeral? Quite the opposite: it's the marble of permanence, the great storehouse of the written word. And the friend, therefore, of reflection.[45]

By the standards of French intellectuals' comprehension of the Internet, Bernard-Henri Lévy is certainly rather advanced. In a milieu where the Web is often seen as a threat, the essayist deserves credit for never echoing that point of view or demonizing the Internet, unlike many other members of the French intelligentsia.

Nevertheless, when for example the question arises of the 'philosophy of transparency' championed by Wikileaks, he reverts to type: 'This is not a good philosophy, for two reasons. One, because information is never raw, it has to be processed. And two, because I am not sure we should enter a universe of absolute transparency where there would no longer be any secrets at all.' He concedes that there is some information which states should be forced to disclose, but 'to think that diplomacy ought to be some sort of glasshouse, that is totally wrong.'[46] Where it is apparent that the ultimate logic of the Internet could upset certain power relations, Bernard-Henri Lévy sides with the dominant discourse.

What he understands very well, on the other hand, is the use he can make of the Web for himself and the causes he wants to defend. In practical terms, however, this apprenticeship is quite recent. When we wrote the first version of this book in 2003–4, there was just one website dedicated to Bernard-Henri Lévy. It was run by an American academic, Liliane Lazar, who had painstakingly compiled and scanned all articles by, and about, the Master, established a chronology and produced some book reviews: touching and loyal, but a little amateurish. As for the man himself, he almost never mentioned digital matters, apart from confessing to a Google Alert on his name (which tells him every time there is new mention of his name on the search engine), to a taste for the best-seller lists on Amazon, and to his perplexity in dealing with the ranking of information in the online press. The tipping point came in 2009, after the failure of *Public Enemies*, his correspondence with Houellebecq. 'The book was very well received by the press, but slaughtered by the blogs in twenty-four hours. If you declare war on the Internet, you're dead; you can't attack a system like that, you have to get it on your side.'[47] And that is what Bernard-Henri Lévy has striven to do since then.

By 2011, the bernard-henri-levy.com site had had a complete makeover. Equipped with the latest content-sharing links (Twitter, Facebook, RSS), it gives access to a video or an article with a click or two. The content is wholly centred on Bernard-Henri Lévy. 'His news', 'His biography', 'His oeuvre' (with a link to fnac.com for easy book ordering), 'His philosophy'... Puzzled by this last tab, we clicked on it and were taken to a page with three new options: 'His universities', 'His teachers' and 'His concepts'; clicking randomly on 'concepts', we found a blank page with the words 'notices forthcoming'.[48] Good luck to whoever has the job of writing them. More links: 'His struggles', a 'Photo gallery' – most entertaining, especially the 'Unusual' section which includes three pix of Bernard-Henri Lévy with members of the New Zealand rugby team – and a 'video gallery', not forgetting the 'wikiBHL' containing small snippets on his connection to celebrated characters who have crossed his path directly or indirectly over thirty-five years. Under 'That day...'

we find sporadic accounts of some important day in Bernard-Henri Lévy's life (there are a lot of these). The home page is very regularly updated with the boss's latest op-ed piece, or the video of his latest TV appearance.

A second website, belonging to the review *La Règle du jeu*, serves as a backup platform for diffusing the latest interventions from Bernard-Henri Lévy (they are posted online jointly by both sites), leavened with a few efforts from collaborators (including 'Suivez Moix', the writer Yann Moix's extraordinarily barmy-seeming blog). Of the *Règle du jeu* site, the essayist told the *Herald Tribune* that it 'is in the process, on the Web, of becoming one of the very top online magazines of ideas in Europe, and in any case in France',[49] which is a bit of an overstatement. He was closer to the truth, at least in intention, when he told the journal that the two sites constitute a 'double war machine' for him. They are linked to two active Twitter accounts (@bernardhl and @laregledujeuorg), two Facebook profiles, one for the review and one for Bernard-Henri Lévy (the latter assigned the status of 'local enterprise', displaying considerable modesty), and a 'chain' on Dailymotion, a video-sharing site à la YouTube.

A NEW 'BUSINESS ANGEL'

Bernard-Henri Lévy owes this new lease of life on the Web to a young man he calls his 'friend', Internet whizz-kid Jean-Baptiste Descroix-Vernier: a precocious entrepreneur who now runs Rentabiliweb, a company specializing in the monetization of access to Internet services and data banks. His general style and positions, for example against the Hadopi law seeking to protect copyright on the Net, give him a typical hacker's image; in reality, associated with the billionaire Bernard Arnault, Vivendi boss Jean-Marie Messier and the reality-TV producer Stéphane Courbit, he is an Internet merchant known for his aggressive methods. He and his teams helped set up the two websites. Bernard-Henri Lévy has often sung his praises (for example when the businessman helped him launch an internet campaign against the election of the Egyptian Farouk Hosni as head of UNESCO) and sprung to his defence.

Thus when, in November 2009, a Rentabiliweb subsidiary organized in the middle of Paris, as a promotional event, a handout of banknotes which was cancelled at the last minute, causing a riot, the champion of the oppressed came up with a paragraph in his regular 'bloc-notes' in *Le Point*.

> He [Jean-Baptiste Descroix-Vernier] whose great pride is the foundation he set up to bring aid, in Europe and outside it, to the poorest of the poor, he whose credo posits a more ethical Internet whose honour will be in serving just causes (how many crusades have I embarked on through, in particular, the site he conceived to archive my positions and my texts!): here he is being depicted as a greedy monster, a pornocrat, when he is not being called an 'exploiter of social deprivation'.[50]

The relationship with Descroix-Vernier enabled Bernard-Henri Lévy to acquire yet another new function, as a 'business angel'. In June 2011 the site *owni.fr* was going through a difficult recapitalization. Founded two years earlier, OWNI is a new kind of information site, run by journalists and developers of what is starting to be called 'data-journalism'. From its creation onward the site (edited and developed by social media company 22Mars) attracted attention and generated interest, but its business model, as with much of the online press, is fragile; and early in the summer of 2011, it needed cash.

Here is what Bernard-Henri Lévy said in his 'bloc-notes' of 30 June 2011:

> One swallow doesn't make a summer, but this is a good story. The story of an online medium, OWNI, which is, with others of its kind, the pride of the French-language Internet. ... Its boss, Nicolas Voisin, disclosed one fine morning that his company, although prosperous, was in peril and that its natural investors were dropping out. At once an idea came to me. A simple idea. Very simple. But one that would work. ... And thus it was, without investment banker or stockbroker or any other grasping Godfather, that there swung into action, with a couple of Skype calls and in less time than it takes to tell it, in a spontaneous chain of solidarity, and to tell the truth almost without words, the most fraternal and surely the quickest fundraiser in the history of the Internet. From Xavier Niel to Marc Simoncini and Jean-Baptiste Descroix Vernier, from Patrick Bertrand to Stéphane Distinguin and the boss of Wikio, all the emblems of the Net were there, its princes and its musketeers, its marshals of the empire to come and its young guard, its rebels and its veterans, its big-hearted corsairs and its institutionalized figures – and the result was that, yes, OWNI pulled through. A lesson in practical fraternity. A lesson for today. And a notice given to yesterday's world.[51]

The OWNI founder let it be known that it was Descroix-Vernier who played the role of intermediary, and that Bernard-Henri Lévy had given 20,000 of the 200,000 euros raked in by the site in the operation. Mere details, however: the point is that Bernard-Henri Lévy saved OWNI.

The story is no trivial anecdote. Bernard-Henri Lévy – shareholder in *Libération*, member of the supervisory boards of *Le Monde* and Arte, diarist in *Le Point* and friend of its proprietor, friend of the founder of *Le Nouvel Observateur*, of the owner of *Paris Match*, *Le Journal du dimanche* and *Elle*, whose diaries are syndicated in the *Huffington Post* and *El País* – Bernard-Henri Lévy, in 'a couple of Skype calls', brings together all the IT millionaires in France and becomes the saviour and one of the shareholders of a news site thought by many to be a possible player in the future of information. The story was all over the French Internet inside a day. Does this tell you anything? The world may change, but Bernard-Henri Lévy remains the same.

CONCLUSION: THE RIDICULOUSNESS OF POWER

This book is not a biography. We are not denouncing a problem of personality, dress style, dishevelled ego or inherited wealth. It is a problem of oligarchy, and it is a French problem: an amazing concentration of power in the hands of a few individuals, placed at the junction of the economic, political and cultural domains. Writer, publisher, businessman, heir, journalist, media intellectual, adviser to politicians: Bernard-Henri Lévy is the fortunate beneficiary of French society's elitism and the mirror of its dysfunctions. By dint of conflicts of interest and cronyism, you scratch my back I'll scratch yours, little compromises and the destruction-testing of weak links, a privileged class maintains dominance over the rest. A national bourgeoisie whose deftness in mobilizing as a social class in pursuit of its own interests was laid bare in 2010 by the sociologists Michel Pinçon and Monique Pinçon-Charlot.[1] The BHLian saga is embedded in that highly specific landscape.

But the writer plays an altogether singular role there. He is both an active member of that world and its 'soul masseur'. His job is to erect a modest partition to screen off from the rest of us that incessant, petty cooking up of arrangements between friends. On that screen he projects the great spectacle of a world in uproar. Diverted attention guaranteed, but there are effects of meaning too: presenting themselves as beavering away in support of Western universalism is a way for the elites of countries in economic and political decline, the former European colonial powers, to continue to imagine they are the centre of the world. And entangled with the blockbusting spectacle of the right to humanitarian intervention, with its unblinking acceptance of such contradictions as war in the name of human rights, is another discourse, more ambiguous and deeply buried: fear of the people, of justice, of rival power sources, of anything that might force an explanation, a reckoning of accounts. This discourse too helps to justify our undemocratic system.

But structures, however dominant, are not the whole story. Bernard-Henri Lévy has not regularly escaped criticism for more than three decades simply because he has the president of the Republic's mobile number and dines with captains of industry. It is also because he is ridiculous. His repeated mistakes, his Botul howler, his comic rage with pie-throwers, his pretentiousness, his sweeping declarations, the way he takes himself so seriously when his oeuvre is as shallow as a puddle ... all that makes people laugh. He's too ludicrous, too trivial to justify public criticism by anyone really up to the job. That relative absence of challenge has helped the ex-New Philosopher to build a media career on the foundation of an overrated – but uncontested – intellectual reputation.

Is there a 'right to make an arse of oneself' (as claimed by the journalist Jean-François Kahn, to excuse himself for having described Dominique Strauss-Kahn's alleged sexual assault on Nafissatou Diallo as 'tumbling a chambermaid')? One can only conclude that there is. The French intellectual elite seem to enjoy a professional impunity of which the common wage-earner can only dream. Their errors of analysis, their wrong predictions, their biased arguments are almost never met with retribution. Getting fired is not a threat in the land of media intellectuals. Nor does the compulsory retirement age apply. Sixty-five, seventy, eighty years old: they shrivel under their sun lamps and still find television programmes and radio shows to welcome them for the space of a sound bite on one of the day's hot stocks in the current-events exchange.

It could go on for ever. 'BHL', a phoenix of the society of the spectacle, has died and risen again several times already. Michel Foucault, in his 1974–5 lectures at the Collège de France, talked about 'clown' government and 'ridiculous authority'. Seeing an essential mechanism of power in the fact of an individual possessing a power for which his intrinsic qualities ought to disqualify him, he gives the example of Roman emperors: 'the person who possessed *majestas*, that is to say, more power than any other power was, at the same time, in his person, his character, and his physical reality, in his costume, his gestures, his body, his sexuality and his way of life, a despicable, grotesque, and ridiculous individual.'[2]

Does that remind you of anyone? An improbably glossy look, white shirt, shades, highly-polished shoes and perfectly pressed suit in the middle of the Libyan desert or among ragged Darfuri refugees? Bare chest bristling under the fabric, whether its owner is calling on Iranian youth to rise against Ahmadinejad or sitting on the supervisory board of *Le Monde*? In Foucault's view, grotesque power is the basis of arbitrary sovereignty, for the absurdity, far from weakening the authority, maximizes its effects. For the king to be a clown demonstrates the 'unavoidable quality', the 'inevitability' of power. Applied to the field of thought, Foucault continues, that boils down to conferring unrestrained power on a parody of scientific discourse. A fake philosopher without a concept to his name, a committed intellectual so often ranged with the big battalions, Bernard-Henri Lévy is made for the parodic register; and his readers play their part willy-nilly in the collective caricature.

EPILOGUE

Bernard-Henri Lévy did not deign to grant any of our requests for interviews, or to answer any of the questions we wanted to put to him. So we have taken the liberty of imagining what he might have said to us.

I predicted their reappearance long ago.

And now they have come. Out of the shadows. The prowlers. The thought police. At last they are showing their true face, the face of a populism one had thought consigned to the darkest hours of History. Make no mistake. These people do not love freedom. How well I know it, having always denounced that petty moralism of facts and precision! How many totalitarianisms would still be flourishing, had we waited to be sure before speaking! I carry the cry of wounded men who fall without knowing where the bullet struck them. We thought we had at last proved that urgency doesn't encumber itself with the pettifogging scruples of all the Norpois of our age.

Am I so naive? Am I so ridiculous? Perhaps, if they say so. But when we were the same age as those sniggering sermonizers, it was the Gulag we were attacking: it was the dumb and cold barbed wire scarring Europe that we were trying to pull out with our bare hands. At the same age that I was looking Barbarism in the eye, they are setting about a man with his back turned and his gaze fixed on darkening horizons where columns of black smoke signal massacres to come.

They don't like my books, that's their right.

Am I hurt? Good God no! Not for myself. I no longer hear, in my own case, the foul murmur of calumny that hisses, swells and grows before my eyes. I no longer see the grinning scorpions preparing to launch their stings. For thirty-five years now they have had it in for me.

But I suffer – I am forced to say it, I who so loathe talking about myself – I suffer for those I care for. For A., whose eyes mist over so quickly when she fears that I am faltering. For J., whom I had hoped would be spared the poisonous darts of her father's enemies for somewhat longer. For J.-P. E. who, had he been in my place – but life, alas, decided otherwise – would have confronted with panache those low blows that are the common lot of intellectuals.

For the reproaches levelled at me today had already been levelled at others. Michel Foucault, Jean-Paul Sartre, Romain Gary, all of them before me had to endure the gaze of a bloodthirsty crowd standing on tiptoe to miss none of the execution. Terrorists of the gaze, eternally will we be hated for pointing out the truth. All intellectuals know this.

Needless to say I will not trouble to respond to this heap of filthy calumnies and infamous gossip. The injunction to transparency is the first law of totalitarianism. I will not buckle. But there is the truth of History, and on some points at least I would like, if it please the court, to explain myself. You want facts? You shall have them.

One charge is that I never met Massoud in 1981. That I embellished on reality. That I 'reconstructed', as they say in their all too recognizable lingo of people who have done-a-year-of-psychology-then-a-master's-in-sociology-and-who-adore-Bourdieu-because-he-talks-of-the-world-we-live-in. Yes, it's true, on my return from Afghanistan, it was commander Amin who designated me – one night, huddled around a flickering candle, as he drew in the sand the advance of the Russian troops – the bearer of a message for France: 'Say my name,' he whispered, in a voice strangely reminiscent of that of Jean Moulin. 'Tell your people that far, far from Paris live men who will roll back the tanks of Barbarism with rifles from ancient wars. Tell that to your people, Bernard-Henri my friend.'

Back in France, I therefore talked about Amin. I spoke of the battles of those men, those Afghan peasants transformed into heroes by the death of a friend or loved one, those near-bandits who, in their bare and arid mountains, fight on by throwing stones when they are out of cartridges. I explained and I believe, in all modesty, that I was heard a little. But what I did not say was that, on the same night that Amin gave me the message, as the lugubrious booms of Russian mortars still resounded in the distance, sitting in the shadows hardly touched by the wavering light, the gaze of another man was seeking mine. In his hands he held the *Mémoires* of General de Gaulle that I had given him some hours earlier upon emerging from an ambush during which – yes, I admit it – I had been afraid, and there had appeared to me fleetingly in the dust kicked up by a bullet the bared shoulder of D., whom I feared for the space of an instant I would not see again. The man staring at me so intensely, with the piercing gaze of a bird of prey accustomed to spotting a Russian uniform hidden among the rocks of the Afghan mountains, that man to whom, in the four days we spent with the mujahideen, I had hardly spoken – that man who on our departure took me in his arms as one clasps a brother – that man was Ahmad Shah Massoud.

And even, even if sometimes it has, perhaps, happened that, betrayed by memory in which wars mingle and meld together, I have confused two places, two men, two facts: would I deserve such opprobrium? I think again of Lazareff asking Blaise Cendrars, author of *The Prose of the Trans-Siberian*: 'But Blaise, did you ever really take the Trans-Siberian?' And I can still hear Cendrars answering in his shrill and cheerful voice: 'Who cares, if I've made millions of other people take it!'

On pain of their displeasure, I am a philosopher of truth. Not Kant's truth, which as Jean-Pierre Lapeste demonstrated in a lecture delivered on a nudist beach in Caracas on the eve of the First World War, is a post-transcendental exactitude. Not the totalitarian truth of Plato at the time of the *Republic*. My truth, the truth I insist is effective in the sense that a gesture is effective, is that of Nietzsche in his last days starting to doubt the reality of the real and entrusting himself to the 'reality of the dream', that of Lacan when he was talking about the 'truth of the false', the truth whose existence Althusser revealed to me one day when, as we were conversing beside the pool at the École normale supérieure from which some goldfish thoughtfully observed our conversation, he told me with a sigh in which I sensed the foreshadowing of a future frightful crime: 'Turn it into a weapon, give it the form suitable to that employment.'

NOTES

PREFACE

1 Philippe Cohen, *BHL, une biographie*, Fayard, Paris, 2005; Nicolas Beau and Olivier Toscer, *Une imposture française*, Les Arènes, 2006; Richard Labévière and Bruno Jeanmart, *Bernard-Henri Lévy ou la règle du je*, Le Temps des cerises, Paris, 2007; Daniel Bensaïd, *B-H Lévy, un nouveau théologien*, Lignes, Paris, 2008.

2 Katha Pollitt, 'Dear France, we're so over', *Nation*, 13 June 2011.

1 THE POPE OF SAINT-GERMAIN-DE-PRÉS

1 bernard-henri-levy.com.

2 Marc Villemain, *Monsieur Lévy*, Plon, Paris, 2003.

3 'La *RDJ* par Bernard-Henri Lévy', laregledujeu.org.

4 Laurent Dispot, 'L'évitement "Lévy te ment"', *La Règle du jeu*, 20th anniversary issue, 2010.

5 'Anniversaire de *La Règle du jeu*: les dessous de la fête', laregledujeu.org, 2 December 2010.

6 'Les vingt ans de *La Règle du jeu*, *TV Saint-Germain*, pariswebtvquartier.fr, December 2010.

7 Joan Juliet Buck, 'France's prophet provocateur', *Vanity Fair*, January 2003.

8 Bertrand Monnard, 'BHL et Arielle Dombasle: la fin d'une belle histoire?', *Le Matin dimanche*, 5 June 2010.

9 Derek Blasberg, 'The Real Daphne Guinness', *Harper's Bazaar*, 11 February 2011.

10 Ibid.

11 *Voici*, 14 April 2011.

12 'Exclusif', TF1, 1 October 2001.

13 Bernard-Henri Lévy, *Le Lys et la Cendre: Journal d'un écrivain au temps de la guerre en Bosnie*, Grasset, Paris, 1996, p. 20.

14 Bernard-Henri Lévy, *Récidives*, Grasset, Paris, 2004, p. 914.

15 See the survey by Béatrice Peyrani, 'Marrakech, l'argent et le plaisir', *Le Point*, 22–28 July 2004.

16 Benoît Jacquot, 'Andrée Putman, une maison à Tanger', documentary broadcast on France 5, 7 June 2007.

17 'Vivement dimanche', France 2, 11 November 2001.

18 On 20 June 1993.

19 *Paris Match*, 25 June–1 July 1993.

20 Quoted by Marie-Dominique Lelièvre, 'Une romance', *Libération*, 9 August 1996.

21 Quoted in Bernard-Henri Lévy, *Comédie*, Grasset, Paris, 1997 (reprinted Livre de poche, Paris, 2000, p. 32).

22 *Paris Match*, 7–13 February 1986.

23 Ibid., 20 March 1987.

24 Ibid., 17 August 1984.

25 Ibid., 29 June 1989.

26 See notably: *Comédie*; *Réflexions sur la guerre, le mal et la fin de l'Histoire*; *Récidives*.

27 Lévy, *Comédie*, p. 111.

28 Ibid., p. 71.

29 Lévy, *Récidives*, p. 911.

30 Lelièvre, 'Une romance'.

31 *Paris Match*, 26 September–2 October 2002.

32 'Vivement dimanche', presented by Michel Drucker, France 2, 11 November 2001.

33 'Pourquoi j'épouse BHL', interview by Guillemette de Sairigne, *Le Figaro Madame*, 19–25 June 1993.

34 On PBS, 13 September 2006.

35 *Libération*, 23 September 2006.

36 Stephen Holden, 'A French singer arrives, trailing a Big Band and a lot of buildup', *New York Times*, 21 September 2006.

37 Maurice Clavel, 'Ces "nouveaux philosophes" dont je suis le "tonton"', *Paris Match*, 17–23 June 1977.

38 'Justine Lévy et Raphaël Enthoven, vingt ans chacun et l'amour pour la vie', *Paris Match*, 3–9 October 1996.

39 Virginie Lewis, 'Le grand rendez-vous de Justine Lévy', *Le Figaro*, 19 September 1996.

40 Justine Lévy, *Rien de grave*, Stock, Paris, 2004.

41 *Paris Match*, 4–10 March 2004.
42 *Le Nouvel Observateur*, 18–24 March 2004.
43 'Vol de nuit', presented by Patrick Poivre d'Arvor, TF1, 22 March 2004.
44 *La Revue des deux mondes*, July–August 2004.
45 Lévy, *Rien de grave*, p. 115.
46 Ariane Chemin, 'La littérature, arme d'une douce vengeance', *Le Monde*, 9 April 2004.
47 Nicolas Sarkozy, *Georges Mandel, le moine de la politique*, Grasset, Paris, 1994.
48 *Le Journal du dimanche*, 5 December 2010.
49 Quoted in Nicolas Baulieu, *Grasset, un combat*, documentary broadcast on La Cinquième, 3 February 2002.
50 Marc Lambron, 'BHL: les feux de la rampe', *Le Point*, 14–20 November 1992.
51 Alexis Liebaert, 'Un homme d'influence sort de l'ombre', *L'Évènement du jeudi*, 26 September–2 October 1996.
52 'Le bloc-notes de Bernard-Henri Lévy', *Le Point*, 31 August–6 September 2001.
53 See Lambron, 'BHL: les feux de la rampe', an article that, ten days before the première of Bernard-Henri Lévy's play *Le Jugement dernier*, speaks of the excited rumours in the Paris air and delivers a long paean to the play, which (hardly surprisingly) he has not yet seen. See also *Le Point* of 10–16 February 1996.
54 'Le bloc-notes de Bernard-Henri Lévy', *Le Point*, 6–12 September 2002.
55 Ibid.
56 Ibid., 5–11 September 2003.
57 Ibid., 15–21 February 2002.
58 Ibid., 2–8 November 2001.
59 Ibid., 16–22 March 2001.
60 Ibid., 8–14 February 2002 and 16–22 May 2003.
61 Ibid., 18–24 October 2002.
62 Ibid., 14–20 November 2003.
63 Ibid., 13–19 December 2002.
64 Ibid., 18–24 June 1999.

2 AN IMPRESSIVE NETWORK OF INFLUENCE

1 Bernard-Henri Lévy, *Barbarism with a Human Face*, Harper and Row, 1979, p. 193.
2 'Quel avenir pour les intellectuels?', conversation between Alain Peyrefitte and Bernard-Henri Lévy, *Le Figaro Littéraire*, 6 April 1987.

3 Nicolas Beau, 'Dans les cuisines du Bernard-Henri-Lévisme', *Le Nouvel Économiste*, 7–13 January 1994.
4 Lévy, *Le Lys et la Cendre*, p. 29.
5 Lévy, *Récidives*, p. 538.
6 'The *Playboy* Interview: Bernard-Henri Lévy, interview with the leading light of young French philosophy', *Playboy*, May 1977.
7 Ibid.
8 *Le Point*, 11–17 March 1991.
9 Statement by deputy spokesman at the Quai d'Orsay, Paris, 15 February 2002.
10 Lévy, *Récidives*, p. 835.
11 'Le bloc-notes de Bernard-Henri Lévy', *Le Point*, 22–28 February 2002.
12 Interview with the authors, June 2004.
13 Raphaëlle Bacqué and Ariane Chemin, *La Femme fatale*, Albin Michel, Paris, 2007, p. 160.
14 Bernard-Henri Lévy, 'Les deux destins de Ségolène Royal', *Le Point*, 23 November 2006.
15 Lévy, *Ce grand cadavre à la renverse*, p. 157.
16 Bernard-Henri Lévy, 'Dinner with Ségolène', *Wall Street Journal*, 8 February 2007 (in French in Bernard-Henri Lévy, *Pièces d'identité*, Grasset, Paris, 2010, p. 977).
17 Lévy, *Ce grand cadavre à la renverse*, p. 159 (JH trans).
18 Lévy, 'Dinner with Ségolène' (*Pièces d'identité*, p. 92).
19 Bacqué and Chemin, *La Femme fatale*, p. 161.
20 The AFP cable announcing the appointment is dated 30 June 1993.
21 Sophie Coignard, *La Vendetta française*, Albin Michel, Paris, 2003, p. 222.
22 Ibid.
23 'Le bloc-notes de Bernard-Henri Lévy', *Le Point*, 2–8 January 2004.
24 Ibid., 5–11 February 2004.
25 Devorah Lauter, 'Philosopher Bernard-Henri Lévy speaks of his role in France's push against Kaddafi', *Los Angeles Times*, 17 April 2011.
26 Lévy, *Left in Dark Times*, p. 10.
27 Ludovic Vigogne, 'BHL-Sarkozy, réconciliation pour la Libye', *Paris Match*, 24 March 2011.
28 Lévy, *Left in Dark Times*, p. 10.
29 Ibid., p. xiv. (Tr. note: incorrectly rendered as 'pitchfork' in the Random House English translation.)
30 Ibid., p. xv.
31 Eric Aeschimann, 'Le roi de l'arène', *Libération*, 8 October 2007.

32 'BHL face à *Marianne*', *Marianne*, 6 February 2010.
33 Nicolas Sarkozy, *Testimony: France in the Twenty-First Century*, Pantheon Books, New York, 2007.
34 Bernard-Henri Lévy, 'New-Look Bonaparte', *New York Times*, 22 July 2007.
35 Ibid.
36 Julien Martin, 'Pour Guaino, BHL est un "petit con prétentieux"', *Rue89*, 9 October 2007.
37 Notably in his 'bloc-notes', *Le Point*, 9 October 2007.
38 Sylvie Santini, 'La plume du président jette le masque', *Paris Match*, 31 October 2007.
39 *Le Monde*, 2 September 2009.
40 *Le Monde*, 4 September 2009.
41 'Henri Guaino: les dessous de l'attaque', linternaute.com, October 2007.
42 Quoted by *Le Monde*, 24 June 2009.
43 Ibid.
44 Quoted by Beau, 'Dans les cuisines du Bernard-Henri-Lévisme'.
45 Quoted by Antoine De Baecque, 'Héraut de l'histoire', *Libération*, 22 July 2004.
46 Xavier Debontride, 'Bernard-Henri Lévy défend l'indépendance de Becob', *Les Échos*, 27 November 1995.
47 Beau and Toscer, *Une imposture française.*
48 Ibid., p. 71.
49 Bertrand Fraysse, 'La vérité sur ... les amis providentiels de BHL', *Challenges*, no. 191, 12 December 2002.
50 'Matériaux + Becob racheté par Pinault-Printemps-Redoute', *La Tribune*, 3 September 1997.
51 Press release from the Pinault-Printemps-Redoute group, 2 September 1997.
52 Quoted by Frédéric Dupuis, *Enquête de personnalité*, documentary broadcast on Canal Plus, 27 January 2003.
53 Pascal Tournier, 'BHL, ombre et lumière', *VSD*, 13–18 May 2004.
54 Fraysse, 'La vérité sur... les amis providentiels de BHL'.
55 Michel Frois, *La Révélation de Casablanca*, Atlantica, Biarritz, 1999, p. 147.
56 Extract K(2), registry of the Paris Tribunal de commerce.
57 Ibid.
58 Ibid.
59 Figure given by Fraysse, 'La verité sur ... les amis providentiels de BHL'.
60 François Vignolle, 'Délit d'initié: B.-H.L. se défend', *Le Parisien*, 22 November 2000.
61 Tournier, 'BHL, ombre et lumière'.

62 In May 1995 PPR had made a takeover bid for the Suez group, aborted in the face of objections by Suez shareholders and government opposition. Jacques Chirac and his economy minister Alain Madelin were against it.
63 'Le bloc-notes de Bernard-Henri Lévy', *Le Point*, 17 June 1995.
64 Pierre-Angel Gay and Caroline Monnot, *François Pinault, les secrets d'une incroyable fortune*, Balland, Paris, 1999, p. 184.
65 Comment made by François Pinault on the programme 'Vivement dimanche', France 2, 11 November 2001.
66 Gay and Monnot, *François Pinault*, pp. 185–6.
67 Ibid., p. 184.
68 Ibid., p. 186.
69 For more details, see ibid.
70 'Vivement dimanche', France 2, 11 November 2001.
71 Lévy, 'Pour saluer Jean-Luc Lagardère', *Récidives*, p. 677.
72 'Le bloc-notes de Bernard-Henri Lévy', *Le Point*, 9–15 November 1996.
73 Ibid., 5–11 May 2000.
74 'Le bloc-notes de Bernard-Henri Lévy'. *Le Point*, 4–10 October 2002.
75 Dupuis, *Enquête de personnalité*.
76 Ibid.
77 Erwan Poiraud, 'Chronique d'un retour en grâce médiatique: à propos de Bernard-Henri Lévy', *Les Cahiers de LaRA*, no. 1, March 2004.
78 'En Éthiopie, l'Occident est cocu', interview with Gilles Hertzog, *Paris Match*, 24–30 October 1986.
79 'BHL: il faut ressusciter Kaboul', interview with Jérôme Béglé, *Paris Match*, 4–10 April 2002.
80 'The *Playboy* Interview: Bernard-Henri Lévy'.
81 See the critical deciphering of the campaign written in the heat of the moment by Emmanuel Poncet, 'Un "promauteur" surexposé', *Libération*, 14 February 1997.
82 *Paris Match*, 30 January–5 February 1997.
83 *Le Figaro Magazine*, 1–7 February 1997.
84 *Le Point*, 1–7 February 1997.
85 *L'Évènement du jeudi*, 13–19 February 1997.
86 Quoted in Poncet, 'Un "promauteur" surexposé'.
87 *La Règle du jeu*, no. 23, October 2003.
88 Alain Delon was on TF1's '7 sur 7' programme on 2 February. On 9 February, Bernard-Henri Lévy was the guest on FR3's '19/20'. A few minutes later Arielle Dombasle was on France 2 in Jean-Luc Delarue's 'Déjà le retour'. On Monday 11 February Bernard-Henri Lévy was the guest of 'Nulle part ailleurs' on Canal Plus. The same evening, Arielle Dombasle participated

in 'Cercle de minuit' on France 2. The next morning, Bernard-Henri Lévy was the guest of Pierre Bouteiller on France Inter. A few days later, Jacques Chancel received him in 'Ligne de mire' on France 3.

89 Source: Bibliothèque du film, bifi.fr .

90 Françoise Giroud, 'La cabale contre BHL', *Le Figaro*, 17 February 1997.

3 IN SEARCH OF THE LOST OEUVRE

1 Geneviève Brisac, 'La collection comme cheval de Troie', *Le Monde*, 21 March 1985.

2 'L'être, c'est la lettre', interview with Marianne Dubertret, *La Vie*, 1–7 July 2004.

3 Bernard-Henri Lévy, *Bangla-Desh, nationalisme dans la révolution*, Maspero, Paris, 1973, p. 7.

4 Bernard-Henri Lévy, *L'Idéologie française*, Le Livre de poche, Paris, 1999, p. 15.

5 Pierre Milza, *Fascisme français, passé et présent,* Flammarion, 'Champs' collection, Paris, 1987.

6 Raymond Aron, *Mémoires*, Robert Laffont, Paris, 2003 (reprint), p. 706. The allusion is to the public prosecutor during the Great Terror.

7 Lévy, *L'Idéologie française*, p. 13.

8 Tr. note: a charity founded by the comedian Coluche that distributes food to the poor.

9 Alain Finkielkraut, *La Défaite de la pensée*, Gallimard, Paris, 1987.

10 See on this matter Dupuis, *Enquête de personnalité.*

11 Bernard-Henri Lévy, *American Vertigo*, Livre de poche, Paris, 2007, p. 76.

12 Glyn Morgan, 'Bernard-Henri Lévy en Amérique, le récit touristique d'un voyageur poli', *Le Monde diplomatique*, March 2006.

13 Quoted in *Le Figaro*, 2 March 2006.

14 *Vogue Hommes*, November 1984.

15 Michel Houellebecq and Bernard-Henri Lévy, *Public Enemies*, trans. M. Frendo and F. Wynne, Random House, New York (paperback), 2011, p.3.

16 Lévy, *Le Lys et la Cendre*, p. 7.

17 On 13, 20, and 27 March, and 3 April, 1991.

18 *Les Aventures de la liberté*, *IV*, 'La fin des prophètes', broadcast on Antenne 2 on 3 April 1991 (quoted in Poiraud,'Chronique d'un retour en grâce médiatique').

19 Bernard-Henri Lévy, *Les Aventures de la liberté. Une histoire subjective des intellectuels*, Livre de poche, Paris, 1993, p. 11. *Adventures on the Freedom Road: The French Intellectuals in the 20th Century*, translated by Richard Vaisey, Harvill, London, 1995, p. 2.

20 Lévy, *Comédie*, p. 70.
21 Bernard-Henri Lévy, *Réflexions sur la guerre, le mal et la fin de l'Histoire*, Grasset, Paris, 2001 (reprinted Livre de poche, Paris, 2003).
22 Bernard-Henri Lévy, *War, Evil and the End of History*, Melville House Publishing, New York, 2004; Duckworth, London, 2004.
23 'Le bloc-notes de Bernard-Henri Lévy', *Le Point*, 4–10 January 2002.
24 For example, 'Conversation avec Frédéric Beigbeder' (in Lévy, *Pièces d'identité. Questions de principe XI,* Grasset, Paris, 2010). In fact it is a reprint of an interview published by the magazine *GQ* in February 2009.
25 *Elle*, 3 May 2004.
26 Quoted by Nicolas Beau, 'Dans les cuisines du Bernard-Henri-Lévisme', *Le Nouvel Economiste*, 7–13 January 1994.
27 Lévy, *Récidives*, p. 206.
28 Bernard-Henri Lévy, *La Pureté dangereuse*, Grasset, Paris, 1994
29 Françoise Giroud and Bernard-Henri Lévy, *Les Hommes et les femmes*, Olivier Orban, Paris, 1993.
30 Pierre Bourdieu, *Les Règles de l'art. Genèse et structure du champ littéraire*, Seuil, Paris, 1992, p. 544.
31 Lévy, *Bangla-Desh, nationalisme dans la révolution*, p. 84.
32 Quoted in Lévy, *Récidives*, p. 507.
33 'Pierre Vidal-Naquet réplique à Bernard-Henri Lévy', *Le Nouvel Observateur*, 25–30 June 1979.
34 Bernard-Henri Lévy, 'La nostalgie des clercs', *Le Nouvel Observateur*, 16–21 July 1979.
35 Interview with the authors, May 2004.
36 'Le bloc-notes de Bernard-Henri Lévy', *Le Point*, 21–27 June 2001.
37 Lévy, *Récidives*, p. 845.
38 Bernard-Henri Lévy, 'Des armes pour la Bosnie', *Le Monde*, 23 December 1992.
39 Lévy, *Le Lys et la Cendre*, p. xxx.
40 Under the heading 'La honte', in Lévy, *Récidives*, p. 577.
41 'Le bloc-notes de Bernard-Henri Lévy', *Le Point*, 8–14 November 2003.
42 Lévy, *Comédie*, p. 41.
43 Bernard-Henri Lévy, 'Nous vivons dans une époque non héroïque', interview with Danièle Brison and Daniel Riot, *Les Dernières Nouvelles d'Alsace*, 10 November 1984.
44 'Le Masque et la Plume', France Inter, 13 May 2004.
45 See everywhere. Tr. note: Commonplace in French, such phrases generally read badly in English when the word 'me' is used, even with a suitable inversion of order e.g. 'Me, I believe that …' So they sometimes appear in

translation with words like 'personally' or 'myself' inserted. In fact, since the 'me' is usually superfluous, it can often simply be omitted.

46 Lévy, *Adventures on the Freedom Road*, p. 131.

47 Lévy, *Comédie*, chapter 5.

48 Lévy, *Récidives*, pp. 525–6.

49 Bernard-Henri Lévy, *Les Indes rouges*, Le Livre de poche, 'Biblio Essais' collection, Paris, 1985, p. 7.

50 'The *Playboy* Interview'.

51 Lévy, *Les Indes rouges*, p. 7.

52 Interview with the authors, May 2004.

4 THE PHONEY PHILOSOPHER

1 Quoted in *Le Nouvel Observateur*, 12–18 May 1994.

2 'Arrêt sur image', La Cinquième, 23 March 1996.

3 'En aparté', Canal Plus, 3 November 2001.

4 Claude Jannoud, 'La grande colère des nouveaux philosophes', *Le Figaro*, 16 May 1977.

5 Lucien Bodard, 'Bernard-Henri Lévy ne veut pas du bon côté du manche', *France-Soir*, 6 July 1977.

6 André Frossard, 'La Barbarie à visage humain', *Le Point*, 2–8 May 1977.

7 Pierrette Rosset and Françoise Ducout, 'Vous aimez lire?', *Elle*, 25–31 July 1977.

8 'L'Homme en question', presented by Anne Sinclair, FR3, November 1977.

9 Maurice Clavel, 'Ces "nouveaux philosophes" dont je suis le "tonton"', *Paris Match*, 17–23 June 1977.

10 Maurice Clavel, 'Un inquiétant jeune homme', *Le Nouvel Observateur*, 5–11 December 1977.

11 Open letter to Bernard-Henri Lévy and published in *Les Nouvelles Littéraires*, 26 May–1 June 1977.

12 Graf Zeppelin, 'Misère de la philosophie', *Rouge*, 28 May 1977.

13 Max Gallo, 'Le Maître, le Mal, Marx et Mao', *L'Express*, 16–22 May 1977.

14 Louis Pauwels, 'Nouveaux philosophes et vieilles questions', *Le Figaro*, 16 May 1977.

15 *Libération*, 27 May 1977.

16 Jean-Marie Benoist, *Marx est mort*, Gallimard, Paris, 1970.

17 André Glucksmann, *La Cuisinière et le mangeur d'hommes*, Seuil, Paris, 1975.

18 Christian Jambet and Guy Lardreau, *L'Ange*, Grasset, Paris, 1976.

19 Raymond Aron, *Mémoires*, Robert Laffont, Paris, 2003 (reprint), p. 705.

20 Broadcast on 30 July 1977.
21 Or so Bernard-Henri Lévy claims in 'Autobiography, four: Mexico' (in *War, Evil and the End of History*). True story or massaged memory? The point here is the legend of an impassioned polemic, a new Battle of Hernani.
22 Extract from the dust-jacket blurb of the Livre de poche reprint edition.
23 Lévy, *Barbarism with a Human Face*, p. 1.
24 Guy Lardreau, *Singe d'or*, Mercure de France, Paris, 1973.
25 'The *Playboy* interview: Bernard-Henri Lévy'.
26 François Aubral and Xavier Delcourt, *Contre la nouvelle philosophie*, Gallimard, Paris, 1977.
27 *Le Nouvel Observateur*, 26 January–1 February 1981.
28 'Boîte aux lettres', broadcast presented by Jérôme Garcin, FR3, 1 May 1983.
29 *États généraux de la philosophie, 16 et 17 Juin 1979*, Flammarion, 'Champs' collection, Paris, 1979, p. 40.
30 Ibid., p. 205.
31 See Claude Lefort, *Un homme en trop. Réflexions sur* L'Archipel du Goulag, Seuil, Paris, 1976; and Cornelius Castoriadis, *L'Institution imaginaire de la société*, Seuil, Paris, 1975.
32 Jean-Pierre Le Goff, *Mai 68, l'héritage impossible*, La Découverte, Paris, 1998, pp. 397–8 (paperback reprint, 2002).
33 Ibid., p. 408.
34 '19-20', France 3, 4 August 2008.
35 Philippe Cohen, *BHL, une biographie*, Fayard, Paris, 2005.
36 LCI, 4 August 2008.
37 Lévy, *Barbarism with a Human Face*, p. ix.
38 Interview with the authors, June 2004.
39 On this topic, see Rémi Rieffel, 'L'édition de sciences humaines et sociales', in Pascal Fouche (ed.), *L'Édition française depuis 1945*, Éditions du Cercle de la Librairie, Paris, 1998.
40 Quoted in Nicolas Baulieu, *Grasset, le combat*, documentary broadcast by La Cinquième, 3 February 2002.
41 Ibid.
42 Lévy, *Bangla-Desh, nationalisme dans la révolution*.
43 Quoted in Baulieu, *Grasset, le combat*.
44 Beau, 'Dans les cuisines du Bernard-Henri-Lévisme'.
45 Quoted by Guillemette de Sairigne, 'BHL: en toutes libertés', *Le Point*, 11–17 March 1991.
46 Gilles Deleuze, *À propos des nouveaux philosophes et d'un problème plus général*, supplement of *Minuit*, no. 24, May 1977 (reprinted in Gilles Deleuze, *Deux régimes de fous: Textes et entretiens 1975–1995*, collection

edited by David Lapoujade, Minuit, Paris, 2003; *Two Regimes of Madness*, Semiotext(e), Cambridge, MA, 2007.

47 Ibid.

48 Ibid.

49 Bernard-Henri Lévy, *Le Testament de Dieu*, Grasset, Paris, 1979.

50 Cornelius Castoriadis, 'L'Industrie du vide', *Le Nouvel Observateur*, 25–30 June 1979.

51 Bernard-Henri Lévy, 'Réponse de Bernard-Henri Lévy', *Le Nouvel Observateur*, 18 June 1979.

52 'Pierre Vidal-Naquet réplique à Bernard-Henri Lévy', *Le Nouvel Observateur*, 25–30 June 1975.

53 Interview with the authors, May 2004.

54 Castoriadis, 'L'Industrie du vide'.

55 In *Comédie*, a book written after the failure of his film *Le Jour et la Nuit* (1996), Bernard-Henri Lévy imagines himself following through the streets of Tangiers his 'old teacher', easily recognizable as Jacques Derrida, with the vague intention of having it out with him. When *Comédie* was mentioned to him, Derrida replied in a tone of some distress: 'Ah, yes, *Comédie* …'

5 THE WORLD IS MY SPECTACLE

1 'The *Playboy* interview: Bernard-Henri Lévy'.

2 Ibid.

3 *Le Matin*, 27 May 1977.

4 Bernard-Henri Lévy, *Le Monde*, 5 January 1993 (reprinted in Lévy, *Récidives*, p. 550).

5 *Le Figaro Magazine*, 15 May 2004.

6 Tournier, 'BHL, ombre et lumière'.

7 Interview with the authors, September 2004.

8 Bernard-Henri Lévy, 'Écrivain-journaliste? Conversation avec Jean Hatzfeld', *Le Magazine Littéraire*, May–June 2003 (reprinted in *Récidives*, p. 371).

9 Lévy, *Récidives*, p. 550.

10 Lévy, *Le Lys et la Cendre*, p. 119.

11 Lévy, *Récidives*, p. 15.

12 Ibid., p. 22.

13 Ibid.

14 Lévy, *Le Lys et la Cendre*, p. 271.

15 Bernard-Henri Lévy, *Sartre, the Philosopher of the Twenty-First Century*, Polity Press, Cambridge, 2003, p. 4.

16 Ibid.

17 Lévy, *Comédie*, p. 124.
18 Lévy, *War, Evil and the End of History*, pp. 136–7.
19 Lévy, *Comédie*, p. 7.
20 Bernard-Henri Lévy, 'Attention à l'anti-américanisme', *Le Figaro Magazine*, 15 May 2004.
21 Ibid.
22 Ibid.
23 'Now with Bill Moyers', PBS, 26 September 2003.
24 'Vous pouvez dire la vérité à un barbare, il ne sera pas moins barbare', ('You can tell the truth to a barbarian, it won't make him any less barbarian'), interview with Annette Lévy-Willard, *Libération*, 24 April 2004.
25 Bernard-Henri Lévy, 'Choses vues en Algérie', *Le Monde*, 8 and 9 January 1998.
26 Nicolas Beau, 'Les généraux d'Alger préfèrent un reportage de BHL à une enquête internationale', *Le Canard enchaîné*, 14 January 1998.
27 Pierre Sané, 'Qui profite de cette situation?', *Libération*, 7 May 1997.
28 See Lounis Aggoun and Jean-Baptiste Rivoire, *Françalgérie, crimes et mensonges d'États*, La Découverte, Paris, 2004, p. 505; on the massacres and generally on the manipulation of radical Islamism by the Algerian secret services, this book contains a mass of very accurate information and analyses that have never been refuted.
29 See notably Patrick Forestier, 'Derrière les nouveaux massacres, y aurait-il le clan des militaires éradicateurs?', *Paris Match*, 25 September–1 October 1997.
30 Bruno Étienne, 'Ce sont les généraux qui se déchirent', *Le Figaro*, 31 August 1997.
31 A quote recorded on 23 September 1997 by a young Algerian cameraman in a report intended for the 1 p.m. news on France 2, but censored by the Algerian authorities, and finally included in the documentary *Bentalha: autopsie d'un massacre*, by Jean-Baptiste Rivoire, Jean-Paul Billault, Thierry Thuillier and Bruno Girodon and broadcast by Télévision Suisse Romande on 8 April 1999 and France 2 on 23 September 1999.
32 Lévy, 'Choses vues en Algérie'.
33 See Aggoun and Rivoire, *Françalgérie*, p. 502.
34 John Sweeney, 'We were murderers who killed for the state', the *Observer*, 11 January 1998.
35 In televised documentaries, like those covering the assassination of the Kabyle singer Lounes Matoub (Michel Despratx, Jean-Baptiste Rivoire, Lounis Aggoun and Marina Ladous, *Algérie, la grande manipulation*, documentary broadcast by '90 Minutes', Canal Plus, 31 October 2000) or the

manipulation of the GIA by the Algerian secret services, notably in the attacks in the Parisian RER in 1995 (Jean-Baptiste Rivoire and Romain Icard, *Attentats de Paris: enquête sur les commanditaires*, documentary broadcast by '90 Minutes', Canal Plus, 4 November 2002. And also in books, for example the one written by a survivor of the Bentalha massacre: Nesroulah Yous (as told to Salima Mellah), *Qui a tué à Bentalha? Algérie, chronique d'un massacre annoncé*, La Découverte, Paris, 2000; and those by dissident Algerian military: Habib Souaida, *La sale guerre*, La Découverte, Paris, 2001; Mohammed Samraoui, *Chronique des années de sang. Algérie: comment les services secrets ont manipulé les groupes islamistes*, Denoël, Paris, 2003.

36 See Salah-Eddine Sidhoum and Algeria-Watch, Algérie: la machine de mort, algeria-watch.org/fr, October 2003. Set up in 1997, the site of the NGO Algeria-Watch contains thousands of documents attesting to these human rights violations.

37 Aggoun and Rivoire, *Françalgérie*, p. 502.

38 Nesroulah Yous (with Salima Mellah), *Qui a tué à Bentalha?*.

39 'Le bloc-notes de Bernard-Henri Lévy', *Le Point*, 27 October–2 November 2000.

40 See notably 'Le bloc-notes de Bernard-Henri Lévy', *Le Point*, 4–10 October 1997: 'Islamists, however bloodthirsty they may be, have a right to a trial; they too have the right not to be tortured or massacred; by answering terror with counter-terror we end by ruining democracy and making the bed of fascislamism.'

41 François Gèze and Pierre Vidal-Naquet, 'L'Algérie et les intellectuels français', *Le Monde*, 4 February 1998.

42 Aggoun and Rivoire, *Françalgérie*, p. 536.

43 Malik Aït-Aoudia, *Ce que j'ai vu en Algérie. Carnets de route d'André Glucksmann*, documentary broadcast by France 3, 6 March 1998.

44 Tournier, 'BHL, ombre et lumière'. On this episode, see the account by Aggoun and Rivoire, *Françalgérie*, pp. 544–5.

45 Reported by Hassane Zerrouky, *L'Humanité*, 28 January 1998.

46 Ibid.

47 Quoted by Jean-Pierre Tuquoi, 'Les succès de communication du pouvoir algérien', *Le Monde*, 20 February 1998.

48 Pierre Bourdieu, *Sur la télévision*, Liber éditions, Paris, 1996, p. 63.

49 Pierre Bourdieu, *Contre-feu*, Raisons d'agir, Paris, 1998, pp. 105–6.

50 Ibid.

51 Gèze and Vidal-Naquet, 'L'Algérie et les intellectuels français'.

52 Bernard-Henri Lévy, 'Algérie: gare au syndrome Timisoara', *Le Monde*,

12 February 1998. See the reply from François Gèze and Pierre Vidal-Naquet, 'L'Algérie de Bernard-Henri Lévy', *Le Monde*, 5 March 1998.

53 'The *Playboy* Interview: Bernard-Henri Lévy'.
54 Ibid.
55 'Vivement dimanche', France 2, 11 November 2001.
56 Lévy, 'The Death of Massoud', in *War, Evil and the End of History*, p. 317.
57 Bernard-Henri Lévy included this event in his report to the president.
58 Alain Guillo appears in Christophe de Ponfilly's film *Vies clandestines, nos années afghanes* (Arte, 2002).
59 Interview with the authors, July 2004.
60 Ibid.
61 Lévy, *Récidives*, p. 840.
62 Ibid., p. 833.
63 Ibid., p. 837.
64 'Vivement dimanche', France 2, 11 November 2001.
65 Michael Barry, *Le Royaume de l'insolence*, Flammarion, Paris, 2001, p. 108.
66 Bernard-Henri Lévy, 'Avec Massoud', *Le Monde*, 13 October 1998.
67 *Le Monde*, 22 October 1998.
68 Interview with the authors, July 2004.
69 Interview with the authors, May 2004.
70 Lévy, 'Avec Massoud'.
71 Interview with the authors, 23 February 2011.
72 Interview with the authors, by email, 16 and 17 February 2011.
73 Interview with the authors, 25 February 2011.
74 Interview with the authors, 23 February 2011.
75 Mikheil Saakashvili (with Raphaël Glucksmann), *Je vous parle de liberté*, Hachette Littératures, Paris, 2008.
76 'BHL n'a pas vu toutes ses "choses vues" en Géorgie', *Rue89*, August 2008.
77 Alain Minc, 'Géorgie: SOS raison!', *Libération*, 18 August 2008.
78 Véronique Maurus, 'Gori brûle-t-il?', *Le Monde*, 31 August 2008.

6 THE MURDER OF DANIEL PEARL

1 'Le bloc-notes de Bernard-Henri Lévy', *Le Point*, 19–25 April 2002.
2 Ibid., 25 April–1 May 2002.
3 Ibid., 24–30 May 2002.
4 Oriana Fallaci, *La Rage et l'orgueil*, Plon, Paris, 2002.
5 'Le bloc-notes de Bernard-Henri Lévy', *Le Point*, 16–22 August 2002.
6 Ibid., 6–12 December 2002.
7 Daniel Lindenberg, *Le Rappel à l'ordre*, Seuil, Paris, 2002.
8 'Le bloc-notes de Bernard-Henri Lévy', *Le Point*, 6–12 September 2002.

9 Ibid., 13–19 September 2002.

10 Ibid., 15–20 November 2002.

11 Olivier and Patrick Poivre d'Arvor, *Courriers de nuit*, Place des Victoires, Paris, 2002.

12 'Le bloc-notes de Bernard-Henri Lévy', 15–21 November 2002.

13 Ibid., 19–25 July 2002.

14 Ibid., 24–30 January 2003.

15 Ibid., 3–9 January 2003.

16 Ibid., 17–23 January 2003.

17 Ibid., 14–20 February 2003.

18 Marie-Claire Pauwels, *Fille à Papa*, Albin Michel, Paris, 2003.

19 'Le bloc-notes de Bernard-Henri Lévy', *Le Point*, 7–13 February 2003.

20 The 'bloc-notes' were interrupted between 22 February and 8 March 2002, then between 8 March and 12 April, the period of BHL's Afghanistan mission. There were interruptions from 7 to 24 May, from 22 November to 6 December, and between 20 December and 3 January 2003. A further interruption took place between 14 February and 4 April 2003.

21 Bernard-Henri Lévy, *Who Killed Daniel Pearl?*, translated by James Mitchell, Duckworth, London, 2003, p. xv. All pagination refers to this edition.

22 Bernard-Henri Lévy, 'Écrivain-journaliste? Conversation avec Jean Hatzfeld', *Magazine littéraire*, May 2003.

23 Interview with Sébastien le Fol, *Le Figaro littéraire*, 24 April 2003.

24 Marianne Pearl, *Un cœur invaincu*, Plon, Paris, 2003.

25 Bernard-Henri Lévy, *Who Killed Daniel Pearl?*, Melville House, New York, 2003; Duckworth, London, 2003.

26 Interview with the authors, July 2004 (original transcript lost: retranslated by JH).

27 Ibid.

28 Lévy, *Who killed Daniel Pearl?*, p. 16.

29 Ibid.

30 Interview with the authors, July 2004.

31 Lévy, *Who killed Daniel Pearl?*, p. 13.

32 Ibid., p. 16.

33 Ibid., pp. 19–20.

34 Interview with the authors, July 2004.

35 'Le bloc-notes de Bernard-Henri Lévy', *Le Point*, 1–7 August 2003.

36 Quotations from the dust jacket of *Qui a tué Daniel Pearl?*

37 Lévy, 'Ecrivain-journaliste?'.

38 Jean Hatzfeld, *Dans le nu de la vie*, Seuil, Paris, 2000; *Une saison de machettes*, Seuil, Paris, 2003.

39 Most notably on France Culture, a special programme devoted to Daniel Pearl, 28 April 2003: 'What threw me in BHL's book was the investigation.'
40 *Le Monde*, 25 April 2003.
41 *Libération*, 2 May 2003.
42 *Marianne*, 28 April–4May 2003.
43 *Le Point*, 25 April-1 May 2003.
44 Arlette Chabot, 'Mots croisés', France 2, 28 April 2003.
45 Edwy Plenel, '*Le Monde* des idées', LCI, 26 April 2003.
46 List made by Poiraud, 'Chronique d'un retour en grâce médiatique'.
47 Pierre Assouline, 'Les Carnets', *Lire*, June 2003.
48 William Dalrymple, 'Murder in Karachi', *New York Review of Books*, 4 December 2003.
49 Philippe Lançon, 'De sang chaud', *Libération*, 2 May 2003.
50 Didier François, 'Dans les pas de Daniel Pearl', *Libération*, 2 May 2003.
51 France Culture, 28 April 2003.
52 Alain Frachon, 'Daniel Pearl, l'enquête', *Le Monde*, 24 April 2003.
53 Lévy, *Who Killed Daniel Pearl?*, p. 175.
54 Mariam Abou Zahab, 'Bernard-Henri Lévy: *Qui a tué Daniel Pearl?*', *Maghreb-Machrek* 178, winter 2003–2004.
55 Interview with the authors, 8 January 2004.
56 Lévy, *Who Killed Daniel Pearl?*, p. xix.
57 Chapter title in *Who Killed Daniel Pearl?*
58 Ibid., p. xvii.
59 'Sheikh Omar Saeed in fact turned himself in at the home of Ejaz Shah, interior minister of the Punjab government and former ISI officer' – Mariam Abou Zahab and Olivier Roy, *Réseaux islamiques. La connexion afghano-pakistanaise*, Autrement/Ceri, Paris, 2002, p. 60.
60 Interview with the authors, June 2004.
61 Ibid.
62 Interview with the authors, July 2004.
63 Ibid.
64 On France Culture, during the special programme on Pearl, 28 April 2003.
65 Beau and Toscer, *Une imposture française*, p. 167.
66 Ibid.
67 Interview with the authors, July 2004.
68 Quoted in Jacques Derrida and Élisabeth Roudinesco, *De quoi demain...*, Flammarion, Paris, 2001, p. 129, note 3.
69 Interview with the authors, July 2004.
70 'Les Matins de France Culture', France Culture, 6 November 2003.
71 Ibid.

72 'Pakistan is an easy place for a journalist to work', first sentence of the preface to Owen Bennett Jones, *Pakistan: Eye of the Storm*, Yale University Press, New Haven, 2003.

73 In his book Bernard-Henri Lévy places Muzaffarabad, the capital of the Pakistani part of Kashmir, in India; locates the Akora Khattack *madrassa* in Peshawar, when it is eighty miles away, not far from the Indus; describes the town of Saharanpur as a suburb of Delhi, when it is four hours by road from the Indian capital; and gets the London address of Omar Sheikh's family wrong (see William Dalrymple, 'Murder in Karachi', *New York Review of Books*, 4 November 2003).

74 The camp called Salman al-Farsi becomes Salam Fassi (see Abou Zahab, 'Bernard-Henri Lévy: *Qui a tué Daniel Pearl?*'.)

75 Bernard-Henri Lévy describes Abdul Ghani Lone, a moderate Kashmiri leader assassinated on 21 May 2002 (probably by Islamists under ISI protection), as a leading light of hard-line Islamism collaborating with the Pakistani secret services; and the All Parties Hurriyat Conference, a political formation with a moderate line on Kashmir, as a fundamentalist Islamist NGO (see Dalrymple, 'Murder in Karachi').

76 Bernard-Henri Lévy, 'Réponse à un "spécialiste"', *Le Monde diplomatique*, February 2004. *Le Monde diplomatique* published BHL's right-to-reply with a further response from William Dalrymple, 'Perseverare diabolicum …', which pulls no punches.

77 William Dalrymple, *Xanadu*, Flamingo, London, 1989; *The Age of Kali*, Flamingo, London, 1998; *From the Holy Mountain*, Flamingo, London, 1997.

78 Lévy, *Who Killed Daniel Pearl?*, p. 453.

79 *Boston Globe*, 6 January 2002.

80 Reid, a British national, had attempted to blow up an American Airlines Boeing between Paris and Miami with explosives concealed in his shoe, on 22 December 2001.

81 Many of Lévy's interlocutors call the terrorist 'Sheikh Omar' instead of 'Omar Sheikh' like Lévy. The writer sees this, mistakenly, as a mark of respect or deference. In reality 'Sheikh' is a caste name, a sort of surname that has nothing to do with the function or status of a 'sheikh'. Some of these caste names are placed after the first name, others before it, as with 'Sheikh', so that it should be 'Sheikh Omar Saïd' and not 'Omar Saïd Sheikh'. 'Omar Sheikh' is also acceptable, but for reasons of custom, not those advanced by Bernard-Henri Lévy.

82 Peter Bergen, *Holy War, Inc. Inside the Secret World of Osama bin Laden*, Weidenfeld & Nicolson, London, 2001.

83 Interview with the authors by email, 29 August 2004.

84 Robert Mackey, 'New report on Daniel Pearl's murder reveals forensic analysis of killer's veins', *The Lede*, thelede.blogs.nytimes.com, 20 January 2011.

85 Center for Public Integrity, 'The Pearl project', treesaver.publicintegrity.org.

86 *Prospect*, October 2003.

87 Olivier Roy, *Généalogie de l'islamisme*, Hachette, Paris, 1995.

88 France-Culture, 28 April 2003.

89 Ibid.

90 Jason Burke, *Al-Qaeda: Casting a Shadow on Terror*, IB Tauris, London/New York, 2004.

91 Interview with the authors, June 2004.

92 Abou Zahab and Roy, *Réseaux islamiques*, p. 60.

93 Dalrymple, 'Murder in Karachi'.

94 Burke, *Al-Qaeda*, p. 91.

95 Abou Zahad and Roy, *Réseaux islamiques*, p. 64.

96 Ibid., p. 33.

97 Ibid., p. 76.

98 Ibid., p. 30.

99 Interview with the authors, July 2004.

100 Interview with the authors, August 2004.

101 See Dalrymple, 'Murder in Karachi'.

102 Interview with the authors, July 2004.

103 'Mots croisés', France 2, 28 April 2003.

104 'Émission spéciale Daniel Pearl', France Culture, 28 April 2003.

105 'Mots croisés', France 2, 28 April 2003.

106 'Valerie and I are very pro-France. We like to think we are heading the anti-anti-French movement' – Dennis Loy Johnson, director of Melville House, and his wife Valerie Merians, interviewed by the journalist Véronique Dupont.

107 Roy, *Généalogie de l'islamisme*, pp. 29–30.

108 François Burgat, *L'Islamisme au Maghreb. La voix du Sud,* Karthala, Paris, 1988; *L'Islamisme en face*, La Découverte, Paris, 1995; *L'Islamisme à l'heure d'Al-Qaïda*, La Découverte, Paris, 2005.

109 *Livres Hebdo*, 30 January 2004.

110 Interview with the authors, July 2004.

111 Interview with the authors, July 2004.

112 To use the verb employed by Alexandre Adler on France Culture, 17 July 2004.

113 Olivia de Lamberterie, books editor of *Elle*, 'Le Masque et la Plume', France Inter, 13 May 2004.

7 WAGING WAR FOR DEMOCRACY

1 *Elle*, 3 May 2004.
2 Quoted in Lévy, *Récidives*, pp. 803–4.
3 *Der Spiegel*, 3 September 2001.
4 Lévy, 'Algérie: gare au syndrome Timisoara'.
5 Olivier Roy, *Généalogie de l'islamisme*, Hachette littératures, 'Pluriel' collection, Paris, 2001.
6 Pierre Milza, *Fascisme français*, Flammarion, 'Champs' collection, Paris, 1987.
7 Ibid., p. 52.
8 Title of the chapter on his efforts against the FN, in *Récidives*, p. 461.
9 Talk given on 15 January 2002 at the École de management de Bordeaux, published on the website forum-events.com.
10 'Le bloc-notes de Bernard-Henri Lévy', *Le Point*, 9–15 May 2003.
11 Milza, *Fascisme français*, p. 10.
12 Lévy, *La Pureté dangereuse*, p. 80; see also *Récidives*, p. 803.
13 Lévy, *Récidives*, p. 811.
14 Ibid., p. 834.
15 Serrou, 'Pour BHL, la pureté, c'est le mal'.
16 Bernard-Henri Lévy, 'Egypte, année zéro', *Libération*, 26 February 2011.
17 Lévy, *Le Jugement dernier*.
18 'BHL, mes vérités', interview by Didier Jacob, *Le Nouvel Observateur*, 29 April–5 May 2004.
19 On this specific question of the mobilization of French intellectuals during the war in former Yugoslavia, see Erwan Poiraud and Thierry Teboul, 'Des intellectuels en cause: de Vukovar à Sarajevo', in Francis James and David Buxton (eds), *Intellectuels et Médias*, INA-L'Harmattan, forthcoming.
20 Interview with the authors, July 2004.
21 Interview with the authors, June 2004.
22 Michel Floquet and Bertrand Coq, *Les Tribulations de Bernard K. en Yougoslavie*, Albin Michel, Paris, 1993, p. 33.
23 On France 2, 20 June 1993, at 1 p.m.
24 On TF1, 21 November 1992, at 8 p.m.
25 'Arrêt sur image', La Cinquième, 23 March 1996.
26 Lévy, *Le Lys et la Cendre*, p. 25.
27 Bernard-Henri Lévy, 'Les Bosniaques n'ont pas perdu la guerre', *Le Figaro*, 1 January 1994.

28 Bernard-Henri Lévy, 'Sarajevo: arrêtez le massacre', *Le Point*, 27 June–3 July 1992.

29 From the voice-over commentary in *Bosna!* (see the text of this commentary in *Récidives*, pp. 157–8).

30 Ibid.

31 Editorial in *La Règle du jeu*, number 10, 20 April 1993.

32 Interview with the authors, July 2004.

33 Interview with Jean-Marie Colombani, *Le Monde*, 5 January 1993.

34 Bernard-Henri Lévy, 'La Yougoslavie au cœur', *Politique internationale*, number 57, Autumn 1992.

35 See in particular Tournier, 'BHL, ombre et lumière'.

36 Dupuis, *Enquête de personnalité.*

37 This article, filled with errors, was severely criticized by the researcher Jérôme Tubiana, a specialist in the region, in a long article, 'Choses (mal) vues au Darfour', published on 9 June 2007 on the website mouvements.info. *Le Monde* and *Libération* had both refused to publish the researcher's text.

38 *Le Monde*, 13 March 2007.

39 Richard Rossin, 'Droit d'asile pour le chef rebelle du Darfour', *Libération*, 26 December 2007.

40 Bernard-Henri Lévy, 'Sarkozy et Kouchner oseront-ils expulser le représentant du Darfour à Paris?', *Le Point*, 20 December 2007.

41 Interview with the authors, 21 January 2011.

42 *Le Point*, 15 April 2010.

43 Interview with the authors, 21 January 2011.

44 Report of the Panel of Experts on the Sudan established pursuant to resolution 1591 (2005).

45 Bernard-Henri Lévy, 'Pourquoi soutenir l'âme de la résistance au Darfour', laregledujeu.org, 14 April 2011.

46 Rony Brauman, 'Darfur, une mobilisation tapageuse et fragile', interview published on mouvements.info, 9 June 2007.

47 Lévy, 'Choses vues au Darfour'.

48 Speech by Bernard-Henri Lévy to the general assembly of Urgence Darfour, 9 January 2010, youtube.com, 12 January 2010.

49 Roland Marchal, 'Le conflit au Darfour, point aveugle des négociations nord-sud au Soudan', *Politique africaine*, number 95, June 2004.

50 Tubiana, 'Choses (mal) vues au Darfour'.

51 'Don't let our nightmare become reality! Protest against the stoning of our mother!', missionfreeiran.org, 26 June 2010.

52 Bernard-Henri Lévy, 'Il faut sauver Sakineh Mohammadi-Ashtiani', *Libération*, 16 August 2010.

53 'On s'est acharné sur elle de toute les manières possibles', *Libération*, 10 December 2010.

54 Bernard-Henri Lévy, 'Le dégoût et encore l'espérance', *Libération*, 10 December 2010.

55 'BHL ne veut pas croire à l'exécution imminente de Sakineh et lance un nouvel appel', laregledujeu.org, 2 November 2010.

56 See for example 'Sarkozy aurait exigé de surseoir à l'exécution de Sakineh, selon BHL', 20minutes.fr, 3 November 2010.

57 Interview with the authors, 1 March 2011.

58 Interview with the authors, 23 March 2011.

59 Ghazal Golshiri and Pierre Puchot, 'Shirin Ebadi: "Les sanctions économiques contre le peuple iranien n'ont aucun sens"', mediapart.fr, 26 November 2010.

60 Bernard-Henri Lévy, 'Un Hitler iranien? Une BD sur Ben Laden, Farouk Hosni, dernière', *Le Point*, 17 September 2009.

61 Interview with the authors, 23 March 2011.

62 Interview with the authors, 31 March 2011.

63 See the video 'En direct ici: un débat unique avec l'opposition iranienne', laregledujeu.org, 11 June 2010.

64 'Bernard-Henri Lévy rencontre en Libye des responsables de l'insurrection', AFP, 5 March 2011.

65 Interview with the authors, 31 March 2011.

66 See for example this extract from the TV news on France 2, a public service broadcaster: 'BHL sur France 2 journal de 20 heures (10 mars 2011)', dailymotion.com.

67 Natalie Nougayrède and Philippe Ricard, 'Le jour où BHL est devenu le porte-parole de l'Élysée', *Le Monde*, 11 March 2011.

68 Bernard-Henri Lévy, 'Quand Sarkozy lâche Khadafi: coulisses', laregledujeu.org, 11 March 2011.

69 Renaud Girard, 'La campagne libyenne de Bernard-Henri Lévy', *Le Figaro*, 18 March 2011.

70 Saïd Mahrane, 'BHL, l'autre ministre des Affaires étrangères', *Le Point*, 24 March 2011.

71 Laurent Dispot, 'Lettre ouverte à Karl-Theodor zu Guttenberg sur la question libyenne', laregledujeu.org, 21 March 2011.

72 Nicolas Bourcier, 'L'insolite cheminement de la mission française', *Le Monde*, 15 March 2011.

73 'Europe 1 soir', Europe 1, 10 March 2011.

74 Pierre Cherruau, 'BHL: Ne pas intervenir "serait à pleurer de rage"', slateafrique.com, 15 March 2011.

75 Photo published in the weekly *Marianne*, 23–29 April 2011, pp. 16 and 17.
76 Bernard-Henri Lévy, 'Enlisement, vous avez dit enlisement?', *Le Monde*, 18 April 2011.
77 *Le Point*, 31 March 2011.
78 Patrick Haimzadeh, 'Les dix erreurs de l'Otan en Libye', *Mediapart*, 23 June 2011.
79 'SOS Syrie', *Le Monde*, 26 May 2011.
80 Burhan Ghalioun, Subhi Hadidi and Farouk Mardam Bey, 'Bernard-Henri Lévy, épargnez aux Syriens votre soutien', *Mediapart*, 27 May 2011.
81 Hala Kodmani, 'Des opposants syriens rejettent le soutien encombrant de BHL', *Rue 89*, 3 July 2011.

8 IS BERNARD-HENRI LÉVY LEFT-WING?

1 'The *Playboy* interview: Bernard-Henri Lévy'.
2 Lévy, *Left in Dark Times*, p. 24.
3 Paul Thibaud, 'La censure érigée en méthode intellectuelle', *Esprit*, Nos 148–9, 1989.
4 'BHL face à *Marianne*', *Marianne*, 6 February 2010.
5 See Lilian Mathieu, *Comment lutter? Pour une sociologie combative des mouvements sociaux*, Textuel, Paris, 2004.
6 'Petit stream entre amis', Europe 1, 28 October 2010.
7 Bernard-Henri Lévy, 'Défense de Dominique Strauss-Kahn', *Le Point*, 16 May 2011.
8 Bernard-Henri Lévy, 'Bernard-Henri Lévy defends accused IMF director', *The Daily Beast*, 16 May 2011.
9 Matt Welch, 'BHL: France's national disgrace', *Reason Magazine*, 16 May 2011.
10 Amy Davidson, 'Arnold, BHL and DSK', *New Yorker*, 17 May 2011.
11 Tom Scocca, '"A subject of justice like any other": Bernard-Henri Lévy makes the case for prosecuting Dominique Strauss-Kahn', *Slate*, 17 May 2011.
12 Joseph Goldberg, 'Bernard-Henri Lévy lashes himself to Strauss-Kahn', *National Review*, 16 May 2011.
13 Scocca, '"A subject of justice like any other"'.
14 Lévy, 'Défense de Dominique Strauss-Kahn'.
15 Jon Stewart, *La Cage aux fools*, 'Daily Show', Comedy Central, 19 May 2011.
16 Pascale Clark, 'Comme on nous parle', France Inter, 17 May 2011.
17 Bernard-Henri Lévy, 'Affaire Strauss-Kahn, question de principe', *Le Point*, 23 May 2011.
18 'Semaine critique', France 2, 20 May 2011.

19 Clark, 'Comme on nous parle'.
20 Riz Khan, Al-Jazeera English, 11 March 2011.
21 Bernard-Henri Lévy, 'BHL, un journal américain', *Le Monde* 2, 4 March 2006.
22 Carl Swanson, 'American Psychoanalyst', *New York Magazine*, 14 January 2006.
23 Claire Avril, 'Bernard-Henri Lévy: le désespoir pour tout espoir', *Nice-Matin*, 2 October 1977.
24 François Ducout, 'Je crois à la guerre des sexes', *Elle*, 17 September 1984.
25 Jacqueline Rémy, 'Les hommes, les femmes et l'amour', *L'Express*, 22 April 1993.
26 Sylvie Metzelard, 'Bernard-Henri Lévy: dire je t'aime n'a plus de sens', *Le Parisien*, 1993.
27 'Vie privée, vie publique', France 3, 8 December 2008.
28 Bernard-Henri Lévy, 'Requiem pour Hillary', *Le Point*, 12 June 2008.
29 Frédéric Beigbeder, 'J'écris généralement nu', *GQ*, February 2009.
30 Bernard-Henri Lévy, 'Pourquoi je défends Polanski', *Le Point*, 8 October 2009.
31 Bernard-Henri Lévy, 'Libération de Polanski: BHL se réjouit', laregledujeu.org, 25 November 2009.
32 'There are moments when everything focuses on a single face. Dreyfus was one. Or the great dissidents in the former Soviet Union. The Polanski affair is of the same dimensions.' Interview with Sefi Henedler, 'Feisty on all fronts', *Haaretz*, 27 May 2010.
33 Lévy, 'Pourquoi je défends Polanski'.
34 '*La Règle du jeu* s'engage aux côtés de Roman Polanski', laregledujeu.org, 10 November 2009.
35 Bernard-Henri Lévy, '24 heures dans la vie de Roman Polanski', *Le Point*, 18 December 2009.
36 Lévy, 'Pourquoi je défends Polanski'.
37 Eve Ensler, 'Does the brotherhood of fame endow you with a lifetime exemption from accountability?' *Huffington Post*, 30 September 2009.
38 'NTC chairman's speech on Mr. Levy's comments', NTC Mediagroup, 5 June 2011.
39 Riz Khan, Al-Jazeera English, 11 March 2011.
40 Interview with the authors, May 2004.
41 Bernard-Henri Lévy, 'À l'heure de Gaza', *Le Journal du dimanche*, 18 January 2009; *The Huffington Post*, 20 January 2009; *Corriere della Sera*, 20 January 2009; *El Mundo*, 21 January 2009; *Frankfurter Allgemeine Zeitung*, 24 January 2009; *Haaretz*, 23 January 2009.

42 Benjamin Barthe, *Ramallah Dream. Voyage au cœur du mirage palestinien*, La Découverte, Paris, 2011.
43 Bernard-Henri Lévy, 'La guerre, vue d'Israël', *Le Monde*, 27 July 2006; *New York Times Magazine*, 6 August 2006; *Expressen*, 28 July 2006; *Corriere della Sera*, 28 July 2006; *Frankfurter Allgemeine Zeitung*, 30 July 2006.
44 Interview with the authors, 13 June 2011.
45 Rafowicz did not follow up our request for an interview.
46 Gideon Levy, 'Go Home Mofaz', *Haaretz*, 30 April 2006.
47 Gili Izikovich, 'IDF's "purity of arms" being eroded, former Mossad chief Zvi Zamir warns', *Haaretz*, 10 June 2011.
48 France-Israel forum on democracy held at the Suzanne Dellal theatre, 30 May 2010.
49 Gideon Alon, 'PM: IDF still most moral army in world', *Haaretz*, 9 December 2004.
50 Bernard-Henri Lévy, 'Pourquoi je défends l'Israël', *Libération*, June 2010.
51 Christophe Ayad, 'Si BHL était allé au Gaza', *Libération*, 23 June 2010.
52 Gideon Levy, 'In response to Bernard-Henri Lévy', *Haaretz*, 10 June 2010.
53 Interview with the authors, May 2004.
54 Ibid.
55 Quoted in Jade Lindgaard, 'Des accords pour quelle paix?, *Les Inrockuptibles*, 2–8 June 2004.
56 Interview with the authors, May 2004.
57 Interview with the authors, March 2011.
58 Bernard-Henri Lévy, 'Pourquoi l'appel au boycott d'Israël est une saloperie', *Le Point*, 27 January 2011.

9 THE NIGHTMARE OF ENDLESS NEW BEGINNINGS

1 Jacques Julliard and Michel Winock (eds), *Dictionnaire des intellectuels français*, Seuil, Paris, 2002 (reprint).
2 *Livres Hebdo*, 1–7 March 1985.
3 Ibid., 11–17 January 1988.
4 Ibid., 5–11 January 1990.
5 Ibid.
6 Ibid., 30 January–4 February 2004.
7 The professional weekly *Livres Hebdo* produces annual lists of the previous year's best-sellers on the basis of voluntary information from selected outlets, subject to error but giving some indication of sales levels.
8 Figures obtained from Ipsos: estimates derived from actual sales up to 12 June 2011 in metropolitan France, from a panel of representative outlets – first- and second-tier bookshops, large cultural retail centres, hypermarkets,

and online sales after January 2010 – but excluding exports, sales in French overseas dependencies, sales to wholesalers and club sales.

9 Marie-Laure Delorme, 'Le livre secret enfin révélé', *Le Journal du dimanche*, 21 September 2008.

10 Jérôme Béglé, 'Houellebecq-BHL: l'impossible rencontre', *Paris Match*, 9 October 2008.

11 Jérôme Garcin, 'Nous, ennemis publics', *Le Nouvel Observateur*, 2 October 2008.

12 Claire Devarrieux, 'BHL-Houellebecq, le duo des bêtes noires', *Libération*, 1 October 2008.

13 Marie-Laure Delorme, 'Splendeurs et misères des écrivains', *Le Journal du dimanche*, 5 October 2008.

14 Nelly Kaprielian, 'Splendeurs et misères des écrivains', *Les Inrockuptibles*, 7 October 2008.

15 Jacques-Pierre Amette, 'BHL contre Houellebecq', *Le Point*, 2 October 2008.

16 Donald Morrison, 'In search of lost time', *Time*, 21 November 2006.

17 Véronique Richebois, 'Chronique de cinq flops (non) annoncés', *Les Échos*, 8 December 2008.

18 Quoted by Daniel Garcia, 'Vendre sous X', *Livres Hebdo*, 3 October 2008.

19 Ibid.

20 Ian Buruma, 'Two guys from Paris', *New York Times*, 14 January 2011.

21 Bernard-Henri Lévy, *De la guerre en philosophie*, Grasset, Paris, 2010, p. 9.

22 Ibid., p. 123.

23 All these texts published by Éditions des Mille et une nuits, in the 'Petite collection' series.

24 Roger-Pol Droit, 'Enclume, camembert et valise à roulettes', *Le Monde des livres*, 2 July 2007.

25 'Le Grand Journal de Canal Plus', 8 February 2010.

26 'Le bloc-notes de Bernard-Henri Lévy', *Le Point*, 11 February 2010.

27 'Matinale de France Inter', 19 February 2010.

28 Christophe Barbier, 'BHL discrédité? Retour sur l'affaire Botul', *L'Express*, 12 February 2010.

29 Philippe Boggio, 'BHL victime de délit de faciès', *slate.fr*, 17 February 2010.

30 Ibid.

31 Ibid.

32 Jean Daniel, 'À propos de Bernard-Henri Lévy', jean-daniel.blogs.nouvelobs.com.

33 Communiqué from the Society of *Le Nouvel Observateur*, 10 February 2010.

34 Lévy, *De la guerre en philosophie*, p. 18.
35 Bernard-Henri Lévy, 'Adieu Régis Debray', *Le Monde*, 14 May 1999.
36 Source: Ipsos.
37 Michel Onfray, *Le Ventre des philosophes, critique de la raison diététique*, Grasset, Paris, 1989.
38 'Le bloc-notes de Bernard-Henri Lévy', *Le Point*, 29 April 2010.
39 Onfray is referring here to the fact that the 'bloc-notes' in which Bernard-Henri Lévy attacked him was also published in the *Huffington Post* on 28 April, the *Corriere della Sera* on the 29th, and *El País* on 2 May.
40 *Le Point*, 6 May 2010.
41 Michel Onfray, 'Pour ou contre BHL?', *Le Nouvel Observateur*, 10 April 2007.
42 Ibid.
43 Michel Onfray, 'Je choisis la pureté', *Libération*, 19 October 2009.
44 Alain Badiou, *De quoi Sarkozy est-il le nom?*, Nouvelles Editions Lignes, Paris, 2007. English translation: Alain Badiou, *The Meaning of Sarkozy*, London, Verso, 2009.
45 Source: Ipsos.
46 Lévy, *Left in Dark Times*, p. 144.
47 Frédéric Pagès, 'De quoi Badiou est-il le renom?', *Le Canard enchaîné*, 2 June 2010.
48 Eric Conan, 'La star de la philo est-il un salaud?', *Marianne*, 27 February 2010.
49 *Libération*, 27 January 2009.
50 Sylvia Zappi, 'La seconde jeunesse d'Alain Badiou, le nouveau héraut de l'antisarkozysme', *Le Monde*, 12 January 2008.
51 Saïd Mahrane, 'Le gourou de l'antisarkozie', *Le Point*, 1 June 2009.
52 Ibid., p. 29.
53 'Le bloc-notes de Bernard-Henri Lévy', *Le Point*, 27 March 2008.
54 Bernard-Henri Lévy, 'De quoi Siné est-il le nom?', *Le Monde*, 21 July 2008.
55 See Alain Badiou and Eric Hazan, *L'Antisémitisme partout. Aujourd'hui en France*, La Fabrique, Paris, 2011.
56 Alain Badiou, *The Meaning of Sarkozy*, p. 6.
57 Émilie Lanez, 'De Badiou à BHL, itinéraire d'un repenti', *Le Point*, 25 July 2008.
58 Mehdi Belhaj Kacem, *Après Badiou*, Grasset, Paris, 2011.
59 Lanez, 'De Badiou à BHL'.

10 BHL WORLDWIDE

1 Jérôme Béglé, 'BHL, vedette américaine', *Paris Match*, 19 May 2004.
2 Joan Juliet Buck, 'France's prophet provocateur', *Vanity Fair*, January 2003.
3 Quoted in Béglé, 'BHL, vedette américaine'.
4 Ibid.
5 Lila Azam Zanganeh, 'Bernard-Henri Lévy en Amérique', *Le Monde*, 20 May 2005.
6 Corinne Lesnes, 'France – États-Unis, le match Lévy-Kristol', *Le Monde*, 26 January 2006.
7 Philippe Coste, 'Les vertiges américains de BHL', *L'Express*, 16 February 2006.
8 Jean-Louis Turlin, 'Bernard-Henri Lévy s'immisce dans le débat politique américain', *Le Figaro*, 28 January 2006.
9 Jean-Louis Turlin, 'BHL en vedette américaine', *Le Figaro*, 2 March 2006.
10 Quoted by Philippe Boulet-Gercourt, 'Pince-fesses et coup de bâton', *Le Nouvel Observateur*, 2–8 March 2006.
11 Coste, 'Les vertiges américains de BHL'.
12 Ibid.
13 Ibid.
14 'BHL: une émeute à Boston', *Le Figaro*, 18 February 2006.
15 'BHL, un journal américain', *Le Monde* 2, 4 March 2006.
16 'Bernard-Henri Lévy à la conquête du nouveau monde', *VSD*, 15–21 March 2006.
17 Quoted in Zanganeh, 'Bernard-Henri Lévy en Amérique'.
18 Quoted in Coste, 'Les vertiges américains de BHL'.
19 Preface to Nick Foulkes, *The Carlyle*, Assouline Publishing, New York, 2007 (reprinted in Lévy, *Pièces d'identité*, p. 1204).
20 Quoted in Laurent Mauriac, 'BHL raconte l'Amérique aux Américains', *Libération*, 18 January 2006.
21 Lévy, 'BHL, un journal américain'.
22 'Bernard-Henri Lévy et Diane von Fürstenberg', bernard-henri-levy.com, January 2010.
23 Coste, 'Les vertiges américains de BHL'.
24 Quoted in Zanganeh, 'Bernard-Henri Lévy en Amérique'.
25 Quoted in Coste, 'Les vertiges américains de BHL'.
26 *Le Point*, 2 March 2006.
27 Tunku Varadarajan, 'French kiss', *Wall Street Journal*, 21–22 January 2006.
28 William Grimes, 'A modern-day Tocqueville finds an uncertain America', *New York Times*, 4 February 2006.

29 Glyn Morgan, 'Bernard-Henri Lévy en Amérique', *Le Monde diplomatique*, March 2006.

30 As at the 'Popular Participative University' run by the Désirs d'avenir group, 5 October 2009.

31 Bernard-Henri Lévy, 'L'Amérique a des leçons à nous donner', *Le Parisien*, 7 March 2006.

32 Bernard-Henri Lévy, 'L'Amérique? Un jour on adore, le lendemain on déteste', *Le Point*, 2 March 2006.

33 Bernard-Henri Lévy, 'Je préfère la gauche américaine', *Le Parisien*, 8 October 2007.

34 *Village Voice*, 29 October 2008 (reprinted in Lévy, *Pièces d'identité*, p. 738).

35 Quoted in Béglé, 'BHL, vedette américaine'.

36 Marianne Wiggins, 'The accidental tourist', *Los Angeles Times*, 22 January 2006.

37 Adam Cohen, 'Democracy in America, then and now, a struggle against majority tyranny', *New York Times*, 22 January 2006.

38 Grimes, 'A modern-day Tocqueville finds an uncertain America'.

39 Alex Beam, 'Suffering from American Vertigo', *Boston Globe*, 25 January 2006.

40 Garrison Keillor, 'On the Road Avec M. Lévy', *New York Times*, 29 January 2006.

41 Christopher Hitchens, 'Garrison Keillor vulgarian. In defense of Bernard-Henri Lévy', slate.com, 13 February 2006.

42 Keillor, 'On the Road Avec M. Lévy'.

43 Lévy, 'BHL, un journal américain'.

44 Ibid.

45 Bernard-Henri Lévy, 'Internet? Un allié?', *International Herald Tribune Magazine*, 9 December 2010.

46 'Matinale' on France Info, 29 November 2010.

47 'L'e-BHL arrive', *L'Express*, 31 July 2009.

48 Last consulted on 7 September 2011. Among the fervid comments at the bottom of the page: 'Who needs concepts, when the postulate is love for humanity?'

49 Lévy, 'Internet? Un allié?'.

50 'Le bloc-notes de Bernard-Henri Lévy', *Le Point*, 26 November 2009.

51 Ibid., 30 June 2011.

CONCLUSION

1 Michel Pinçon and Monique Pinçon-Charlot, *Le Président des riches. Enquête sur l'oligarchie dans la France de Nicolas Sarkozy*, Zones, Paris, 2010.

2 Michel Foucault, *Abnormal: Lectures at the Collège de France 1974–1975*, Picador, New York, 2003.